REAL PHILOSOPHY

JACOB NEEDLEMAN is Professor of Philosophy at San Francisco State University and former Director of the Center for the Study of New Religions at Graduate Theological Union, Berkeley. He was educated in philosophy at Harvard, Yale and the University of Freiburg, Germany. He has also served as Research Associate at the Rockefeller Institute for Medical Research and was a Research Fellow at Union Theological Seminary. He is the author of *The New Religions, A Sense of the Cosmos, Lost Christianity, The Heart of Philosophy, The Way of the Physician*, and was General Editor of the Penguin Metaphysical Library. In addition to his teaching and writing he serves as a consultant in the fields of psychology, education, medical ethics, philanthropy and business, and is increasingly well known as an organizer and moderator of conferences in these fields. His most recent book, *Sorcerers*, is a novel about magic and the search for one's inner self.

DAVID APPELBAUM is Professor of Philosophy at State University College in New Paltz. He has also been a Teaching Fellow at Harvard University, Visiting Professor at Brooklyn College and an Instructor at New Asia College, the Chinese University of Hong Kong. He gained his MA in Psychology, Philosophy and Physiology in 1966 from Exeter College, Oxford, and his Ph.D. in 1973 from Harvard University. He is the author of *Contact and Attention* (1986), *Making the Body Heard* (1988), *Bringing the Body to Touch* (1988) and *Ethics and the Professions* (with Sarah Lawton, 1990). He has also written numerous philosophical articles, papers and book reviews, and has been series editor, with Peter Lang, of *Revisioning Philosophy*.

REAL PHILOSOPHY

An Anthology of
the Universal Search for Meaning

with introduction and commentary by
Jacob Needleman and David Appelbaum

ARKANA

ARKANA

Published by the Penguin Group
27 Wrights Lane, London W8 5TZ, England
Viking Penguin, a division of Penguin Books USA Inc.,
375 Hudson Street, New York, New York 10014, USA
Penguin Books Australia Ltd, Ringwood, Victoria, Australia
Penguin Books Canada Ltd, 2801 John Street, Markham, Ontario, Canada L3R 1B4
Penguin Books (NZ) Ltd, 182–190 Wairau Road, Auckland 10, New Zealand

Penguin Books Ltd, Registered Offices: Harmondsworth, Middlesex, England

First published 1990
10 9 8 7 6 5 4 3 2 1

Selection, introductions and notes
Copyright © Jacob Needleman and David Appelbaum, 1990
All rights reserved
The acknowledgements on pp. 8–10 constitute an extension of this copyright page
The moral rights of the authors have been asserted

Filmset in 11 on 12 pt Palatino
Made and printed in England by Clays Ltd, St Ives plc

CONTENTS

CONTENTS

ACKNOWLEDGEMENTS

Permission to reproduce the following copyright material is gratefully acknowledged.

Part 1

Extract from *The Philosophical Works of Descartes*, translated by E. Haldane and G. R. T. Ross, reproduced by the kind permission of Cambridge University Press

Extract from *The Thirteen Principal Upanishads*, translated by R. E. Hume, reprinted by kind permission of Oxford University Press

Extract from *The Sickness unto Death* by Soren Kierkegaard, translated by Alistair Hannay, reproduced by kind permission of Penguin Books

Extract from *The Tales of the Dervishes* by Idries Shah, reproduced by kind permission of the publisher, E. P. Dutton, a division of Penguin Books USA Inc., and A. P. Watt Ltd

Part 2

'The Hymn of the Pearl', retold by Anne Twitty, *Parabola*, Winter 1985, and reproduced with her kind permission

Extract from *The Brothers Karamazov* by Fyodor Dostoyevsky, translated by Constance Garnett and reproduced by kind permission of William Heinemann Limited

Extract from St Augustine's *Confessions*, translated by E. Pusey and reproduced by kind permission of Thomas Nelson and Sons Ltd

Extract from *The Nichomachean Ethics* by Aristotle, translated by W. D. Ross and reprinted by kind permission of Oxford University Press

Part 3

Extract from Maimonides's *The Guide for the Perplexed*, translated by M. Friedlander and reproduced by kind permission of Dover Publications, Inc.

Extract from Kant's *Religion within the Limits of Reason Alone*, translated by Greene and Hudson and reproduced by kind permission of The Open Court Publishing Company, La Salle, Illinois

Extract from Attar's *The Conference of the Birds*, translated by C. S. Nott and reproduced by kind permission of Penguin Books Ltd

Extract from *The Thirteen Principal Upanishads*, translated by R. E. Hume and reproduced by kind permission of Oxford University Press

ACKNOWLEDGEMENTS

Part 4

Extract from *Being and Nothingness* by Jean-Paul Sartre, translated by H. Barnes and reproduced by kind permission of Philosophical Library Publishers

Excerpt from *Being and Time* by Martin Heidegger, translated by J. Macquarrie and E. Robinson, copyright © 1962 by SCM Press Ltd, reprinted by permission of Harper & Row, Publishers, Inc.

Extract from *Buddhist Texts through the Ages*, edited by E. Conze and published by Bruno Cassirer, reproduced by kind permission of M. Conze

Extract from *The Lives of a Cell* by Lewis Thomas, copyright © 1973 by The Massachussetts Medical Society, originally published in *The New York Journal of Medicine*, reprinted by kind permission of Viking Penguin, Inc.

Part 5

Extract from *Heraclitus* by Philip Wheelwright, copyright © 1959 Princeton University Press, reproduced by kind permission of Princeton University Press

Extract from *A Source Book in Chinese Philosophy*, translated by Wing-Tsit Chan, copyright © 1963 by Princeton University Press, reproduced by kind permission of Princeton University Press

Extract from Nietzsche's *The Birth of Tragedy and the Genealogy of Morals*, translated by F. Golffing, copyright © 1956 by Doubleday & Company, Inc., reprinted by kind permission of the publisher

Part 6

Extract from *The Mystery of Being*, I, by Gabriel Marcel, translated by G. S. Fraser and reproduced by kind permission of Regnery Gateway, Inc., publishers of Regnery Books and Gateway Editions

Extract from *The Nichomachean Ethics* by Aristotle, translated by W. D. Ross and reproduced by kind permission of Oxford University Press

Extract from *Sadhana* by Rabindanath Tagore, reprinted by kind permission of Macmillan, London and Basingstoke

Extract from *Freedom from the Known* by Jiddu Krishnamurti, copyright © 1969 by the Krishnamurti Foundation Trust, reprinted by kind permission of Harper & Row, Publishers, Inc., and the Krishnamurti Foundation Trust Ltd

Part 7

Extract from *The Myth of Sisyphus and Other Essays* by Albert Camus, translated by Justin O'Brien, reprinted by kind permission of Alfred A. Knopf, Inc., and Hamish Hamilton

Extract from *A Source Book in Indian Philosophy* edited by Sir Sarvepalli Radhakrishnan and Charles A. Moore, copyright © 1957 by Princeton University Press, renewed © 1985, reprinted by kind permission of Princeton University Press.

Extract from *Time and Free Will* by Henri Bergson, translated by F. L. Pogson and reproduced by kind permission of Unwin Hyman Ltd

ACKNOWLEDGEMENTS

Extract from *The Epic of Gilgamesh*, translated by N. K. Sandars and reproduced by kind permission of Penguin Books Ltd

Part 8

Extract from *Tractatus Logico-Philosophicus* by Wittgenstein, translated by D. F. Pears and B. F. McGuiness and reproduced by kind permission of Humanities Press International, Inc., Atlantic Highlands, NJ, and Routledge

Extract from *The Phenomenology of Perception* by Maurice Merleau-Ponty, translated by C. Smith and reproduced by kind permission of Humanities Press International Inc., Atlantic Highlands, NJ, and Routledge

Extract from *A Source Book in Chinese Philosophy*, translated by Wing-Tsit Chan, copyright © 1963 by Princeton University Press, reproduced by kind permission of Princeton University Press

Extract from *The Sermons* by Meister Eckhart, translated by R. B. Blakney, copyright 1941 by Harper & Row, Publishers, Inc., and reprinted by kind permission of the publisher

'The Wall of Mystery', retold by Anne Twitty, *Parabola*, Spring 1986, and reproduced with her kind permission

Part 9

Extract from *The Portable Nietzsche*, edited by W. Kaufmann, copyright © 1954 by the Viking Press, Inc., renewed © 1982 by Viking Penguin Inc., and reproduced by kind permission of Viking Penguin Inc.

Extract from *Mount Analogue* by René Daumal, translated by R. Shattuck, translation copyright © 1959 by Vincent Stuart Ltd, reprinted by kind permission of Pantheon Books, a division of Random House, Inc.

Extract from *Myths and Symbols in Indian Art and Civilization* by Heinrich Zimmer, edited by Joseph Campbell, Bollingen Series VI, copyright 1946, © 1973 renewed by Princeton University Press, reprinted by kind permission of Princeton University Press

Extract from *Tertium Organum*, by P. D. Ouspensky, translated by Nicholas Bessaraboff and Claude Bragdon, copyright 1922 and renewed 1950 by Henry W. Bragdon, reprinted by kind permission of Alfred A. Knopf, Inc.

Extract from *The Selected Poetry of Rainer Maria Rilke*, edited and translated by Stephen Mitchell, copyright © 1982 by Stephen Mitchell, reprinted by kind permission of Random House, Inc.

INTRODUCTION

One of the most dramatic and important psychological truths of the twentieth century was discovered by the Austrian psychiatrist Viktor Frankl who, as a prisoner in a Nazi concentration camp during the Second World War, lived through unimaginable pain, fear and prolonged degradation. Few came out of these camps alive, and even fewer survived with heart and soul intact. As one of these very few, Frankl asked himself what it was that had enabled him and a small number of others to retain their humanity; his inquiry led him to a vision of human nature fundamentally opposed to the prevailing Freudian view, a view which still exerts considerable influence on how we think about ourselves. What Frankl proposed was that there is a fundamental drive within the human psyche which is not connected with the sexual instinct, nor with any other biological or socially conditioned impulse. Frankl felt, from his own experience, that the deepest moving force within himself and within every human being is *the need for meaning*. Without meaning, men and women lose their chief source of strength and become something other, something far less, than their potential. Whereas, Frankl felt, if one remains open to the possibility of meaning, even great suffering cannot destroy the human spirit. In short, no one can live without meaning. Indeed the need for meaning is what defines our very humanity and distinguishes us from all other beings on earth.

The selections in this book are a testimony to the search for meaning that has marked the human species in all ages and in all cultures including our own. *Philosophy*, the 'love of wisdom', is one of the names we give to this search. This book is meant to be

11

more than a survey of humanity's quest for the meaning of existence, however; it is also, and primarily, meant to serve a new awakening that is taking place throughout our threatened civilization. In almost every area of our culture, the realization is dawning that material progress and scientific achievement cannot of themselves lead us towards an understanding of the meaning of our lives and that, unless scientific progress is balanced by another kind of inquiry, it will inevitably become an instrument of self-destruction.

Every civilization directs most of its creative energies towards specific forms of activity, thereby focusing on or expressing some particular aspect of the human mind. Our modern contemporary civilization is characterized by its fascination with the technological application of scientific discovery and its neglect of those aspects of our nature that require other kinds of perceptions, other kinds of 'food', and that cannot be satisfied by the products of technology. These parts of our mind, these aspects of our selves, are starving, and if they die, we will die with them. This is not speculation: it is an obvious truth that we are all beginning to sense.

The extracts collected here are examples of how some of the great philosophers have struggled with questions that are the life-blood of our moral and spiritual selves, questions of human identity, purpose and ethics that have now become compellingly necessary to our very survival as we face the threats of nuclear war and ecological disaster. This potential horror, the extinction of *all* life, makes the lesson learned by Dr Frankl desperately relevant to every one of us.

Lacking the guidance of philosophy, more and more people are beginning to turn towards other approaches to meaning – institutional religion, science, psychiatry, political ideology, popular mysticism – but these often seem unable entirely to respond to the need. Religion, cut off from its ancient, traditional sources, is vulnerable to the confusion of the present day. Psychiatry, for its part, has long since lost its messianic aura; the hope it once seemed to offer has dissolved in the face of its self-confessed factionalism and inability to satisfy man's inherent need for ultimate values. Ideology has spawned mass movements and 'true believers', and has thus led people away from, rather than towards, the individual search for meaning; it depends upon the crowd, with its herd instinct, and has played on man's suggestibility rather than serving his wish to inquire and question. Finally, the current influx of mystical teachings (both from the East and from native Western traditions) has often proved antagonistic to the impulse to search, tending to sedate rather than to foster the individual qualities of anyone who turns towards them. The popularity of such movements, which are often examples of cultism, as in the mass suicide at Jonestown, shows how hungry we are for guidance and how little our culture now offers us in this respect.

What is *real philosophy*? It is neither science, nor religion, nor psychiatry, nor ideology, nor mysticism. Real philosophy is a separate force in human life that partakes of both an inner search (religion) and an outer discovery process (science). It covers the broad middle-ground between intimate self-questioning and ordinary, everyday interactions with others. In the Western tradition, it is represented by the figure of Socrates, who personifies the questioning attitude, brought to life, given flesh and blood and made to breathe. Following the Socratic method, real philosophy ponders the fundamental questions of human life. The quest does not forsake the market-place for some private sanctuary or specialized laboratory. On the contrary, real philosophy is born in a mind in search of itself, within the actual environment of day-to-day choice. It concerns itself equally with ordinary action and with the mysterious configuration of existence. It aims to guide us in the art of living, which was once called *wisdom*. It seeks to comprehend this art, to make the hidden heart of thinking known and felt. It addresses itself to the whole person, galvanized by philosophical activity, aware both of his conflicting desires and of the unity given by his calling, his sense of purpose.

This book is intended for everyone who wants to practise the art of wisdom, those who cannot give themselves wholly to science, religion, psychiatry, ideology, or any mass movement. It is for people who recognize the attraction of traditional human values in this time of historical crisis – people who want to remain engaged in their special life-pursuits, while at the same time responding to the call for real meaning.

Many people, in all walks of life, are realizing that they literally cannot live without philosophy and are returning to the philosophy classroom in search of the guidance philosophy can give them. They come with an impulse to question, sometimes with their questions still unformulated. It is hoped that they will find the selections in this book useful. They will not provide 'answers', but they will deepen and intensify the questioning process.

In the absence of real philosophy, other areas of knowledge tend to expand into the void, becoming more reflective, more 'philosophical'. We see this tendency in the contemporary physical sciences, which sometimes blend Eastern thought with the theories of the 'new physics'. There are now alternative views of health and illness, which try to treat the whole person. Institutional religion often attempts to mine the mystical or esoteric veins of the Judeo-Christian tradition. The social sciences have incorporated new concepts of consciousness and brain function; anthropology is sensitive to the mystery of man's origin and the power of myth and symbol; educational theory has begun to be critical of rote learning and vocational training. Even in the realms of business and finance the value of work, wealth and leadership is often questioned. The moral and intellectual foundations of every form of human activity are now being scrutinized, yet this still does not reach to the core of real philosophy.

The questions of real philosophy have a special quality that commands our attention. We must identify and nurture this quality; our hearts must be touched by these questions. The great questions of philosophy arise from somewhere deep inside us, from the child within us, and we long to think or dream about them. They have a compelling, magical quality, which is reflected in many of the extracts in this book.

The questions of real philosophy have a different 'taste' from those of academic philosophy, as it is officially taught. When it is too 'professionalized', philosophy recognizes only a limited canon of issues as 'problems of philosophy': there is, for instance, the 'mind–body problem', the 'problem of the external world', the 'problem of free will', and the like. These formulations are like the tracks in the forest left by a living creature, while the creature itself, the real question, is still alive and moving somewhere else. To approach the living question with the mind alone is impossible. The intellect must be coupled with feeling in order to stir a person to authentic inquiry. Real philosophy recognizes that ideas have sensations and emotions connected with them, and that one responds to them with the whole of oneself.

Each of us, as individuals, has at one time or another hungered to know what life is about. In every aspect of everyday living – in family life, on the job, in relationships, in health and illness – this need may make itself felt, often uninvited. When we are stirred by a scene of great beauty, upset by a turn in a friendship, astonished by some fact of science or history, or jolted out of our comfortable assumptions by some moral dilemma, then we become aware of the *power* of the philosophical impulse, because we are compelled to explore beyond the surface of things. Not knowing how to respond to this philosophical impulse leaves us frustrated, restless, unsatisfied. Much of what is called culture is simply a distraction from this unfulfilled yearning for philosophy; culture too often becomes an over-the-counter drug, a palliative that mitigates the symptoms of our need.

Real Philosophy is thus a compendium of the 'wider tradition' of philosophy. This has two essential characteristics. First, it is a world tradition, one that cuts across cultural frontiers. It knows no one place of origin, and so is particularly appropriate for our time, when 'world' and 'global village' have become synonymous. We are becoming more aware of the essential interdependence of one culture with another and the mutual support that different traditions give each other: any attempt to force philosophy into the mould of a single tradition or a single cultural perspective would therefore be self-defeating. Only a world tradition can show the strength of the guiding thread of philosophy, which operates similarly even in diverse cultural settings: only a world tradition can bring philosophy into focus in today's multi-cultural perspective.

Secondly, this wider tradition goes back to the basic function of philosophy as an essential stepping-stone on the way to self-knowledge and self-transformation. In Western culture, Socrates' injunction, 'Know thyself', stands at the beginning of this path of investigation. Platonic thought goes on to construct a vast system of reminders — mythic, speculative, logical, dramatic — that self-examination is our first task. After Plato, however, the emphasis on experiential self-knowledge becomes less important in what is usually considered to be 'mainstream' philosophy. The wider tradition, real philosophy, bypasses much of Aristotle, scholastic thought, and the rational-empirical philosophies of the modern era, but includes thinkers such as Scotus Erigena, Nicolas of Cusa, Spinoza, and Kierkegaard, and can also be recognized in the Hermetic and Neoplatonic schools of thought and in certain 'alchemical' philosophers of the Renaissance.

Real Philosophy includes readings from many spiritual traditions: Hindu, Buddhist, Taoist, Islamic, Sufi, Jewish and Christian. All contribute to the essential function of philosophy, that of guidance. Through the selections, we attempt to reassess this neglected stream of thought, and at the same time to counterbalance both modern humanism and 'mainstream' philosophy.

The 'wider tradition' centres on the ability *to ask*; not in *knowing* but in *asking* does the real activity of philosophy lie. Only by heartfelt questioning can we cut through the irrelevancies of our contemporary preoccupation with information. Our technocentric age depends on modern science for its survival and turns to empty ritual or the irrational for solace. We need to break the spell of both 'scientism' and 'religionism' to rediscover our own moral worth. It is the aim of *Real Philosophy* to assist in this quest.

PART ONE

Who am I?

In moments of emotional crisis, extreme physical duress, or penetrating reflection, people often sense a fundamental uncertainty about their lives. In such times, the ideas by which a person understands himself or herself collapse, revealing a new depth of existence. Habitually accepted self-images fall to one side and one begins to question one's identity. More exactly, that identity has become a question. One asks, with deep feeling, 'Who am I?'

The crisis reveals a condition of existence that is unnoticed until the veils — the deceptions, false beliefs, unfounded expectations, unrealizable ideals — behind which one hides are rent in two. Like a movement seen out of the corner of the eye, the unheeded question has from time to time impinged, leaving one disquieted. It is the task of understanding to address this situation squarely, to see illusion as such. 'But the task appeared enormous,' Descartes, whose approach to it revolutionized an entire tradition of thought, confessed, 'and I put it off till I should reach such a mature age that no increased aptitude for learning anything was likely to follow.' The crisis may begin with the recognition of the disparity between how one appears to be and what one really is. As Descartes discovered, a kind of doubt arises that has the power to penetrate one's most cherished beliefs and reveal them in a new, questioning light. With this illumination, inquiry is born, inquiry into the self. For Descartes, the mind is repeatedly distracted by matters of peripheral interest but eventually concentrates on one central point, the self. His aim was to find something which 'was so certain and so evident that all of the most extravagant suppositions of the sceptics were not capable of shaking it' on which to found his philosophy.

The nature of self-knowledge can be compared to the nature of visual perception, which may be affected by a malfunction of one's eye. If, for instance, the corneal lens is scratched, the image of everything seen is distorted by the injury. In the same way, if a person's view of himself or herself is unclear, everything thought, felt, or perceived is equally unprecise. Ordinarily, we tend to reason from what is outside ourselves back to the self, saying, 'The sunset inspired me,' or 'My friend hurt me.' But in fact this order reverses the one inherent in reality. As the Hindu philosopher Ramana Maharishi (1879–1950) puts it, 'It is after the appearance of the first personal pronoun that the second and third personal pronouns appear.'

Because the attention is habitually drawn to the external, a whole new orientation is needed to explore the self. 'I am bewildered,' Descartes reports, 'as though I had suddenly fallen into a deep sea, and could neither plant my foot on the bottom nor swim up to the top.' How is one to navigate the unfamiliar waters, once one has apprehended the disparity between how one appears to be and what one really is? This is a question of method and approach. In general, it can be said that there are two major approaches, that of inclusion and that of negation. Both Descartes and the *Upanishads* practise the second. For Descartes, it is a matter of rejecting 'whatever admits of the least doubt'. According to the *Upanishads*, each particular thought or experience is to be met with the assertion that it is 'not this, not that' (*neti, neti*). In both cases, one resolves not to accept any state, condition, or event as definitive of the self; the self is open-ended, a process or an unfolding. By analogy, one may 'catch' a river in a bucket, but what one has in the bucket is not the river, but a pailful of water.

Kierkegaard views the stuff of selfhood as activity, the activity of relating parts of oneself (thoughts, desires, passions, sensations) to a whole. To stop this activity by saying, 'I am angry,' or 'I am sure you're wrong,' is to miss the self, to accept a very partial account for the whole. Kierkegaard's method is to include each aspect of every moment; one is continually trying to enlarge the boundaries of one's identity, never to say, 'I am only this and no more.'

Whether a person embarks on an inquiry into the self from an abrupt, raw confrontation with an unknown reality or by careful intellectual assessment of his or her situation, the question of man's ultimate nature arises. 'Who am I?' leads one to ask, 'What kind of being am I?' 'What kind of nature do I have?' Three kinds of answers emerge from the widely varying schools of thought.

The first holds that we have a dual nature, each aspect of which has equal claim to reality and knowledge. One side of us lives by habit, mechanically, accepting the values prescribed by the prevailing social ideals. This side of us, directed towards pleasure-seeking, is, according to Plato, earth-bound. It tends to become attached now to this thing, now to that; fixed opinions, assertive statements, aggressiveness, and closed-mindedness are its marks. It is ceaselessly entangled in disputes, with an air of self-justification. The other aspect of us, the *psyche* or soul, is, as Plato says, 'immortal, for that which is ever in motion is immortal'. It embodies an unending search for a knowledge of 'the good, the true, and the beautiful'. It has the power to see through illusion and to form an objective view of the forces affecting human life. Because it does not diminish us as our subjective biases do, Plato refers to this principle as the divine in man. Although we all partake of both natures, it would be wrong to think the two coexist peacefully. Rather, the contradictions, revealed in moments of crisis, result from the never-ending clash between these two aspects.

A second school of thought sees our nature as single, not dual. Man's composition is unmixed because ultimately the self and the whole universe enjoy the same undifferentiated being, and the self is enlarged to include everything that exists. In this view, the only true oneness is wholeness. Unity is totality. In the *Upanishads*, this is expressed as '*atman* is *Brahman*', or self *is* all existence. In addition, the reason why one appears to want so many conflicting things, to hold contrary views, and to entertain inconsistent

21

thoughts about oneself and the world, is explained: the creative but as-yet undisciplined power of thought is the culprit. Ramana Maharishi draws an analogy: 'Just as the spider emits the thread out of itself and again withdraws it into itself, likewise the mind projects the world out of itself and again resolves it into itself.' The path of self-inquiry clarifies the distinction between what is merely imagined and what actually is. It lessens our adherence to the myth of our separateness from nature, the assumption that we stand apart from nature and that nature is there for our exploitation and private enjoyment. It causes us to wonder whether our fascination with diversity is a distraction from seeking the single-mindedness that a unitary nature implies.

The third response to the question 'What kind of nature do I have?' is more abrupt. According to this response, there is no nature because there is no self: the self is a convenient fiction, a belief that vanishes like a mirage when subjected to closer inspection. The words 'I' or 'myself' refer to nothing, but by repeating them we create and perpetuate for ourselves an elaborate biography, a physical identity, a future history. We come to place our trust in the verbal formulas, not questioning the underlying reality. Reality – mental, emotional, or physical – is unaffected by the habit that says, 'This is me', 'This is mine', but the thought of self obscures the true nature of experience from us. Buddhism affirms the non-existence of the self, and holds that the idea of the self is the cause of our felt frustrations, anguish, despair, and doubt. For the Buddhist, a person is truly without self-nature, but only a strong commitment to the examination of ongoing experience can root out the notion of self and reveal things as they actually are. The Buddhist views freedom as the eradication of the idea of self and believes that our arrogance, self-importance, and callousness to the pain of others will disappear if we concentrate on the pure and uncontaminated experiences of living.

Agreement on how best to approach the nature of the self is notably lacking. Some thinkers, including early critics of Descartes, have held that the proper sequel to the question 'Who am I?' is not 'What kind of being am I?', but rather 'Am I?' The call to verify one's existence, to cease to hold it as a given, is part of Kierkegaard's thought. One becomes, in Plato's striking image, midwife to one's own birthing. The crisis which marks one's first questioning of one's identity is, to this way of thinking, like birth-pangs – the precursor of birth – rather than an illness. 'Even as a teething child feels an aching and pain in its gums when a tooth has just come through,' Plato says, 'so does the soul of him who is beginning to grow his wings feel a ferment and painful irritation.' The very act of questioning the nature of his existence allows a person to begin to participate in a more organic process, the growth of a 'something' whose essence transcends fleeting experience and which therefore has special claims to existence. Though this 'something' can be named and described, language can only give an approximation, as it does of the subtle sensations inspired by a mountain sunset. For these thinkers, thought is not exhausted by language, for in its higher reaches it has the power to bring a person closer to being. Thought discerns, at the core of one's life, the seed or potential for becoming.

Our Western intellects are strongly attracted to systems and formulations; our pure sciences, technological insights, and industrial organization all testify to this. It therefore needs to be emphasized that self-inquiry defies all systemization. The traces that other thinkers have left are best described, not by a straight path, but by a circuitous and winding route. However, pursuing the question 'Who am I?' does not mean entering a lawless land where no truth endures for long. On the contrary, as Plato warns us, necessity rules everything. The laws are everywhere the same, but difficult to determine, demanding a personal effort from those who want to discover them. The *Upanishads* remind us that self-knowledge 'is not to be obtained by instruction, nor by intellect, nor by much learning'. In the pursuit of self-knowledge, there is room for what to the ordinary mind appears irrational and ungrounded. When journeying over the shifting sands of inquiry, perseverance and resourcefulness count for more than instructions learned by rote.

How can the unknown ever become known? How does one recognize it? For if it is recognizable, the fact must in a sense have been known already. The paradox of inquiry is heightened in the case of the self. The one who raises the question 'Who am I?', is the very same person who is the object of the investigation. It is as if the eye were supposed to include itself in the field of vision. That this is possible is an indication of the enigmatic or mysterious element in self-inquiry. Suddenly, quite unexpectedly, one is confronted with the fact of one's existence. Abstract analysis or speculation is suddenly seen to be of limited use; a childlike naïvety is a more effective attitude in the presence of the unknownness surrounding one's own self. Myths, fables, and teaching tales provide a rich source of material that can turn the mind in a new direction. The ability to appreciate 'crazy wisdom', the unconventional, intuitive approach – as the Turkish folk hero Mulla Nasrudin does – marks the beginnings of thought's new quest.

PLATO, *THE PHAEDRUS*

From *The Dialogues of Plato*, translated by B. Jowett, New York, Random House, 1920

Plato (427?–347 BC), born of an aristocratic family of Athens, was the foremost student of Socrates. His writings, in the form of dialogues, open almost all the great questions of Western thought, from metaphysics to ethics, from aesthetics to politics. He founded a school of philosophy, the Academy, and taught Aristotle.

Plato maintains that a human being has two natures. One has upward tendencies, the second, downward. Each is inescapable and necessary. Self-mastery, or the acceptance of one's real identity, consists not in denying the lower in favour of the higher, but in training, educating, and influencing it. Plato uses the memorable image of two horses pulling a chariot.

As I said at the beginning of this tale, I divided each soul into three — two horses and a charioteer; and one of the horses was good and the other bad: the division may remain, but I have not yet explained in what the goodness or badness of either consists, and to that I will proceed. The right-hand horse is upright and cleanly made; he has a lofty neck and an aquiline nose; his colour is white, and his eyes dark; he is a lover of honour and modesty and temperance, and the follower of true glory; he needs no touch of the whip, but is guided by word and admonition only. The other is a crooked, lumbering animal, put together anyhow; he has a short, thick neck; he is flat-faced and of a dark colour, with grey eyes and blood-red complexion;* the mate of insolence and pride, shag-eared and deaf, hardly yielding to whip and spur. Now when the charioteer beholds the vision of love, and has his whole soul warmed through sense, and is full of the prickings and ticklings of desire, the obedient steed, then as always under the government of shame, refrains from leaping on the beloved; but the other, heedless of the pricks and of the blows of the whip, plunges and runs away, giving all manner of trouble to his companion and the charioteer, whom he forces to approach the beloved and to remember the joys of love. They at first indignantly oppose him and will not be urged on to do terrible and unlawful deeds; but at last, when he persists in plaguing them, they yield and agree to do as he bids them. And now they are on the spot and behold the flashing beauty of the beloved; which, when the charioteer sees,

*Or, with grey and blood-shot eyes. (Trans.)

his memory is carried to the true beauty, whom he beholds in company with Modesty like an image placed upon a holy pedestal. He sees her, but he is afraid and falls backwards in adoration, and by his fall is compelled to pull back the reins with such violence as to bring both the steeds on their haunches, the one willing and unresisting, the unruly one very unwilling; and when they have gone back a little, the one is overcome with shame and wonder, and his whole soul is bathed in perspiration; the other, when the pain is over which the bridle and the fall had given him, having with difficulty taken breath, is full of wrath and reproaches, which he heaps upon the charioteer and his fellow-steed, for want of courage and manhood, declaring that they have been false to their agreement and guilty of desertion. Again they refuse, and again he urges them on, and will scarce yield to their prayer that he would wait until another time. When the appointed hour comes, they make as if they had forgotten, and he reminds them, fighting and neighing and dragging them on, until at length he, on the same thoughts intent, forces them to draw near again. And when they are near he stoops his head and puts up his tail, and takes the bit in his teeth and pulls shamelessly. Then the charioteer is worse off than ever; he falls back like a racer at the barrier, and with a still more violent wrench drags the bit out of the teeth of the wild steed and covers his abusive tongue and jaws with blood, and forces his legs and haunches to the ground and punishes him sorely. And when this has happened several times and the villain has ceased from his wanton way, he is tamed and humbled, and follows the will of the charioteer, and when he sees the beautiful one he is ready to die of fear. And from that time forward the soul of the lover follows the beloved in modesty and holy fear.

And so the beloved who, like a god, has received every true and loyal service from his lover, not in pretence but in reality, being also himself of a nature friendly to his admirer, if in former days he has blushed to own his passion and turned away his lover because his youthful companions or others slanderously told him that he would be disgraced, now, as years advance, at the appointed age and time, is led to receive him into communion. For fate, which has ordained that there shall be no friendship among the evil, has also ordained that there shall ever be friendship among the good. And the beloved, when he has received him into communion and intimacy, is quite amazed at the goodwill of the lover; he recognizes that the inspired friend is worth all other friends or kinsmen; they have nothing of friendship in them worthy to be compared with his. And when his feeling continues and he is nearer to him and embraces him in gymnastic exercises and at other times of meeting, then the fountain of that stream, which Zeus when he was in love with Ganymede named Desire, overflows upon the lover, and some enters into his soul, and some when he is filled flows out again; and as a breeze or an echo rebounds from the smooth rocks and returns whence it came, so does the stream of beauty, passing through the eyes, which are the windows of the soul, come back to the beautiful one; there arriving and quickening the passages of the wings, watering them and inclining them to grow, and filling the soul of the beloved also with love. And thus he loves, but he knows not what; he does not understand and cannot explain his own state; he appears to have caught the infection of blindness from another; the lover is his mirror in which he is beholding himself, but he is not aware of this. When he is with the lover, both cease from their pain, but when he is away then he longs as he is longed for, and has love's image, love for love [*Anteros*], lodging in his breast, which he calls and believes to be not love but friendship only, and his desire is as the desire of the other, but weaker; he wants to see him, touch him, kiss, embrace him, and probably not long afterwards his desire is accomplished. When they meet, the wanton steed of the lover has a word to say to the charioteer; he would like to have a little pleasure

in return for many pains, but the wanton steed of the beloved says not a word, for he is bursting with passion which
he understands not; he throws his arms round the lover and
embraces him as his dearest friend; and, when they are side by
side, he is not in a state in which he can refuse the lover
anything, if he ask him; although his fellow-steed and the charioteer oppose him with the arguments of shame and reason.
After this their happiness depends upon their self-control; if the
better elements of the mind which lead to order and philosophy
prevail, then they pass their life here in happiness and harmony
— masters of themselves and orderly — enslaving the vicious
and emancipating the virtuous elements of the soul; and when
the end comes, they are light and winged for flight, having
conquered in one of the three heavenly or truly Olympian victor-
ies; nor can human discipline or divine inspiration confer any
greater blessing on man than this. If, on the other hand, they
leave philosophy and lead the lower life of ambition, then
probably, after wine or in some other careless hour, the two
wanton animals take the two souls when off their guard and
bring them together, and they accomplish that desire of their
hearts which to the many is bliss; and this having once en-
joyed they continue to enjoy, yet rarely, because they have
not the approval of the whole soul. They too are dear, but
not so dear to one another as the others, either at the time of
their love or afterwards. They consider that they have given and
taken from each other the most sacred pledges, and they may
not break them and fall into enmity. At last they pass out of
the body, unwinged, but eager to soar, and thus obtain no
mean reward of love and madness. For those who have once
begun the heavenward pilgrimage may not go down again to
darkness and the journey beneath the earth, but they live in
light always; happy companions in their pilgrimage, and when
the time comes at which they receive their wings they have the
same plumage because of their love.

DESCARTES, *THE MEDITATIONS*

From René Descartes, *The Philosophical Works of Descartes*, translated by E. Haldane and G. R. T. Ross, Cambridge University Press, 1911

René Descartes (1596–1650) is acknowledged to be a founder of modern thought. He rejected scholasticism and returned philosophy to its basic quest for the self, as well as discovering principles of geometry, algebra, optics, and earth sciences. His philosophical importance derives from his original method, and his placing of his own experience at the centre of the stage.

Descartes sets off in a new direction, questioning his own nature. To ask 'Who am I?' is to initiate a broad inquiry into one's own experience. It is to cast doubt on all the assumptions one holds about oneself and the world. Coming to this point, Descartes makes his famous discovery that 'I think, therefore I am.'

*It is now some years since I detected how many were the false beliefs that I had from my earliest youth admitted as true, and how doubtful was everything I had since constructed on this basis; and from that time I was convinced that I must once for all seriously undertake to rid myself of all the opinions which I had formerly accepted, and commence to build anew from the foundation, if I wanted to establish any firm and permanent structure in the sciences. But as this enterprise appeared to be a very great one, I waited until I had attained an age so mature that I could not hope that at any later date I should be better fitted to execute my design. This reason caused me to delay so long that I should feel that I was doing wrong were I to occupy in deliberation the time that yet remains for me for action. Today, then, since very opportunely for the plan I have in view I have delivered my mind from every care [and am happily agitated by no passions] and

*Phrases in square brackets are from Descartes's first edition published in Paris in 1641; the bulk of the translation is made from the second edition, published in Holland.

since I have procured for myself an assured leisure in a peaceable retirement, I shall at last seriously and freely address myself to the general upheaval of all my former opinions.

Now for this object it is not necessary that I should show that all of these are false — I shall perhaps never arrive at this end. But inasmuch as reason already persuades me that I ought no less carefully to withhold my assent from matters which are not entirely certain and indubitable than from those which appear to me manifestly to be false, if I am able to find in each one some reason to doubt, this will suffice to justify my rejecting the whole. And for that end it will not be requisite that I should examine each in particular, which would be an endless undertaking; for owing to the fact that the destruction of the foundations of necessity brings with it the downfall of the rest of the edifice, I shall only in the first place attack those principles upon which all my former opinions rested.

All that up to the present time I have accepted as most true and certain I have learned either from the senses or through the senses; but it is sometimes proved to me that these senses are deceptive, and it is wiser not to trust entirely to any thing by which we have once been deceived.

But it may be that although the senses sometimes deceive us concerning things which are hardly perceptible, or very far away, there are yet many others to be met with as to which we cannot reasonably have any doubt, although we recognize them by their means. For example, there is the fact that I am here, seated by the fire, attired in a dressing-gown, having this paper in my hands and other similar matters. And how could I deny that these hands and this body are mine, were it not perhaps that I compare myself to certain persons, devoid of sense, whose cerebella are so troubled and clouded by the violent vapours of black bile that they constantly assure us that they think they are kings when they are really quite poor, or that they are clothed in purple when they are really without covering, or who imagine that they have an earthenware head or are nothing but pumpkins or are made of glass. But they are mad, and I should not be any the less insane were I to follow examples so extravagant.

At the same time I must remember that I am a man, and that consequently I am in the habit of sleeping, and in my dreams representing to myself the same things or sometimes even less probable things than do those who are insane in their waking moments. How often has it happened to me that in the night I dreamt that I found myself in this particular place, that I was dressed and seated near the fire, whilst in reality I was lying undressed in bed! At this moment it does indeed seem to me that it is with eyes awake that I am looking at this paper; that this head which I move is not asleep, that it is deliberately and of set purpose that I extend my hand and perceive it; what happens in sleep does not appear so clear nor so distinct as does all this. But in thinking over this I remind myself that on many occasions I have in sleep been deceived by similar illusions, and in dwelling carefully on this reflection I see so manifestly that there are no certain indications by which we may clearly distinguish wakefulness from sleep that I am lost in astonishment. And my astonishment is such that it is almost capable of persuading me that I now dream.

Now let us assume that we are asleep and that all these particulars, e.g. that we open our eyes, shake our head, extend our hands, and so on, are but false delusions; and let us reflect that possibly neither our hands nor our whole body are such as they appear to us to be. At the same time we must at least confess that the things which are represented to us in sleep are like painted representations which can only have been formed as the counterparts of something real and true, and that in this way those general things at least, i.e. eyes, a head, hands, and a whole body, are not imaginary things, but things really existent. For, as a matter of fact, painters, even when they study with the greatest skill to represent sirens and satyrs by forms the most strange and extraordinary, cannot give them natures which are entirely new, but merely make a certain medley of the members of different animals; or if their imagination is extravagant enough to invent something so novel that nothing similar has ever before been seen, and that then their work represents a thing purely fictitious and absolutely false, it is certain all the same that the colours of which this is composed are necessarily real. And for the same reason, although these general things, to wit, [a body], eyes, a head, hands, and such like, may be imaginary, we are bound at the same time to confess that there are at least some other objects yet more simple and more universal, which are real and true; and of these just in the same way as with certain real colours, all these images of things which dwell in our thoughts, whether true and real or false and fantastic, are formed.

To such a class of things pertains corporeal nature in general, and its extension, the figure of extended things, their quantity of magnitude and number, as also the place in which they are, the time which measures their duration, and so on.

That is possibly why our reasoning is not unjust when we conclude from this that Physics, Astronomy, Medicine and all other sciences which have as their end the consideration of composite things, are very dubious and uncertain; but that Arithmetic, Geometry and other sciences of that kind which only treat of things that are very simple and very general, without taking great trouble to ascertain whether they are actually existent or not, contain some measure of certainty and an element of the indubitable. For whether I am awake or asleep, two and three together always form five, and the square can never have more than four sides, and it does not seem possible that truths so clear and apparent can be suspected of any falsity [or uncertainty].

Nevertheless I have long had fixed in my mind the belief that an all-powerful God existed by whom I have been created such as I am. But how do I know that He has not brought it to pass that there is no earth, no heaven, no extended body, no magnitude, no place, and that nevertheless [I possess the perceptions of all these things and that] they seem to me to exist just exactly as I now see them? And, besides, as I sometimes imagine that others deceive themselves in the things which they think they know best, how do I know that I am not deceived every time that I add two and three, or count the sides of a square, or judge of things yet simpler, if anything simpler can be imagined? But possibly God has not desired that I should be thus deceived, for He is said to be supremely good. If, however, it is contrary to His goodness to have made me such that I constantly deceive myself, it would also appear to be contrary to His goodness to permit me to be sometimes deceived, and nevertheless I cannot doubt that He does permit this.

There may indeed be those who would prefer to deny the existence of a God so powerful, rather than believe that all other things are uncertain. But let us not oppose them for the present, and grant that all that is here said of God is a fable; nevertheless in whatever way they suppose that I have arrived at the state of being that I have reached – whether they attribute it to fate or to accident, or make out that it is by a continual succession of antecedents or by some other method – since to err and deceive oneself is a defect, it is clear that the greater will be the probability of my being so imperfect as to deceive myself ever, as is the Author to whom they assign my origin the less powerful. To these reasons I have certainly nothing to reply, but at the end I feel constrained to confess that there is nothing in all that I formerly believed to be true, of which I cannot in some measure doubt, and that not merely through want of thought or through levity, but for reasons which are very powerful and maturely considered; so that henceforth I ought not the less carefully to refrain from giving credence to these opinions than to that which is manifestly false, if I desire to arrive at any certainty [in the sciences].

But it is not sufficient to have made these remarks; we must also be careful to keep them in mind. For these ancient and commonly held opinions still revert frequently to my mind, long and familiar custom having given them the right to occupy my mind against my inclination and rendered them almost masters of my belief; nor will I ever lose the habit of deferring to them or of placing my confidence in them, so long as I consider them as they really are, i.e. opinions in some measure doubtful, as I have just shown, and at the same time highly probable, so that there is much more reason to believe in than to deny them. That is why I consider that I shall not be acting amiss, if, taking of set purpose a contrary belief, I allow myself to be deceived, and for a certain time pretend that all these opinions are entirely false and imaginary, until at last, having thus balanced my former prejudices with my latter [so that they cannot divert my opinions more to one side than to the other], my judgement will no longer be dominated by bad usage or turned away from the right knowledge of the truth. For I am assured that there can be neither peril nor error in this course, and that I cannot at present yield too much to distrust, since I am not considering the question of action, but only of knowledge.

I shall then suppose, not that God who is supremely good and the fountain of truth, but some evil genius not less powerful than deceitful, has employed his whole energies in deceiving me; I shall consider that the heavens, the earth, colours, figures, sound, and all other external things are nought but the illusions and dreams of which this genius has availed himself in order to lay traps for my credulity; I shall consider myself as having no hands, no eyes, no flesh, no blood, nor any senses, yet falsely believing myself to possess all these things; I shall remain obstinately attached to this idea, and if by this means it is not in my power to arrive at the knowledge of any truth, I may at least do what is in my power [i.e. suspend my judgement], and with firm purpose avoid giving credence to any false thing, or being imposed upon by this arch deceiver, however powerful and deceptive he may be. But this task is a laborious one, and insensibly a certain lassitude leads me into the course of my ordinary life. And just as a captive who in sleep enjoys an imaginary liberty, when he begins to suspect that his liberty is but a dream, fears to awaken, and conspires with these agreeable illusions that the deception may be prolonged, so insensibly of my own accord I fall back into my former opinions, and I dread awakening from this slumber, lest the laborious wakefulness which would follow the tranquillity of this repose should have to be spent not in daylight, but in the excessive darkness of the difficulties which have just been discussed.

The Meditation of yesterday filled my mind with so many doubts that it is no longer in my power to forget them. And yet I do not see in what manner I can resolve them; and, just as if I had all of a sudden fallen into very deep water, I am so disconcerted that I can neither make certain of setting my feet on the bottom, nor can I swim and so support myself on the surface. I shall nevertheless make an effort and follow anew the same path as that on which I yesterday entered, i.e. I shall proceed by setting aside all that in which the least doubt could be supposed to exist, just as if I had discovered that it was absolutely false; and I shall ever follow in this road until I have met with something which is certain, or at least, if I can do nothing else, until I have learned for certain that there is nothing in the world that is certain. Archimedes, in order that he might draw the terrestrial globe out of its place, and transport it elsewhere, demanded only that one point should be fixed and immoveable; in the same way I shall have the right to conceive high hopes if I am happy enough to discover one thing only which is certain and indubitable.

I suppose, then, that all the things that I see are false; I persuade myself that nothing has ever existed of all that my fallacious memory represents to me. I consider that I possess no senses; I imagine that body, figure, extension, movement and place are but the fictions of my mind. What, then, can be esteemed as true? Perhaps nothing at all, unless that there is nothing in the world that is certain.

But how can I know there is not something different from those things that I have just considered, of which one cannot have the slightest doubt? Is there not some God, or some other being by whatever name we call it, who puts these reflections into my mind? That is not necessary, for is it not possible that I am capable of producing them myself? I myself, am I not at least something? But I have already denied that I had senses and body. Yet I hesitate, for what follows from that? Am I so dependent on body and senses that I cannot exist without these? But I was persuaded that there was nothing in all the world, that there was no heaven, no earth, that there were no minds, nor any bodies: was I not then likewise persuaded that I did not exist? Not at all; of a surety I myself did exist since I persuaded myself of something [or merely because I thought of something]. But there is some deceiver or other, very powerful and very cunning, who ever employs his ingenuity in deceiving me. Then without doubt I exist also if he deceives me, and let him deceive me as much as he will, he can never cause me to be nothing so long as I think that I am something. So that after having reflected well and carefully examined all things, we must come to the definite conclusion that this proposition: *I am, I exist*, is necessarily true each time that I pronounce it, or that I mentally conceive it . . .

'SIR LAUNCELOT'S DREAM'

From Howard Pyle, *The Story of the Grail and the Passing of Arthur*, New York, Charles Scribner's Sons, 1910

The legend of King Arthur's search for the Holy Grail is well known. The meaning of that vessel, and what is contained therein, gives us a vibrant symbol of the mystery of our being. In this excerpt, we read of Sir Launcelot's encounter with the object of his quest. Because of an earlier betrayal, however, he is unable to seize on that moment and bring his quest to a successful conclusion.

Sir Launcelot rode for the rest of the day without meeting further adventure, until about evening time, when he came to a bare and naked knoll covered with furze bushes. Here, in the midst of that wild, he beheld an ancient ruined chapel, and he said to himself, 'Here will I rest me for the night.' So he rode around that chapel, seeking for the door thereof, but he could find no door upon any side of the chapel, but only windows, very high raised from the ground. Then Sir Launcelot said, 'This is a very strange chapel that it should have no doors, but only windows so high that I cannot enter by them. Now I will rest here and see what is the meaning of this place.'

So saying, he dismounted from his horse, and lay down beneath a thorn-bush that was not far distant from the chapel.

Now, as Sir Launcelot lay there, a drowsiness began to descend upon him, and though he could not sleep yet it was as though he did sleep, for he could move nor hand nor foot. Yet was he conscious of all that passed about him as though he had been wide awake. For he was conscious of the dark and silent vaults of sky, sprinkled all over with an incredible number of stars, and he was conscious of his horse cropping the herbage beside him in the darkness, and he was conscious of the wind that blew across his face, and that moved the corner of his cloak in the silence of the night time. Of all these things was he conscious, and yet he could not move of his own will so much as a single hair.

Anon, whilst he lay in that wise he was presently aware that some people were approaching the chapel in the darkness, for he heard the sound of voices and of the feet of horses moving upon the road. So, in a little while, there came to that place a knight and an esquire. And the knight was very sorely wounded, for his armour was broken and shattered by battle, and the esquire sustained him in the saddle so that, except for the upholding of the esquire's arm and hand, he would have fallen prostrate down upon the ground.

Then Sir Launcelot, as he lay in that waking sleep, heard the knight say to the esquire, 'Floradaine, is the chapel near at hand, for mine eyes are failing and I cannot see?' And the esquire wept and he said, 'Yea, Lord, it is here. Sustain yourself but for a little and you will be there.'

Therewith the esquire drew rein and he dismounted from his horse and he lifted the knight down from his charger, and the knight groaned very dolorously as the esquire lifted him down. Then, breathing very heavily and with great labour, the knight said, 'Floradaine, is there a light?' And the esquire said, 'Not yet, Messire.' Again, after a little, the knight said, 'Is there yet a light?' And again the esquire answered, 'Not yet, Messire.' And again, after awhile, the knight said for the third time, 'Floradaine, is there yet a light?' And this time the knight breathed the words, as in a whisper of death. Then of a sudden the esquire called out in a loud and joyful voice, 'Yea, Lord, now I behold a light!'

All this Sir Launcelot beheld in that waking dream, and though it was in the darkness of night, yet he beheld it very clearly, as though it were by the sun of noonday. For he beheld the face of the knight that it was white as of pure wax, and that the sweat of death stood in beads upon his forehead. And he beheld that the esquire was young and fair, and that he had long ringlets of yellow hair that curled down upon his shoulder. Then when the esquire said that he beheld a light, Sir Launcelot beheld the windows of the chapel that they were illuminated from within with a pale blue lustre, as though the dawn were shining in that chapel. And he heard the sound of chanting voices, at first very faint and far away, but anon ever growing stronger and stronger as the light from the chapel grew stronger. And those voices chanted a melody that was so sweet and ravishing that it caused the heart to melt as with an agony.

Then the walls of that chapel opened like a door and a light shone forth with a remarkable lustre so that it illuminated the face of that dying knight, and of the page who upheld him. And at the same time the song burst forth in great volume, as it were a thunder of chanting.

Then forthwith there came out of the chapel a bright shining spear, and two fair hands held the spear by the butt, yet Sir Launcelot could not behold the body to whom those two hands belonged. And after the spear there came forth a chalice, and two fair, white hands held that chalice, but neither could Sir Launcelot behold any body to which those hands belonged. And the chalice seemed to send forth a light of such dazzling radiance that it was as though one looked at the bright and shining sun in his glory.

Then Sir Launcelot was aware that this was the Holy Grail of which he was in search, and he strove with all his might to arouse himself, but he could not do so. Then the tears burst out from his eyes and traced down his cheeks in streams, but still he could not arouse himself, but lay chained in that waking sleep.

So the chalice advanced towards that knight, but the knight had not the strength to reach forth and touch it. Then the esquire took the arm of the knight and raised it, and he raised the hand of the knight so that the hand touched the chalice.

Then it was as though Sir Launcelot beheld the virtue of the Grail go forth from it, and that it passed through the hand of the wounded knight, and that it passed through his arm and penetrated into his body. For he beheld that the blood ceased to flow from the wounded knight, and that the colour flooded back into his cheeks and that the light came back into his eyes and that the strength returned to his body.

Then the knight arose and he kneeled down before the Grail, and he set his palms together and he prayed before the Grail.

Then, slowly, the light that had been so bright from the Grail began to wane. First the spear disappeared, and then the hands that held it disappeared. Then, for a while, the Grail glowed with a faint, pallid light, and then it, too, vanished, and all was dark as it had been before.

So Sir Launcelot beheld the vision of the Grail, but as in the vision of a dream as I have told it here to you. And still the tears rained from his eyes, for he could not rouse himself to behold it with his waking eyes.

After this the knight and the esquire approached to the place where Sir Launcelot lay asleep, and the esquire said to the knight, 'Messire, who is this man, and why sleepeth he here whilst all these wonders pass him by?' And the knight said, 'This knight is a very sinful man, and his name is Sir Launcelot of the Lake.' Quoth the esquire, 'How hath he sinned?' To which the knight replied, 'He hath sinned in this way. He had a beautiful and gentle lady, and he deserted that wife for the sake of Queen Guinevere. So his lady went away and left him, and anon she gave birth to Galahad, and in that birth she also gave her life. So Sir Launcelot betrayed his wife, and because of that betrayal he now lieth sleeping, and he cannot waken until after we are gone away from this place.'

Then the esquire said to the knight, 'Messire, behold; here this knight hath a good, strong horse. Take thou this horse and leave thine own in its stead. For this horse is fresh and full of life, and thine is spent and weary with battle.' And the knight said, 'I will take that horse.'

Then, after they had gone, Sir Launcelot bestirred himself and awoke. And he would have thought that all that he had beheld was a dream, but he beheld the worn and weary horse of the knight was there, and that his horse was gone. Then he cried aloud in great agony of soul, 'Lord, my sin hath found me out!' And therewith he rushed about like a madman, seeking to find a way into that chapel, and finding no way.

So when the day broke he mounted the worn and weary horse that the knight had left, and he rode away from that place and back into the forest; and his head hung low upon his breast. When he had come into the forest and to the cell of the hermit thereof, he laid aside his armour and he kneeled down before the Hermit of the Forest, and confessed all his sins to him. And the Hermit of the Forest gave him absolution for these sins, and he said, 'Take peace, my son. For although thou shalt not behold the Grail in thy flesh, yet shall God forgive thee these sins of thine that lie so heavily upon thy soul.'

Then Sir Launcelot arose chastened from his confession. And he left his armour where it lay and assumed the garb of an anchorite. And he went away from that place, into the remoter recesses of the forest. There he dwelt in the caves and in the wilds, living upon the berries and the fruits of the forest. And he dwelt there a long time until he felt assured that God had forgiven him. Then he returned to his kind again; but never after that day was he seen to smile.

KATHA UPANISHAD

From *The Thirteen Principal Upanishads*, translated by R. E. Hume, Oxford University Press, 2nd ed., 1931

The Katha Upanishad *is one of the principal Upanishads, the writings of a philosophical movement of ancient India, beginning around the sixth century BC. In these explorations, the great questions of the meaning of life and the relation of the individual to the cosmos are examined in depth. In toto, they must be ranked with the foremost discoveries in the realm of thought.*

In the Katha Upanishad, *a pathway to the* atman *or soul is indicated in terms of the image of a chariot and its driver. It is implied that self-knowledge involves a certain correct ordering of the components of a person and a recognition of the lack of order in our ordinary situation.*

The Soul revealed to the unstriving elect

20. More minute than the minute, greater than the great,
    Is the Soul [Atman] that is set in the heart of a
      creature here.
    One who is without the active will [a-kratu] beholds
      Him, and becomes freed from sorrow —

The universal and the individual soul

1. There are two that drink of righteousness in the world
    of good deeds;
    Both are entered into the secret place [of the heart],
      and in the highest upper sphere.
    Brahma-knowers speak of them as 'light' and 'shade',
    And so do householders who maintain the five sacrificial
      fires, and those too who perform the triple Naciketas-
      fire.

The Naciketas sacrificial fire as an aid

2. This which is the bridge for those who sacrifice,
    And which is the highest imperishable Brahma
    For those who seek to cross over to the fearless farther
      shore —
    the Naciketas-fire may we master!

Parable of the individual soul in a chariot

3. Know thou the soul [atman, self] as riding in a chariot,
    The body as a chariot.
    Know thou the intellect [buddhi] as the chariot-driver,
    And the mind [manas] as the reins.
4. The senses [indriya], they say, are the horses;
    The objects of sense, what they range over.

The self combined with senses and mind
Wise men call 'the enjoyer' [*bhoktr*].

5. He who has not understanding [*a-vijnana*],
Whose mind is not constantly held firm –
His senses are uncontrolled,
Like the vicious horses of a chariot-driver.

6. He, however, who has understanding,
Whose mind is constantly held firm –
His senses are under control,
Like the good horses of a chariot-driver.

Intelligent control of the soul's chariot needed to arrive beyond reincarnation

7. He, however, who has not understanding,
Who is unmindful and ever impure,
Reaches not the goal,
But goes on to reincarnation [*samsara*].

8. He, however, who has understanding,
Who is mindful and ever pure,
Reaches the goal
From which he is born no more.

9. He, however, who has the understanding of a chariot-driver,
A man who reins in his mind –
He reaches the end of his journey,
That highest place of Vishnu.

The order of progression to the supreme Person

10. Higher than the senses are the object of sense.
Higher than the objects of sense is the mind [*manas*];

And higher than the mind is the intellect [*buddhi*].
Higher than the intellect is the Great Self [*Atman*].

11. Higher than the Great is the Unmanifest [*avyakta*].
    Higher than the Unmanifest is the Person.
    Higher than the Person there is nothing at all.
    That is the goal. That is the highest course.

The subtle perception of the all-pervading Soul

12. Though He is hidden in all things,
    That Soul [*Atman*, self] shines not forth.
    But he is seen by subtle seers
    With superior, subtle intellect.

KIERKEGAARD, *THE SICKNESS UNTO DEATH*

**From Soren Kierkegaard, *The Sickness unto Death*,
translated by Alistair Hannay, Penguin Books, 1989**

*Soren Kierkegaard (1815–55), the Danish philosopher, saw philosophy
as the expression of individual existence. Writing under different pseu-
donyms, he remained anti-systematic, believing that the matters of
ultimate concern lie beyond neat conceptualization. Though leading a
solitary and melancholic life, his thinking conveys a passion for the great
questions of the human condition.*

*Like Plato, Kierkegaard thinks of a person's basic identity as twofold.
It is a blending of opposites — finitude and infinitude, eternity and
the passing moment — the thorough mixing of these aspects into
a real unity. The synthesizing activity, he believes, has validity only
when a person takes cognizance of the fact that its source lies above
him, in a power which confers the possibility of actively knowing
the self.*

That despair is the sickness unto death

A

Despair is a sickness of the spirit, of the self, and so can have three forms: being unconscious in despair of having a self (inauthentic despair), not wanting in despair to be oneself, and wanting in despair to be oneself.

The human being is spirit. But what is spirit? Spirit is the self. But what is the self? The self is a relation which relates to itself, or that in the relation which is its relating to itself. The self is not the relation but the relation's relating to itself. A human being is a synthesis of the infinite and the finite, of the temporal and the eternal, of freedom and necessity. In short a synthesis. A synthesis is a relation between two terms. Looked at in this way a human being is not yet a self.

In a relation between two things the relation is the third term in the form of a negative unity, and the two relate to the relation, and in the relation to that relation; this is what is from the point of view of soul for soul and body to be in relation. If, on the other hand, the relation relates to itself, then this relation is the positive third, and this is the self.

Such a relation, which relates to itself, a self, must either have established itself or been established by something else.

If the relation which relates to itself has been established by something else, then of course the relation is the third term, but then this relation, the third term, is a relation which relates in turn to that which has established the whole relation.

Such a derived, established relation is the human self, a relation which relates to itself, and in relating to itself relates to something else. That is why there can be two forms of authentic despair. If the human self were self-established, there would only be a question of one form: not wanting to be itself, wanting to be rid of

45

itself. There could be no question of wanting in despair to be oneself. For this latter formula is the expression of the relation's (the self's) total dependence, the expression of the fact that the self cannot by itself arrive at or remain in equilibrium and rest, but only, in relating to itself, by relating to that which has established the whole relation. Indeed, so far from its being simply the case that this second form of despair (wanting in despair to be oneself) amounts to a special form on its own, all despair can in the end be resolved into or reduced to it. If a person in despair is, as he thinks, aware of his despair and doesn't refer to it mindlessly as something that happens to him (rather in the way someone suffering from vertigo talks through an internally caused delusion about a weight on his head, or its being as though something were pressing down on him, etc., neither the weight nor the pressure being anything external but an inverted image of the internal), and wants now on his own, all on his own, and with all his might to remove the despair, then he is still in despair and through all his seeming effort only works himself all the more deeply into a deeper despair. The imbalance in despair is not a simple imbalance but an imbalance in a relation that relates to itself and which is established by something else. So the lack of balance in that 'for-itself' relationship also reflects itself infinitely in the relation to the power which established it.

This then is the formula which describes the state of the self when despair is completely eradicated: in relating to itself and in wanting to be itself, the self is grounded transparently in the power that established it.

B

The possibility and actuality of despair

Is despair a merit or a defect? Purely dialectically it is both. If one

46

were to think of despair only in the abstract, without reference to some particular despairer, one would have to say it is an enormous merit . . .

Every actual moment of despair is to be referred back to its possibility; every moment he despairs he *brings it upon himself*; the time is constantly the present; nothing actual, past and done with, comes about; at every moment of actual despair the despairer bears with him all that has gone before as something present in the form of possibility.

This is because despair is an aspect of spirit, it has to do with the eternal in a person. But the eternal is something he cannot be rid of, not in all eternity. He cannot rid himself of it once and for all; nothing is more impossible. Every moment he doesn't have it, he must have cast or be casting it off – but it returns, that is, every moment he despairs he brings the despair upon himself. For despair is not a result of the imbalance, but of the relation which relates to itself. And the relation to himself is something a human being cannot be rid of, just as little as he can be rid of himself, which for that matter is one and the same thing, since the self is indeed the relation to oneself.

MILINDAPAHNA

From *Buddhism in Translations*, translated Warren, Cambridge, Harvard University Press, 1896

The Milindapahna, *or the* Questions of King Milinda, *is a text of classical Buddhism. Buddhism is a body of thought and practice which strives, through active study, to free the individual from all the impediments to attaining full human expression. The study begins with suffering and impermanence and ends with the realization that there is no self different from the cosmos as a whole.*

In the following passage, the question of whether the self has a real identity arises. The argument is negative. The conclusion is that we experience a succession of different impressions, but that no underlying unity exists.

17. No continuous personal identity

'*Bhante* Nagasena,' said the king, 'is a person when just born that person himself, or is he some one else?'

'He is neither that person,' said the elder, 'nor is he some one else.'

'Give an illustration.'

'What do you say to this, your majesty? When you were a young, tender, weakly infant lying on your back, was that your present grown-up self?'

'Nay, verily, *bhante*. The young, tender, weakly infant lying on its back was one person, and my present grown-up self is another person.'

'If that is the case, your majesty, there can be no such thing as a mother, or a father, or a teacher, or an educated man, or a righteous man, or a wise man. Pray, your majesty, is the mother of the *kalala** one person, the mother of the *abbuda** another person, the mother of the *pesi** another person, the mother of the *ghana** another person, the mother of the little child another person, and the mother of the grown-up man another person? Is it one person who is a student, and another person who has finished his education? Is it one person who commits a crime, and another person whose hands and feet are cut off?'

'Nay, verily, *bhante*. But what, *bhante*, would you reply to these questions?'

Said the elder, 'It was I, your majesty, who was a young, tender, weakly infant lying on my back, and it is I who am now grown up.

*Various stages of the embryo. (Trans.)

It is through their connection with the embryonic body that all these different periods are unified.'

'Give an illustration.'

'It is as if, your majesty, a man were to light a light – would it shine all night?'

'Assuredly, *bhante*, it would shine all night.'

'Pray, your majesty, is the flame of the first watch the same as the flame of the middle watch?'

'Nay, verily, *bhante*.'

'Is the flame of the middle watch the same as the flame of the last watch?'

'Nay, verily, *bhante*.'

'Pray, then, your majesty, was there one light in the first watch, another light in the middle watch, and a third light in the last watch?'

'Nay, verily, *bhante*. Through connection with that first light there was light all night.'

'In exactly the same way, your majesty, do the elements of being join one another in serial succession: one element perishes, another arises, succeeding each other as it were instantaneously. Therefore neither as the same nor as a different person do you arrive at your latest aggregation of consciousness.'

'Give another illustration.'

'It is as if, your majesty, new milk were to change in process of time into sour cream, and from sour cream into fresh butter, and from fresh butter into clarified butter. And if any one, your majesty, were to say that the sour cream, the fresh butter, and the clarified butter were each of them the very milk itself – now would he say well, if he were to say so?'

'Nay, verily, *bhante*. They came into being through connection with that milk.'

'In exactly the same way, your majesty, do the elements of being join one another in serial succession: one element perishes, another arises, succeeding each other as it were instantaneously. Therefore neither as the same nor as a different person do you arrive at your latest aggregate consciousness.'

'You are an able man, *bhante* Nagasena.'

'NOBODY REALLY KNOWS'

From Idries Shah, *The Tales of the Dervishes*, New York, Dutton, 1967

Idries Shah is a contemporary writer on Sufi philosophy. Sufi thought engages in a search for unifying one's experience of oneself and the world in order to communicate directly with the Absolute. It derives its language from Islam, although it probably pre-dated Muhammad (570–632).

Mulla Nasrudin is a popular Middle Eastern embodiment of 'crazy wisdom'. He here addresses the question of self.

Suddenly realizing that he did not know who he was, Mulla Nasrudin rushed into the street, looking for someone who might recognize him.

The crowds were thick, but he was in a strange town, and he found no familiar face.

Suddenly he found himself in a carpenter's shop.

'What can I do for you?' asked the craftsman, stepping forward.

Nasrudin said nothing.

'Perhaps you would like something made from wood?'

'First things first,' said the Mulla. 'Now, did you see me come into your shop?'

'Yes, I did.'

'Good. Now, have you ever seen me in your life before?'

'Never in my life.'

'Then how do you know it is *me*?'

PART TWO

Why am I Here?

'And lo, I was now in my thirtieth year, sticking in the same mire,' St Augustine writes, 'greedy of enjoying things present, which passed away and wasted my soul; while I said to myself, "Tomorrow I shall find it . . ."' St Augustine, in his *Confessions*, is describing an encounter with the question of life's meaning; he isolates the features — dull repetition, cloying pleasure, the empty passage of time — which characterize the lack of purpose he feels.

There is strong evidence that this kind of confrontation is preceded by a break in one's routine assessment of life and of one's values, desires and dreams. Most of us have not yet discovered a design to our existence, but have lulled ourselves into disregarding the issue. According to the Greek dramatist Sophocles, our situation is governed by forces outside ourselves much greater than those we have at our own disposal, and yet we take no account of them. At moments of particular importance we may have some sense of a fateful collision of influences that changes the whole direction of events; we may become aware of how insignificant, seen on the cosmic scale, are the effects of human will. Oedipus flees from his home in an attempt to avoid committing the terrible crimes which the oracle has foretold, but the more he tries to effect his escape, the more enmeshed he becomes in the events which lead to the fulfilment of the prophesy and the more he is forced to confront his own powerlessness. Only by relinquishing all claims to personal choice and following the course that is laid down for him does Oedipus gain a measure of freedom.

In the Greek view the disparity between the demands of

51

necessity and a person's individual hopes, desires, and aspirations gives rise to a sense of the tragic. The final chorus of *Oedipus Rex* chants, 'We must call no one happy who is of mortal race, until he has crossed life's border, free from pain.' A sense of purpose comes from acknowledging one's submission to higher powers and affirming them throughout the destined course of one's existence; not to recognize this leads to tragedy. A person is then dragged unwillingly to his or her fate, experiencing pain as a consequence. Or it may be that suffering is simply the inability to understand one's place in unfolding events.

Not all thinkers, however, would agree that this lack of acceptance of one's fate has to spell tragedy, or even that acknowledging one's place in the scheme of things necessarily leads to a meaningful life. In the 'Grand Inquisitor' scene from Dostoyevsky's *The Brothers Karamazov*, Alyosha is shown a world in which the people have given up their power to choose. The episode suggests that one's hunger for meaning is in itself a cause of suffering, but this hunger cannot be satisfied, nor can we escape from it. Dostoyevsky, in his relentless probing of our motivation for asking questions, suggests that the universe is without answers. If the aim of our search is to put an end to questioning, then we are bound to be disappointed and a source of our own unhappiness.

Simply asking the question 'What is the meaning of my life?' upsets one's equilibrium. Thinking along these lines soon leads one to the conclusion that in the scheme of things as a whole, the individual is totally unimportant. But if the question is not asked, life from birth and childhood to old age and death is a closed circle, bound always and for all time to repeat itself, without variation. Only the impulse to search for meaning opens our lives to something other than clockwork repetition. This impulse alone allows us to stand apart, at least for an instant, from the mechanical activity of an unquestioning existence. The imperative to search for meaning must, however, include a positive initiative — it is not enough merely to repeat words learned from elsewhere. What is required is an attempt to transform the whole person through questioning.

When we fail to inquire into the source of meaning, our lives, thinkers agree, are condemned to remain on a certain level; our 'aliveness' remains only a partial fulfilment of our potential. There is the danger of never responding to the call, of always taking things for granted. Even if we have once been roused from our easy assumptions, there is the danger that we will fall back again, into drowsiness, hypnosis, sleep. We were warned against this in the *Hymn of the Pearl*, whose hero travels to a foreign land in quest of the pearl of wisdom. Although he has it in his grasp, he becomes distracted, grows unmindful. The prince forgets his mission and his high station. He loses himself in the preoccupations of his new situation. The implication is that we must exert unwavering vigilance to prevent ourselves from being sidetracked. Just as an athlete (Plato is fond of this analogy) gets into training for running a mile, we must practise continually in order to make our minds 'fit'. To see the necessity for training in intellectual rigour is another, more positive, way of understanding the discrepancy between life and thought. It need not be that, as in classical tragedy, despair results from the unavoidable disharmony between our thinking and the course of our life. For the tragedian, thought is essentially both the cause and the expression of our anguish. For someone who places a search for meaning foremost, despair becomes a signal to seek out a new way of thinking, one which corresponds more fully to one's state of being. That we can become deeply involved with our search for meaning and then (as the prince did) doze off, indicates that our road passes through many diverse places. We invariably adapt to conditions which try us – sometimes at the expense of our commitment to inquiry. We are at times closer to understanding, but at other times farther off. Our inquiry is not continuous but an episode among the many episodes of our travels.

Closely related to the question of this chapter is another, 'What makes my life have meaning?' We may answer that it is one's resolve to face courageously the repeated threat of meaninglessness and the anxiety surrounding the loss of meaning. One is rarely able to predict how one will react to any course of events, least of all to suffering. Only by continuing to pursue the search for meaning, *in spite of* fear, confusion, hopelessness, and paralysis, does a person strengthen his capacity to question. Like a hunter who can wait patiently for hours in the same place until his prey appears, the person remains available to his life's meaning. The moment when things all come to 'make sense' — without there being a change in outward circumstance — is the moment in which meaning arises. Though we create all kinds of biographical facts — our careers, relationships, hobbies, interests — we are not creators, at the most fundamental level, of meaning. To believe that one is is to express the arrogance that leads Oedipus to his cataclysmic reversal. Thought guides a person to a basic openness, to a position from which he or she can receive an answer to the question. The force of such knowledge is very great. It can change the course of one's whole life.

The Grand Inquisitor tells Alyosha that 'the craving for universal unity is the third and last anguish of men'. When stripped of its cynicism, this is an instructive lesson. Regardless of emotional stress, physical hardship, or intellectual challenge, if one has a sense of one's wholeness, then life is meaningful. We express this idea when we glibly exclaim of a trivial event, 'That was meaningful for me.' If we are aware of our own integrity and our oneness with others we are convinced that our burden is worth bearing. When that insight is refused, through excruciating pain, undignified suffering (as in the concentration camp), or our own opinions about ourselves, we may feel cut off, isolated in self-interested beliefs. Strangely, precisely at the moment of refusal, the place of choice, of playing our part, is revealed. Even Oedipus, shackled by his fate, eventually chooses to face the fact of his disunity and his lack of meaning.

To ask about the meaning of our lives involves the rational aspect of our intelligence. But what is rationality and how does it fit into a quest for wholeness? We would be short-changing ourselves if we were to confine ourselves to our calculative, analytic, or critical skills. Our intelligence has feeling. It is perceptive. It has an emotional quality which we find at the highest levels of integrated thought. The *feel* of real thinking guides us. Aristotle has this in mind when he speaks of the highest good of man in terms of fulfilling one's function. To be in place: this is where we arrive in a moment of seeing ourselves as we are. Aristotle speaks of the special excellence we experience in such a moment. Things, the passing world, our immediate experience: all is impregnated with importance. We have arrived at the question which invites our response.

Finally we might ask ourselves what it is about the human condition that poses the question of life's meaning. Neither the anxiety nor the growth of understanding involved in such a search exists for animals. We face meaning as both a promise and a threat. When prepared, through diligence or need, to receive this knowledge, we are promised a role in fulfilling our own destiny. Unlike animals, we are something more than the playthings of nature (or of the gods, according to the Greek view). We attain an awareness of ourselves in relation to the world. If we do not succumb to the arrogance of an Oedipus, whose mistake was to feel himself master of his fate, this awareness gives us the opportunity to participate in the unfolding of a life of meaning. The task of understanding is, however, threatening when it overwhelms us with its enormous responsibility, when we sense that the stature of man is far greater than we allow, when we remain passive and unquestioning. From a certain viewpoint, the question itself comes like a cosmic dare: either perfect your situation or feel never-ending remorse because you have not tried.

SOPHOCLES, *OEDIPUS REX*

**Translated by R. C. Jebb, in *Complete Greek Drama*,
ed. W. Oates and E. O'Neill, New York, Random
House, 1938**

*Sophocles (495?–405? BC), Aeschylus and Euripides were the three
greatest writers of ancient Greek tragedy. Born to a wealthy family,
Sophocles showed himself from youth a master of tragic technique. Of
his 125 known plays, only seven are extant. Best known are the three
comprising the Oedipus trilogy.*

*Oedipus Rex is the story of a man who, in trying to avoid his
fate, collides with it. The shock of recognition reveals to him the
impossibility of running from himself. In this moment, his condition
shifts from that of ignorant leadership to wisdom and exile. Oedipus
speaks in this passage, at the very centre of his crisis, with supreme
candour.*

CHORUS: O dread fate for men to see, O most dreadful of all
that have met mine eyes! Unhappy one, what madness hath come
on thee? Who is the unearthly foe that, with a bound of more than
mortal range, hath made thine ill-starred life his prey?

Alas, alas, thou hapless one! Nay, I cannot e'en look on thee,
though there is much that I would fain ask, fain learn, much that
draws my wistful gaze – with such a shuddering dost thou fill me!

OEDIPUS: Woe is me! Alas, alas, wretched that I am! Whither,
whither am I borne in my misery? How is my voice swept abroad
on the wings of the air? Oh my Fate, how far has thou sprung?

CHORUS: To a dread place, dire in men's ears, dire in their sight.

OEDIPUS: O thou horror of darkness that enfoldest me, visi-
tant unspeakable, resistless, sped by a wind too fair!

Ay me! and once again, ay me!

How is my soul pierced by the stab of these goads, and withal by the memory of sorrows!

CHORUS: Yea, amid woes so many a twofold pain may well be thine to mourn and to bear.

OEDIPUS: Ah, friend, thou still art steadfast in thy tendance of me – thou still has patience to care for the blind man! Ah me! Thy presence is not hid from me – no, dark though I am, yet know I thy voice full well.

CHORUS: Man of dread deeds, how couldst thou in such wise quench thy vision? What more than human power urged thee?

OEDIPUS: Apollo, friends, Apollo was he that brought these woes to pass, these my sore, sore woes: but the hands that struck the eyes were none but mine, wretched that I am! Why was I to see, when sight could show me nothing sweet?

CHORUS: These things were even as thou sayest.

OEDIPUS: Say, friends, what can I more behold, what can I love, what greeting can touch mine ear with joy? Haste, lead me from the land, friends, lead me hence, the utterly lost, the thrice accursed, yea, the mortal most abhorred of heaven!

CHORUS: Wretched alike for thy fortune and for thy sense thereof, would that I had never so much as known thee!

OEDIPUS: Perish the man, whoe'er he was, that freed me in the pastures from the cruel shackle on my feet, and saved me from death, and gave me back to life – a thankless deed! Had I died then, to my friends and to thine own soul I had not been so sore a grief.

CHORUS: I also would have had it thus.

OEDIPUS: So had I not come to shed my father's blood, nor been called among men the spouse of her from whom I sprang: but now am I forsaken of the gods, son of a defiled mother, successor to his bed who gave me mine own wretched being: and if there be yet a woe surpassing woes, it hath become the portion of Oedipus.

CHORUS: I know not how I can say that thou hast counselled well: for thou wert better dead than living and blind.

OEDIPUS: Show me not at large that these things are not best done thus: give me counsel no more. For, had I sight, I know not with what eyes I could e'en have looked on my father, when I came to the place of the dead, aye, or on my miserable mother, since against both I have sinned such sins as strangling could not punish. But deem ye that the sight of children, born as mine were born, was lovely for me to look upon? No, no, not lovely to mine eyes for ever! No, nor was this town with its towered walls, nor the sacred statues of the gods, since I, thrice wretched that I am — I, noblest of the sons of Thebes — have doomed myself to know these no more, by mine own command that all should thrust away the impious one — even him whom gods have shown to be unholy — and of the race of Laius!

After bearing such a stain upon me, was I to look with steady eyes on this folk? No, verily: no, were there yet a way to choke the fount of hearing, I had not spared to make a fast prison of this wretched frame, that so I should have known nor sight nor sound; for 'tis sweet that our thought should dwell beyond the sphere of griefs.

Alas, Cithaeron, why hadst thou a shelter for me? When I was given to thee, why didst thou not slay me straightway, that so I might never have revealed my source to men? Ah, Polybus — ah,

Corinth, and thou that wast called the ancient house of my fathers, how seeming-fair was I, you nurseling, and what ills were festering beneath! For now I am found evil, and of evil birth. O ye three roads, and thou secret glen – thou coppice, and narrow way where three paths met – ye who drank from my hands that father's blood which was mine own – remember ye, perchance, what deeds I wrought for you to see – and then, when I came hither, what fresh deeds I went on to do?

O marriage-rites, ye gave me your birth, and when ye had brought me forth, again ye bore children to your child, ye created an incestuous kinship of fathers, brothers, sons – brides, wives, mothers – yea, all the foulest shame that is wrought among men! Nay, but 'tis unmeet to name what 'tis unmeet to do – haste ye, for the gods' love, hide me somewhere beyond the land, or slay me, or cast me into the sea, where ye shall never behold me more! Approach, deign to lay your hands on a wretched man; hearken, fear not, my plague can rest on no mortal beside.

'THE HYMN OF THE PEARL'

Gnostic, retold by Anne Twitty, in *Parabola*, Winter 1985

The Hymn of the Pearl, *from Coptic Gnostic sources dating back to the third century AD, tells the story of a prince's dangerous journey to a foreign land. Sent to bring back a treasure, he lapses into forgetfulness. We are given a clear image for the struggle to attain great knowledge, and the reminder that help is never far away.*

A small child. I was dwelling in my Father's palace, delighting in wealth and luxuries. My parents sent me from our home, the East, putting together a load of treasures. It was large, yet so light I could carry it alone. Gold from the land of Gilan, silver from

Gazzak the Great, chalcedonies from India, iris-hued opals from Kushan, and the hard adamant that cuts iron, they sent with me. They took my robe from me, my robe spangled with gold, and my mantle. And they made a covenant with me, and the covenant was written in my heart. It said:

> If you go down into Egypt
> and bring back the one Pearl
> the Pearl of the Sea
> that lies close to the loud-breathing Serpent
> then you shall wear once again
> your robe and your mantle
> and, with your brother, shall be
> heir to the kingdom.

I came out of the East, and with two guides, I travelled the hard and dangerous road. I passed by the borders of Maishan, the market of eastern merchants, and I reached the Land of Babel, and entered the walls of Sarbug. Further I went, into Egypt, and there my guides left me. At once I went to the Serpent, and settled close to the hole where he lay, waiting to take the Pearl, while he slept. Alone I was there, and lonely, a stranger.

But now a kinsman came to me, a fair young man. He joined me, became my companion. We were wary of of the Egyptians, and I wore their clothing to seem like them. But they offered me food, and by friendship deceived me. I forgot I was the son of a king, and became a slave to their king. I forgot the Pearl my parents had sent me to search for. And I fell into a deep sleep.

But my parents perceived this, and hurried to take counsel. The kings and great ones of the East came to their doors and decided I must not be left down in Egypt. They wrote out a letter for me:

> From the King of Kings, your Father
> and your Mother, Queen of the Dawn-land,
> and from our second son, your brother,

peace. Rise, rise and wake out of sleep
and hear the words of our letter.
Remember you are a king's son.
Whom have you served as a slave?
Remember the Pearl.
Remember your robe of glory
and your mantle of splendour.
Your name is named in the Book of Life
and, with your brother, you shall be
heir to our kingdom.

The letter flew, in the form of an eagle. It flew and it settled beside me, and it became speech. Its voice and the sound of its wingbeats woke me from sleep. I took the letter and kissed it. I loosened its seal and I read it. And I remembered that I was a king's son. I remembered the Pearl.

I began to charm the terrible Serpent. I lulled him to sleep with my chanting, chanting the name of my Father, the name of my brother, the name of my Mother, the Queen of the East. When he was sleeping, I snatched up the Pearl and returned towards the house of my Father. I returned by the way I had taken, to the light of my home, to the Land of the East. I stripped off my filthy garment. On the road I found the letter before me. As it had wakened me with its voice, now with its light it led me. On shining silk, with red letters, it travelled before me. I went through Sarbug, through the Land of Babel, and I reached Maishan, the great meeting place of the merchants.

There my parents sent me my glorious robe, and my mantle. At once, when I saw it, I knew and saw myself through it. We seemed two, yet we were one likeness. The glorious robe, a splendour of colours, gold and beryls, chalcedonies, iris-hued opals, sapphires, was spangled and covered with the image of the King of Kings. All through it, I saw the motions of Gnosis.

Its music spoke to me:

I belong to one more valiant than all men
and my stature grows according to his works.

And the robe poured itself towards me, and I, too, ran towards it, stretched myself to receive it. I clothed myself in its beauty, and wrapped myself in my sparkling mantle. I clothed myself, and ascended to the gate of greeting and homage. I bowed my head and worshipped the brightness of him who had sent it.

There, at the gate, I mingled with princes. And they received me with gladness and promised me I would be sent to the gates of the King, and, taking with me my pearl, I would be received by the King.

DOSTOYEVSKY, 'THE GRAND INQUISITOR'

**From Fyodor Dostoyevsky, *The Brothers Karamazov*,
translated by Constance Garnett, New York, Random
House, and London, Heinemann, 1912**

Fyodor Dostoyevsky (1821–81), the Russian novelist and thinker, wrote Crime and Punishment *and* The Idiot *(both 1866),* The Possessed *(1871), and* The Brothers Karamazov *(1880). The latter ranks as one of the crowns of Western literature, and, like Hamlet and Oedipus Rex, is the story of a parricide.*

In 'The Grand Inquisitor' scene from his novel The Brothers Karamazov, *Dostoyevsky writes of three temptations. Each distracts a person from his search for meaning in this life. Each is a perversion of a question which, when asked truly, can guide one to real knowledge. The third, the will to unity, described here, has clearly gained a foothold in the modern attraction to conformity, patriotism, sloganeering, and the identification of oneself with some organization. In this selection, the Grand Inquisitor addresses the Prisoner, the person over whom he exercises his power.*

'"Listen, then. We are not working with Thee, but with *him* – that is our mystery. It's long – eight centuries – since we have been on *his* side and not on Thine. Just eight centuries ago, we took from him what Thou didst reject with scorn, that last gift he offered Thee, showing Thee all the kingdoms of the earth. We took from him Rome and the sword of Caesar, and proclaimed ourselves sole rulers of the earth, though hitherto we have not been able to complete our work. But whose fault is that? Oh, the work is only beginning, but it has begun. It has long to await completion and the earth has yet much to suffer, but we shall triumph and shall be Caesars, and then we shall plan the universal happiness of man. But Thou mightest have taken even the sword of Caesar.

'"Why didst Thou reject that last gift?

'"Hadst Thou accepted that last counsel of the mighty spirit, Thou wouldst have accomplished all that man seeks on earth – that is, some one to worship, some one to keep his conscience, and some means of uniting all in one unanimous and harmonious antheap, for the craving for universal unity is the third and last anguish of men. Mankind as a whole has always striven to organize a universal state. There have been many great nations with great histories, but the more highly they were developed the more unhappy they were, for they felt more acutely than other people the craving for worldwide union. The great conquerors, Timours and Genghis Khans, whirled like hurricanes over the face of the earth striving to subdue its people, and they too were but the unconscious expression of the same craving for universal unity. Hadst Thou taken the world and Caesar's purple, Thou wouldst have founded the universal state and have given universal peace. For who can rule men if not he who holds their conscience and their bread in his hands?

'"We have taken the sword of Caesar, and in taking it, of course, have rejected Thee and followed *him*.

'"Oh, ages are yet to come of the confusion of free thought, of their science and cannibalism. For having begun to build their tower of Babel without us, they will end, of course, with cannibalism. But then the beast will crawl to us and lick our feet and spatter them with tears of blood. And we shall sit upon the beast and raise the cup, and on it will be written, 'Mystery'. But then, and only then, the reign of peace and happiness will come for men.

'"Thou art proud of Thine elect, but Thou hast only the elect, while we give rest to all. And besides, how many of those elect, those mighty ones who could become elect, have grown weary waiting for Thee, and have transferred and will transfer the powers of their spirit and the warmth of their heart to the other camp, and end by raising their *free* banner against Thee. Thou didst Thyself lift up that banner. But with us, all will be happy and will no more rebel nor destroy one another as under Thy freedom.

'"Oh, we shall persuade them that they will only become free when they renounce their freedom to us and submit to us. And shall we be right or shall we be lying? They will be convinced that we are right, for they will remember the horrors of slavery and confusion to which Thy freedom brought them. Freedom, free thought and science, will lead them into such straits and will bring them face to face with such marvels and insoluble mysteries, that some of them, the fierce and rebellious, will destroy themselves, others, rebellious but weak, will destroy one another, while the rest, weak and unhappy, will crawl fawning to our feet and whine to us: 'Yes, you were right, you alone possess His mystery, and we come back to you, save us from ourselves!'

'"Receiving bread from us, they will see clearly that we take the bread made by their hands from them, give it to them, without any miracle. They will see that we do not change the stones to bread, but in truth they will be more thankful for taking it from our hands than for the bread itself! For they will remember only too well that in the old days, without our help, even the bread they made turned to stones in their hands, while since they have come back to us, the very stones have turned to bread in their hands. Too, too well they know the value of complete submission! And until men know that, they will be unhappy. Who is most to blame for their not knowing it, speak? Who scattered the flock and sent it astray on unknown paths? But the flock will come together again and will submit once more, and then it will be once for all. Then we shall give them the quiet humble happiness of weak creatures such as they are by nature. Oh, we shall persuade them at last not to be proud, for Thou didst lift them up and thereby taught them to be proud. We shall show them that they are weak, that they are only pitiful children, but that childlike happiness is the sweetest of all. They will become timid and will look to us and huddle close to us in fear, as chicks to the hen. They will marvel at us and will be awe-stricken before us, and will be proud at our being so powerful and clever, that we have been able to subdue such a turbulent flock of thousands of millions. They will tremble impotently before our wrath, their minds will grow fearful, they will be quick to shed tears like women and children, but they will be just as ready at a sign from us to pass to laughter and rejoicing, to happy mirth and childish song. Yes, we shall set them to work, but in their leisure hours we shall make their life like a child's game, with children's songs and innocent dance. Oh, we shall allow them even sin, they are weak and helpless, and they will love us like children because we allow them to sin. We shall tell them that every sin will be expiated, if it is done with our permission, that we allow them to sin because we love them, and the punishment for these sins we take upon ourselves. And we shall take it upon ourselves, and they will adore us as their saviours who have taken on themselves their sins before God. And they will have no secrets from us. We shall allow or forbid them to live with their wives and mistresses, to have or not to have children – according to whether they have been obedient or disobedient – and they will submit to us gladly and cheerfully. The most painful secrets of their conscience, all, all they will bring to us, and we shall have an answer for all. And they will be glad to believe our answer, for it will save them from the great anxiety and terrible agony they endure at present in making a free decision for themselves. And all will be happy, all the millions of creatures except the hundred thousand who rule over them. For only we, we who guard the mystery, shall be unhappy.

'"There will be thousands of millions of happy babes, and a hundred thousand sufferers who have taken upon themselves the curse of the knowledge of good and evil. Peacefully they will die, peacefully they will expire in Thy name, and beyond the grave they will find nothing but death. But we shall keep the secret, and for their happiness we shall allure them with the reward of heaven and eternity. Though if there were anything in the other world, it certainly would not be for such as they.

'"It is prophesied that Thou wilt come again in victory, Thou wilt come with Thy chosen, the proud and strong, but we will say that they have only saved themselves, but we have saved all. We are told that the harlot who sits upon the beast, and holds in her hands the *mystery*, shall be put to shame, that the weak will rise up again, and will rend her royal purple and will strip naked her loathsome body. But then I will stand up and point out to Thee the thousand millions of happy children who have known no sin. And we who have taken their sins upon us for their happiness will stand up before Thee and say: 'Judge us if Thou canst and darest.' Know that I fear Thee not. Know that I too have been in the wilderness, I too have lived on roots and locusts, I too prized the freedom with which Thou hast blessed men, and I too was striving to stand among Thy elect, among the strong and powerful, thirsting 'to make up the number'. But I awakened and would not serve madness. I turned back and joined the ranks of those *who have corrected Thy work*. I left the proud and went back to the humble, for the happiness of the humble. What I say to Thee will come to pass, and our domination will be built up. I repeat, tomorrow Thou shalt see that obedient flock who at a sign from me will hasten to heap up the hot cinders about the pile on which

I shall burn Thee for coming to hinder us. For if any one has ever deserved our fires, it is Thou. Tomorrow I shall burn Thee. *Dixi*."'

Ivan stopped. He was carried away as he talked and spoke with excitement; when he had finished, he suddenly smiled.

Alyosha had listened in silence; towards the end he was greatly moved and seemed several times on the point of interrupting, but restrained himself. Now his words came with a rush.

'But . . . that's absurd!' he cried, flushing. 'Your poem is in praise of Jesus, not in blame of Him – as you meant it to be. And who will believe you about freedom? Is that the way to understand it? That's not the idea of it in the Orthodox Church . . . That's Rome, and not even the whole of Rome, it's false – those are the worst of the Catholics, the Inquisitors, the Jesuits! . . . And there could not be such a fantastic creature as your Inquisitor. What are these sins of mankind they take on themselves? Who are these keepers of the mystery who have taken some curse upon themselves for the happiness of mankind? When have they been seen? We know the Jesuits, they are spoken ill of, but surely they are not what you describe? They are not that at all, not at all . . . They are simply the Romish army for the earthly sovereignty of the world in the future, with the Pontiff of Rome for Emperor . . . that's their ideal, but there's no sort of mystery of lofty melancholy about it . . . It's simply lust of power, of filthy earthly gain, of domination – something like a universal serfdom with them as masters – that's all they stand for. They don't even believe in God perhaps. Your suffering Inquisitor is a mere fantasy.'

'Stay, stay,' laughed Ivan, 'how hot you are! A fantasy you say, let it be so! Of course it's a fantasy. But allow me to say: do you really think that the Roman Catholic movement of the last centuries is actually nothing but the lust of power, of filthy earthly gain? Is that Father Paissy's teaching?'

'No, no, on the contrary, Father Paissy did once say something the same as you . . . but of course it's not the same, not a bit the same,' Alyosha hastily corrected himself.

'A precious admission, in spite of your "not a bit the same". I ask you why your Jesuits and Inquisitors have united simply for vile material gain? Why can't there be among them one martyr oppressed by great sorrow and living humanity? You see, only suppose that there was one such man among all those who desire nothing but filthy material gain — if there's only one like my old Inquisitor, who had himself eaten roots in the desert and made frenzied efforts to subdue his flesh to make himself free and perfect. But yet all his life he loved humanity, and suddenly his eyes were opened, and he saw that it is no great moral blessedness to attain perfection and freedom, if at the same time one gains the conviction that billions of God's creatures have been created as a mockery, that they will never be capable of using their freedom, that these poor rebels can never turn into giants to complete the tower, that it was not for such geese that the great idealist dreamt his dream of harmony. Seeing all that he turned back and joined — the clever people. Surely that could have happened?'

'Joined whom, what clever people?' cried Alyosha, completely carried away. 'They have no such great cleverness and no mysteries and secrets ... Perhaps nothing but atheism, that's all their secret. Your Inquisitor does not believe in God, that's his secret!'

'What if it is so! At last you have guessed it. It's perfectly true that that's the whole secret, but isn't that suffering, at least for a man like that, who has wasted his whole life in the desert and yet could not shake off his incurable love of humanity? In his old age he reached the clear conviction that nothing but the advice of the great dread spirit could build up any tolerable sort of life for the feeble, unruly "incomplete, empirical creatures created in jest". And so, convinced of this, he sees that he must follow the council of the wise spirit, the dread spirit of death and destruction, and therefore accept lying and deception, and lead men consciously to death and destruction, and yet deceive them all the way so that they may not notice where they are being led, that the poor blind creatures may at least on the way think themselves happy. And note, the deception is in the name of Him in Whose ideal the old man had so fervently believed all his life long. Is not that tragic? And if only one such stood at the head of the whole army "filled with the lust of power only for the sake of filthy gain" — would not one such be enough to make a tragedy? More than that, one such standing at the head is enough to create the actual leading idea of the Roman Church with all its armies and Jesuits, its highest idea. I tell you frankly that I firmly believe that there has always been such a man among those who stood at the head of the movement. Who knows, there may have been some such even among the Roman Popes. Who knows, perhaps the spirit of that accursed old man who loves mankind so obstinately in his own way, is to be found even now in a whole multitude of such old men, existing not by chance but by agreement, as a secret league formed long ago for the guarding of the mystery, to guard it from the weak and the unhappy, so as to make them happy. No doubt it is so, and so it must be indeed. I fancy that even among the Masons there's something of the same mystery at the bottom, and that that's why the Catholics so detest the Masons as their rivals breaking up the unity of the idea, while it is so essential that there should be one flock and one shepherd ... But from the way I defend my idea I might be an author impatient of your criticism. Enough of it.'

'You are perhaps a Mason yourself!' broke suddenly from Alyosha. 'You don't believe in God,' he added, speaking this time very sorrowfully. He fancied besides that his brother was looking at him ironically. 'How does your poem end?' he asked, suddenly looking down. 'Or was it the end?'

'I meant it to end like this:

'"When the Inquisitor ceased speaking he waited for some time for his Prisoner to answer him. His silence weighed down upon him. He saw the Prisoner had listened intently all the time, looking gently in his face and evidently not wishing to reply. The old man longed for Him to say something, however bitter and terrible. But

He suddenly approached the old man in silence and softly kissed him on his bloodless aged lips. That was His answer. The old man shuddered. His lips moved. He went to the door, opened it, and said to Him: 'Go, and come no more ... Come not at all, never, never!' And he let Him out into the dark alleys of the town. The Prisoner went away."'

'And the old man?'

'The kiss glows in his heart, but the old man adheres to his idea.'

ST AUGUSTINE, *THE CONFESSIONS*

**From St Augustine, *The Confessions*, translated by
E. Pusey, London, Nelson**

St Augustine (354–430), born in North Africa, stands at the meeting-point of the ancient and the medieval worlds. He lived as a cultured and educated member of Roman antiquity until a conversion experience in 386. He was baptized the following year, detailing his experiences in The Confessions *(400). Thereafter he turned to a broader examination of the ultimate questions, which relied heavily on Aristotelean thought; his ideas influenced thinkers for the succeeding millennium. His greatest work is* The City of God.

Life is time. One's own life-time is all that one has. Augustine here asks the question, 'What is time?' He notes that we are attracted to the past (memory) and the future (anticipation), and imagine many things about these times; and we are in the process of experiencing the present, which can include much more than a single 'slice' of time. In addition, we have a sense of eternity, or timelessness. In his most intimate fashion, Augustine tries to find the relation between these different aspects of time.

But if any excursive brain rove over the images of forepassed times, and wonder that Thou the God Almighty and All-creating and All-supporting, Maker of heaven and earth, didst for innumerable ages forbear from so great a work, before Thou wouldest make it; let him awake and consider, that he wonders at false conceits. For whence could innumerable ages pass by, which Thou madest not, Thou the Author and Creator of all ages? Or what times should there be, which were not made by Thee? Or how should they pass by, if they never were? Seeing then Thou art the Creator of all times, if any time was before Thou madest heaven and earth, why say they that Thou didst forgo working? For that very time didst Thou make, nor could times pass by, before Thou madest those times. But if before heaven and earth there was no time, why is it demanded, what Thou then didst? For there was no 'then', when there was no time.

Nor dost Thou by time, precede time: else shouldest Thou not precede all times. But Thou precedest all things past, by the sublimity of an ever-present eternity; and surpassest all things future because they are future, and when they come, they shall be past; but Thou art the Same, and Thy years fail not. Thy years neither come nor go; whereas ours both come and go, that they all may come. The years stand together, because they do stand; nor are departing thrust out by coming years, for they pass not away; but ours shall all be, when they shall no more be. Thy years are one day; and Thy day is not daily, but Today, seeing Thy Today gives not place unto tomorrow, for neither doth it replace yesterday. Thy Today is Eternity; therefore didst Thou beget The Coeternal, to whom Thou saidst, This day have I begotten Thee. Thou hast made all things; and before all times Thou art: neither in any time was time not.

At no time then hadst Thou not made any thing, because time itself Thou madest. And no times are coeternal with Thee, because Thou abidest; but if they abode, they should not be times. For what is time? Who can readily and briefly explain this? Who can even in thought comprehend it, so as to utter a word about it? But what in discourse do we mention more familiarly and knowingly than time? And, we understand, when we speak of it; we understand also, when we hear it spoken of by another. What then is time? If someone asks me, I know: if I wish to explain it to one that asketh, I know not; yet I say boldly that I know that if nothing passed away, time past were not; and if nothing were coming, a time to come were not; and if nothing were, time present were not. Those two times then, past and to come, how are they, seeing the past now is not, and that to come is not yet? But the present, should it always be present, and never pass into time past, verily it should not be time, but eternity. If time present (if it is to be time) only cometh into existence, because it passeth into time past, how can we say that either this is, whose cause of being is, that it shall not be; so, namely, that we cannot truly say that time is, but because it is tending not to be?

And yet we say, 'a long time' and 'a short time'; still, only of time past or to come. A long time past (for example) we call a hundred years since; and a long time to come, a hundred years hence. But a short time past, we call (suppose) ten days since; and a short time to come, ten days hence. But in what sense is that long or short, which is not? For the past, is not now; and the future, is not yet. Let us not then say, 'it is long'; but of the past, 'it hath been long'; and of the future, 'it will be long'. O my Lord, my Light, shall not here also Thy Truth mock at man? For that past time which was long, was it long when it was now past, or when it was yet present? For then might it be long, when there was, what could be long; but when past, it was no longer; wherefore neither could that be long, which was not at all. Let us not then say, 'time past hath been long': for we shall not find, what hath been long, seeing that since it was past, it is no more; but let us say, 'that present time was long'; because, when it was present, it was long. For it had not yet passed away, so as not to be; and therefore there was, what could be long; but after it was past, that ceased also to be long, which ceased to be.

Let us see then, thou soul of man, whether present time can be long: for to thee it is given to feel and to measure length of time. What wilt thou answer me? Are a hundred years, when present, a long time? See first, whether a hundred years can be present. For if the first of these years be now current, it is present, but the other ninety and nine are to come, and therefore are not yet, but if the second year be current, one is now past, another present, the rest to come. And so if we assume any middle year of this hundred to be present, all before it, are past; all after it, to come; wherefore a hundred years cannot be present. But see at least whether that one which is now current, itself is present; for if the current month be its first, the rest are to come; if the second, the first is already past, and the rest are not yet. Therefore, neither is the year now current present; and if not present as a whole, then is not the year present. For twelve months are a year; of which whatever be the current month is present; the rest past, or to come. Although neither is that current month present; but one day only; the rest being to come, if it be the first; past, if the last; if any of the middle, then amid past and to come.

See how the present time, which alone we found could be called long, is abridged to the length scarce of one day. But let us examine that also; because neither is one day present as a whole. For it is made up of four and twenty hours of night and day: of which, the first hath the rest to come; the last hath them past; and any of the middle hath those before it past, those behind it to come. Yea, that one hour passeth away in flying particles. Whatsoever of it hath flown away, is past; whatsoever remaineth, is to come. If an instant of time be conceived, which cannot be divided into the smallest particles of moments, that alone is it, which may be called present. Which yet flies with such speed from future to past, as not to be lengthened out with the least stay. For if it be, it is divided into past and future. The present hath no space. When then is the time, which we may call long? Is it to come? Of it we do not say, 'it is long', because it is not yet, so as to be long; but we say, 'it will be long'. When therefore will it be? For if even then, when it is yet to come, it shall not be long (because what can be long, as yet is not), and so it shall then be long, when from the future which as yet is not, it shall begin now to be, and have become present, that so there should exist what may be long; then does time present cry out in the words above, that it cannot be long.

And yet, Lord, we perceive intervals of times, and compare them, and say, some are shorter, and others longer. We measure also, how much longer or shorter this time is than that; and we answer, 'This is double, or treble; and that, but once, or only just so much as that.' But we measure times as they are passing, by perceiving them; but past, which now are not, or the future, which are not yet, who can measure? Unless a man shall presume to say, that can be measured, which is not. When then time is passing, it may be perceived and measured; but when it is past, it cannot, because it is not.

I ask, Father, I affirm not: O my God, rule and guide me. 'Who will tell me that there are not three times (as we learned when boys, and taught boys), past, present, and future; but present only, because those two are not? Or are they also; and when from future it becometh present, doth it come out of some secret place; and so, when retiring, from present it becometh past? For where did they, who foretold things to come, see them, if as yet they be not? For that which is not, cannot be seen. And they who relate things past, could not relate them, if in mind they did not discern them, and if they were not, they could no way be discerned. Things then past and to come, are.'

Permit me, Lord, to seek further. O my hope, let not my purpose be confounded. For if times past and to come be, I would know where they be. Which yet if I cannot, yet I know, wherever they be, they are not there as future, or past, but present. For if there also they be future, they are not yet there; if there also they be past, they are no longer there. Wheresoever then is whatsoever is, it is only as present. Although when past facts are related, there are drawn out of the memory, not the things themselves which are past, but words which, conceived by the images of the things, they, in passing, have through the senses left as traces in the mind. Thus my childhood, which now is not, is in time past, which now is not: but now when I recall its image, and tell of it, I behold it in the present, because it is still in my memory. Whether there be alike cause of foretelling things to come also; that of things which as yet are not, the images may be perceived before, already existing, I confess, O my God, I know not. This indeed I know, that we generally think before on our future actions, and that that forethinking is present, but the action whereof we forethink is not yet, because it is to come. Which, when we have set upon, and have begun to do what we were forethinking, then shall that action be; because then it is no longer future, but present.

Which way soever then this secret fore-perceiving of things to come be, that only can be seen, which is. But what now is, is not future, but present. When then things to come are said to be seen, it is not themselves which as yet are not (that is, which are to be), but their causes perchance or signs are seen, which already are. Therefore they are not future but present to those who now see that from which the future, being fore-conceived in the mind, is foretold. Which fore-conceptions again now are; and those who foretell those things, do behold the conceptions present before them. Let now the numerous variety of things furnish me some example. I behold the daybreak, I foreshow that the sun is about to rise. What I behold, is present; what I foresignify, to come; not the sun, which already is; but the sun-rising, which is not yet. And yet did I not in my mind imagine the sun-rising itself (as now while I speak of it), I could not foretell it. But neither is that daybreak which I discern in the sky the sun-rising, although it goes before it; nor that imagination of my mind; which two are seen now present, that the other which is to be may be foretold. Future things then are not yet: and if they be not yet, they are not:

and if they are not, they cannot be seen; yet foretold they may be from things present, which are already, and are seen.

Thou then, Ruler of Thy creation, by what way dost Thou teach souls things to come? For Thou didst teach Thy Prophets. By what way dost Thou, to whom nothing is to come, teach things to come; or rather of the future, dost teach things present? For, what is not, neither can it be taught. Too far is this way out of my ken: it is too mighty for me, I cannot attain unto it; but from Thee I can, when Thou shalt vouchsafe it, O sweet light of my hidden eyes.

What now is clear and plain is, that neither things to come nor past are. Nor is it properly said, 'there be three times, past, present, and to come'; yet perchance it might be properly said, 'there be three times; a present of things past, a present of things present, and a present of things future'. For these three do exist in some sort, in the soul, but otherwhere do I not see them: present of things past, memory; present of things present, sight; present of things future, expectation. If thus we be permitted to speak, I see three times, and I confess there are three. Let it be said too, 'there be three times, past, present, and to come', in our incorrect way. See, I object not, nor gainsay, nor find fault, if what is so said be but understood, that neither what is to be, now is, nor what is past. For but few things are there of which we speak properly, of most things improperly; still the things intended are understood.

I said then even now, we measure times as they pass, in order to be able to say, this time is twice so much as that one; or, this is just so much as that; and so of any other parts of time, which be measurable. Wherefore, as I said, we measure times as they pass. And if any should ask me, 'How knowest thou?' I might answer, 'I know, that we do measure, nor can we measure things that are not; and things past and to come, are not.' But time present how do we measure, seeing it hath no space? It is measured while passing; for there will be nothing to be measured. But whence, by what way, and whither passes it while it is a measuring? Whence, but from the future? Which way, but through the present? Whither, but into the past? From that therefore, which is not yet, through that, which hath no space, into that, which now is not. Yet what do we measure, if not time in some space? For we do not say, single and double, and triple, and equal, or any other like way that we speak of time, except of spaces of times. In what space then do we measure time passing? In the future, whence it passeth through? But what is not yet, we measure not. Or in the present, by which it passes? But no space, we do not measure. Or in the past, to which it passes? But neither do we measure that, which now is not.

ARISTOTLE, *NICOMACHEAN ETHICS*

From Aristotle, *Nicomachean Ethics*, translated by W. D. Ross, Oxford University Press, 1954, I, 4–9

Aristotle (384–322 BC), the student of Plato, whose far-reaching explorations of the many aspects of thought have pervaded study since his time. Over two hundred of his works have been preserved. His scientific and analytical mode set the standard for observation and logic for centuries. Books on metaphysics, ethics, psychology, natural history, politics, aesthetics, and rhetoric are included in his corpus.

For Aristotle, to ask why we are here is to question the ultimate goal of human life. This, he says, is happiness, for 'there is agreement' that being happy is what people mostly seek. But what is happiness? Aristotle rejects views which equate it with pleasure, wealth, or fame, and instead locates it in the 'good life', the life filled by well-being. We are well when we are fulfilling that function for which we were created. What that might be requires us to conduct untiring practical research, which he called virtuous activity.

4. Let us resume our inquiry and state, in view of the fact that all knowledge and every pursuit aims at some good, what it is that

we say political science aims at and what is the highest of all goods
achievable by action. Verbally there is very general agreement; for
both the general run of men and people of superior refinement say
that it is happiness, and identify living well and faring well with
being happy; but with regard to what happiness is they differ, and
the many do not give the same account as the wise. For the former
think it is some plain and obvious thing, like pleasure, wealth, or
honour; they differ, however, from one another – and often even
the same man identifies it with different things, with health
when he is ill, with wealth when he is poor; but, conscious of their
ignorance, they admire those who proclaim some great thing that
is above their comprehension. Now some* thought that apart
from these many goods there is another which is good in itself
and causes the goodness of all these as well. To examine all the
opinions that have been held were perhaps somewhat fruitless;
enough to examine those that are most prevalent or that seem
to be arguable . . .

5. Let us, however, resume our discussion from the point at which
we digressed. To judge from the lives that men lead, most men,
and men of the most vulgar type, seem (not without some
ground) to identify the good, or happiness, with pleasure; which is
the reason why they love the life of enjoyment. For there are, we
may say, three prominent types of life – that just mentioned, the
political, and thirdly the contemplative life. Now the mass of
mankind are evidently quite slavish in their tastes, preferring a life
suitable to beasts, but they get some ground for their view from
the fact that many of those in high places share the tastes of
Sardanapallus. A consideration of the prominent types of life
shows that people of superior refinement and of active disposition
identify happiness with honour; for this is, roughly speaking, the
end of the political life. But it seems too superficial to be what we

*The Platonic School. (Trans.)

78

are looking for, since it is thought to depend on those who bestow honour rather than on him who receives it, but the good we divine to be something of one's own and not easily taken from one. Further, men seem to pursue honour in order that they may be assured of their merit; at least it is by men of practical wisdom that they seek to be honoured, and among those who know them, and on the ground of their virtue; clearly, then, according to them, at any rate, virtue is better. And perhaps one might even suppose this to be, rather than honour, the end of the political life. But even this appears somewhat incomplete; for possession of virtue seems actually compatible with being asleep, or with lifelong inactivity, and, further, with the greatest sufferings and misfortunes; but a man who was living so no one would call happy, unless he were maintaining a thesis at all costs. But enough of this; for the subject has been sufficiently treated even in the popular discussions. Third comes the contemplative life, which we shall consider later.

The life of money-making is one undertaken under compulsion, and wealth is evidently not the good we are seeking; for it is merely useful and for the sake of something else. And so one might rather take the aforementioned objects to be ends; for they are loved for themselves. But it is evident that not even these are ends; yet many arguments have been wasted on the support of them. Let us leave this subject, then . . .

7. Let us again return to the good we are seeking, and ask what it can be. It seems different in different actions and arts; it is different in medicine, in strategy, and in the other arts likewise. What then is the good of each? Surely that for whose sake everything else is done. In medicine this is health, in strategy victory, in architecture a house, in any other sphere something else, and in every action and pursuit the end; for it is for the sake of this that all men do whatever else they do. Therefore, if there is an end for all that we do, this will be the good achievable by action, and if there are more than one, these will be the goods achievable by action.

So the argument has by a different course reached the same point; but we must try to state this even more clearly. Since there is evidently more than one end, and we choose some of these (e.g. wealth, flutes,* and in general instruments) for the sake of something else, clearly not all ends are final ends; but the chief good is evidently something final. Therefore, if there is only one final end, this will be what we are seeking. Now we call that which is in itself worthy of pursuit more final than that which is worthy of pursuit for the sake of something else, and that which is never desirable for the sake of something else more final than the things that are desirable both in themselves and for the sake of that other thing, and therefore we call final without qualification that which is always desirable in itself and never for the sake of something else.

Now such a thing happiness, above all else, is held to be; for this we choose always for itself and never for the sake of something else, but honour, pleasure, reason, and every virtue we choose indeed for themselves (for if nothing resulted from them we should still choose each of them), but we choose them also for the sake of happiness, judging that through them we shall be happy. Happiness, on the hand, no one chooses for the sake of these, nor, in general, for anything other than itself.

From the point of view of self-sufficiency the same result seems to follow; for the final good is thought to be self-sufficient. Now by self-sufficient we do not mean that which is sufficient for a man by himself, for one who lives a solitary life, but also for parents, children, wife, and in general for his friends and fellow citizens, since man is born for citizenship. But some limit must be set to this; for if we extend our requirement to ancestors and descendants and friends' friends we are in for an infinite series. Let us examine this question, however, on another occasion; the self-sufficient we now

*Strictly, double-reed instruments. (Trans.)

define as that which when isolated makes life desirable and lacking in nothing; and such we think happiness to be; and further we think it most desirable of all things, not a thing counted as one good thing among others — if it were so counted it would clearly be made more desirable by the addition of even the least of goods; for that which is added becomes an excess of goods, and of goods the greater is always more desirable. Happiness, then, is something final and self-sufficient, and is the end of action.

Presumably, however, to say that happiness is the chief good seems a platitude, and a clearer account of what it is is still desired. This might perhaps be given, if we could first ascertain the function of man. For just as for a flute-player, a sculptor, or any artist, and, in general, for all things that have a function or activity, the good and the 'well' is thought to reside in the function, so would it seem to be for man, if he has a function. Have the carpenter, then, and the tanner certain functions or activities, and has man none? Is he born without a function? Or as eye, hand, foot, and in general each of the parts evidently has a function, may one lay it down that man similarly has a function apart from all these? What then can this be? Life seems to belong even to plants, but we are seeking what is peculiar to man. Let us exclude, therefore, the life of nutrition and growth. Next there would be a life of perception, but *it* also seems to be shared even by the horse, the ox, and every animal. There remains, then, an active life of the element that has a rational principle; of this, one part has such a principle in the sense of being obedient to one, the other in the sense of possessing one and exercising thought. And, as 'life of the rational element' also has two meanings, we must state that life in the sense of activity is what we mean; for this seems to be the more proper sense of the term. Now if the function of man is an activity of soul which follows or implies a rational principle, and if we say 'a so-and-so' and 'a good so-and-so' have a function which is the same in kind, e.g. a lyre-player and a good lyre-player, and so without qualification in all cases, eminence in respect of goodness being added to the name of the function (for the function of a lyre-player is to play the lyre, and that of a good lyre-player is to do so well): if this is the case [and we state the function of man to be a certain kind of life, and this to be an activity or actions of the soul implying a rational principle, and the function of a good man to be the good and noble performance of these, and if any action is well performed when it is performed in accordance with the appropriate excellence: if this is the case], human good turns out to be activity of soul exhibiting excellence, and if there are more than one excellence, in accordance with the best and most complete.

But we must add 'in a complete life'. For one swallow does not make a summer, nor does one day; and so too one day, or a short time, does not make a man blessed and happy . . .

Is happiness acquired by learning or habituation, or sent by God or by chance?

9. For this reason also the question is asked, whether happiness is to be acquired by learning or by habituation or some other sort of training, or comes in virtue of some divine providence or again by chance. Now if there is *any* gift of the gods to men, it is reasonable that happiness should be god-given, and most surely god-given of all human things inasmuch as it is the best. But this question would perhaps be more appropriate to another inquiry; happiness seems, however, even if it is not god-sent but comes as a result of virtue and some process of learning or training, to be among the most godlike things; for that which is the prize and end of virtue seems to be the best thing in the world, and something godlike and blessed.

It will also on this view be very generally shared; for all who are not maimed as regards their potentiality for virtue may win it by a certain kind of study and care. But if it is better to be happy thus than by chance, it is reasonable that the facts should be so, since everything that depends on the action of nature is by nature as good as it can be, and similarly everything that depends on art or any rational cause, and especially if it depends on the best of all causes. To entrust to chance what is greatest and most noble would be a very defective arrangement.

The answer to the question we are asking is plain also from the definition of happiness; for it has been said to be a virtuous activity of soul, of a certain kind. Of the remaining goods, some must necessarily pre-exist as conditions of happiness, and others are naturally cooperative and useful as instruments. And this will be found to agree with what we said at the outset; for we stated the end of political science to be the best end, and political science spends most of its pains on making the citizens to be of a certain character, viz. good and capable of noble acts.

It is natural, then, that we call neither ox nor horse nor any other of the animals happy; for none of them is capable of sharing in such activity. For this reason also a boy is not happy; for he is not yet capable of such acts, owing to his age; and boys who are called happy are being congratulated by reason of the hopes we have for them. For there is required, as we said, not only complete virtue but also a complete life, since many changes occur in life, and all manner of chances, and the most prosperous may fall into great misfortunes in old age, as is told of Priam in the Trojan Cycle; and one who has experienced such chances and has ended wretchedly no one calls happy.

PART THREE

Does God Exist?

Asking a question implies a relation between the one who questions and the object of study. Interrogation also involves communication, since by asking a question a person expresses a willingness to listen to an answer. Within the sphere of philosophical inquiry, we may wonder whether all questions relate to the same level of reality or whether some imply a higher level —whether the responses which they receive arise from the same plane as human life or whether there are higher planes beyond the one which we inhabit.

The ancient world, and traditional societies in all ages, placed man under the authority of powers endowed with a higher order of intelligence than himself, and ascribed a particular importance to experiences which seemed to confirm this view of the world. The created universe comprised an ordered cosmology in which different beings had their own particular place in the workings of things. Humanity was neither at the top nor at the bottom. Modern science, beginning in the sixteenth and seventeenth centuries, has changed all this; it has tended to believe in a 'flat' universe, rejecting the notion of different levels in questions, experiences, and orders of things. It has favoured a view in which the universe is like a clockwork mechanism, some of the parts being more important than others, but none more real, more perfect, more knowing, or more valuable. It has assumed that the same laws apply to phenomena throughout the 'flat' universe, and even that (according to the second law of thermodynamics) differences in energy between things will tend to even out, producing an even flatter universe in the future.

This idea of a single-levelled universe runs counter to the intuitions of people through the ages. Intuitive understanding is possible only if one 'stands under' a reality whose intelligence is as far superior to the human mind as the human mind is to that of a spider. The 'proof' of this intuition takes one of three approaches. 'When I was ten years of age,' Tatanka-ohitika writes, 'I looked at the land and the rivers, the sky above, and the animals around me and could not fail to realize that they were made by some great power.' This is the 'argument from design'; the fact that the universe seems to have a design has led people to conclude that it must have a creator. Thinkers have also reasoned that a first cause or, to use Aristotle's expression, a 'prime mover' must have set the cosmos in motion, have set off the original 'big bang'. This is the 'cosmological argument', which draws on the familiar idea that every effect must have a cause. (Maimonides presents this argument in clear form in the extract quoted here.) Third, there is the argument that since we have an image, concept, or experience of a being belonging to a higher order, then this very fact verifies its existence. This, the 'ontological argument', derives the reality of higher levels from our capacity to conceive of them; the implication is that the human mind is a sensing apparatus or antenna, able to receive signals from a finer plane of existence. To continue the metaphor, when the mind is properly tuned, it enters into communication with an intelligence greater than our own.

Many people have had experiences that seem to indicate knowledge of another reality. A deep, silent communion with nature, the love felt for a child or friend, the sudden alertness great danger brings: all point to another way of knowing. 'There are two knowledges to be known,' the *Mundaka Upanishad* tells us, 'a higher and a lower.' While the lower is subject to systematic analysis, the second borders on mystery. From a religious point of view, it involves the element of faith. Both philosophy and religion speak in terms of a divine being or god (deism), of many gods (polytheism), or of a pervading vital principle (panpsychism);

both hold that behind all our ordinary perception and reflection there stands a more subtle, superior knowledge. Not all philosophers conclude that a finer perception indicates a reality higher than the human one, however. Kant, for example, maintains that 'the highest wonder, when we view it properly, and for which admiration is not only legitimate but even exalting', belongs to our commitment to moral action. The source of our heightened sensitivity lies in our own conscience and we know of higher matters when we are in harmony with its dictates. What else there is, we cannot know. According to Kant, we must remain silent about the existence as well as the non-existence of levels above human reality.

Is the concept or experience of a higher reality an accurate gauge of the way the universe is arranged? Why is it that the moment of truth is so often followed by a moment of doubt? Modern science encourages this natural scepticism. It finds flaws in any approach which attempts to move from a single-level to a multi-level world. Empirical philosophy, which accords with the thinking of modern science, establishes a view of the world derived solely from ordinary sense-experience, sights, sounds, and tactile sensations. Perception, it is argued, builds up an elaborate and complex picture of the way things are, but nowhere does it find an entity or force which corresponds to a higher reality; that idea, therefore, must be merely the mind's own invention.

The plausibility of the view of the universe held by modern science derives from the unmistakable character of sensory experience. Our sense organs provide our only windows on the world. But is it an absolute fact that the senses work only in this way, or do we think that they do because this is how we are accustomed to using them? Plotinus, a Neoplatonist, argued that, by a kind of sensory retraining, one could become sensitive to impressions of another order. New impressions, as he says, 'come forward, on the contrary, as from within, unlike the sense-objects known as from without'. Our sensory conditioning takes place, by imitation and rote learning, in our infancy; a more disciplined reconditioning requires intentional exercise, much as an athlete trains his body. In this way, our awareness of what comes to us through our senses can be enhanced. We see things with new eyes.

If we accept that ordinary sense-perception is only one of the possible forms of perception, a many-levelled view of reality seems more plausible. The question now is one of access or of the accuracy of our reception. When our 'attunement' is better, when we are more attentive to the messages our senses pick up, we can contact a level of reality lying above the one we have uncritically assumed to be unique. This point of view does not contradict modern science. Instead, it expresses a relation between what we see and what we have been led to expect to see. We should remember, in this respect, how we become aware of a new reality when we encounter the unexpected; then, in addition to the familiar sights, sounds, and feels of our everyday world, there is the vivid sense of something more real, more alive, more actual.

The matter of expectation plays a paramount role in the question of multiple levels of reality. Operating in subtle ways, expectation tends to flatten the dimensionality of one's vision. The unexpected in experience and thought, by contrast, ushers in the novel event and serves to remind one that the source of life lies beyond oneself. The sudden entry of joy or death, good fortune, irony, or fatality, serves to challenge the thick skin of engrained habit. But if there is another, superior level of reality, then who or what does this signify for us? This question, arising from the depths of a person's thought, indicates that the only reality is that of the path by which one seeks for an authentic superior authority. Embarking on an unknown quest, we come face to face with the habitual timidity of our thought. Attar, a Persian visionary, in his classic account of how men and women respond to the reality of the quest, has one of his characters say, 'I've never tried a feat like that before./ This valley's endless; dangers lie ahead;/ The first time that we rest I'll drop down dead.' A plural reality is a challenge.

'We've seen and heard so much — what have we learned?' Attar asks us. True learning is the conjunction of the wholly new with the mind ready to receive it. Other sights and sounds are only repetitions of what we already know or expect. Only an unwavering awareness can begin to discern the novel elements which emerge from what we perceive. This awareness reminds one of the openness of the child, Tatanka-ohitika: 'I was so anxious to understand this power that I questioned the trees and the bushes. It seemed as though the flowers were staring at me, and I wanted to ask them, "Who made you?"'

PLOTINUS, *THE ENNEADS*

From Plotinus, *The Ethical Treatises*, vol. 1, translated by S. MacKenna, London Medici Society, 1926

Plotinus (205–70), born and educated in Egypt, was attracted to the thought of Plato. In his rejuvenation of Platonic ideas, Plotinus left an extensive system exhibiting deep metaphysical insights into the nature of the cosmos. The relation between self-knowledge and knowledge of the whole was a theme that drove him to a vision in the Enneads of the comprehensiveness of all things.

Plotinus describes a reality above the one we ordinarily live in as belonging to a purified soul. A pure soul is one sensitive to its inner relation to universal goodness. Plotinus tells us how we can undertake purification by a new kind of vision. As we begin to discern in ourselves the definite marks of our higher origin, we can progress towards a living sense of this other reality. We see, in the simple term Plotinus uses, the beauty within us.

6. For, as the ancient teaching was, moral discipline and courage and every virtue, not even excepting Wisdom itself, all is purification.

Hence the Mysteries with good reason adumbrate the immersion of the unpurified in filth, even in the Nether-World, since the unclean loves filth for its very filthiness, and swine foul of body find their joy in foulness.

What else is Sophrosyne [temperance], rightly so-called, but to take no part in the pleasures of the body, to break away from them as unclean and unworthy of the clean? So too, Courage is but being fearless of the death which is but the parting of the Soul from the body, an event which no one can dread whose delight is to be his unmingled self. And Magnanimity is but disregard for the lure of things here. And Wisdom is but the Act of the Intellectual-Principle withdrawn from the lower places and leading the Soul to the Above.

The Soul, thus cleansed in all Idea and Reason, wholly free of body, intellective, is entirely of that divine order from which the wellspring of Beauty rises and all the race of Beauty.

Hence the Soul heightened to the Intellectual-Principle is beautiful to all its power. For Intellection and all that proceeds from Intellection are the Soul's beauty, a graciousness native to it and not foreign, for only with these is it truly Soul. And it is just to say that in the Soul's becoming a good and beautiful thing is its becoming like to God, for from the Divine comes all the Beauty and all the Good in beings.

We may even say that Beauty *is* the Authentic-Existence and Ugliness is the Principle contrary to Existence; and the Ugly is also the primal evil; therefore its contrary is at once good and beautiful, or is Good and Beauty: and hence the one method will discover to us the Beauty-Good and the Ugliness-Evil.

And Beauty, this Beauty which is also The Good, must be posed as The First: directly deriving from this First is the Intellectual-Principle which is pre-eminently the manifestation of Beauty; through the Intellectual-Principle Soul is beautiful. The beauty in things of a lower order — actions and pursuits for instance — comes by operation of the shaping Soul which is also the author of the beauty found in the world of sense. For the Soul, a divine thing, a fragment as it were of the Primal Beauty, makes beautiful to the fullness of their capacity all things whatsoever it grasps and moulds.

7. Therefore we must ascend again towards the Good, the desired of every Soul. Anyone that has seen This, knows what I intend when I say that it is beautiful. Even the desire of it is to be desired as a Good. To attain it is for those that will take the upward path, who will set all their forces towards it, who will divest themselves of all that we have put on in our descent — so, to those that approach the Holy Celebrations of the Mysteries, there are appointed purifications and the laying aside of the garments worn before, and the entry in nakedness — until, passing, on the upward way, all that is other than the God, each in the solitude of himself shall behold that solitary-dwelling Existence, the Apart, the Unmingled, the Pure, that from Which all things depend, for Which all look and live and act and know, the Source of Life and of Intellection and of Being.

And one that shall know this vision — with what passion of love shall he not be seized, with what pang of desire, what longing to be molten into one with This, what wondering delight! If he that has never seen this Being must hunger for It as for all his welfare, he that has known must love and reverence It as the very Beauty; he will be flooded with awe and gladness, stricken by a salutary terror; he loves with a veritable love, with sharp desire; all other lives than this he must despise, and disdain all that once seemed fair.

This, indeed, is the mood even of those who, having witnessed the manifestation of Gods or Supernals, can never again feel the old delight in the comeliness of material forms: what then are we to think of one that contemplates Absolute Beauty in Its essential integrity, no accumulation of flesh and matter, no dweller on earth or in the heavens — so perfect Its purity — far above all such things in that they are non-essential, composite, not primal but descending from This?

Beholding this Being – the Choragos* of all Existence, the Self-Intent that ever gives forth and never takes – resting, rapt, in the vision and possession of so lofty a loveliness, growing to Its likeness, what Beauty can the soul yet lack? For This, the Beauty supreme, the absolute, and the primal, fashions Its lovers to Beauty and makes them also worthy of love.

And for This, the sternest and the uttermost combat is set before the Souls; all our labour is for This, lest we be left without part in this noblest vision, which to attain is to be blessed in the blissful sight, which to fail of is to fail utterly.

For not he that has failed of the joy that is in colour or in visible forms, not he that has failed of power or of honours or of kingdom has failed, but only he that has failed of only This, for Whose winning he should renounce kingdoms and command over earth and ocean and sky, if only, spurning the world of sense from beneath his feet, and straining to This, he may see.

8. But what must we do? How lies the path? How come to vision of the inaccessible Beauty, dwelling as if in consecrated precincts, apart from the common ways where all may see, even the profane?

He that has the strength, let him arise and withdraw into himself, forgoing all that is known by the eyes, turning away for ever from the material beauty that once made his joy. When he perceives those shapes of grace that show in body, let him not pursue: he must know them for copies, vestiges, shadows, and hasten away towards That they tell of. For if anyone should follow what is like a beautiful shape playing over water – is there not a myth telling in symbol of such a dupe, how he sank into the

*Literally, 'leader of the chorus'.

depths of the current and was swept away to nothingness? So too, one that is held by material beauty and will not break free shall be precipitated, not in body but in Soul, down to the dark depths loathed of the Intellective-Being, where, blind even in the Lower-World, he shall have commerce only with shadows, there as here.

'Let us flee then to the beloved Fatherland': this is the soundest counsel. But what is this flight? How are we to gain the open sea? For Odysseus is surely a parable to us when he commands the flight from the sorceries of Circe or Calypso — not content to linger for all the pleasure offered to his eyes and all the delight of sense filling his days.

The Fatherland to us is There whence we have come, and There is The Father.

What then is our course, what the manner of our flight? This is not a journey for the feet; the feet bring us only from land to land; nor need you think of coach or ship to carry you away; all this order of things you must set aside and refuse to see: you must close the eyes and call instead upon another vision which is to be waked within you, a vision, the birthright of all, which few turn to use.

9. And this inner vision, what is its operation?

Newly awakened it is all too feeble to bear the ultimate splendour. Therefore the Soul must be trained — to the habit of remarking, first, all noble pursuits, then the works of beauty produced not by the labour of the arts but by the virtue of men known for their goodness: lastly, you must search the souls of those that have shaped these beautiful forms.

But how are you to see into a virtuous soul and know its loveliness?

Withdraw into yourself and look. And if you do not find yourself beautiful yet, act as does the creator of a statue that is to be made beautiful: he cuts away here, he smoothes there, he makes this line lighter, this other purer, until a lovely face has grown upon his work. So do you also: cut away all that is excessive, straighten all that is crooked, bring light to all that is overcast, labour to make all one glow of beauty and never cease chiselling your statue, until there shall shine out on you from it the godlike splendour of virtue, until you shall see the perfect goodness surely established in the stainless shrine.

When you know that you have become this perfect work, when you are self-gathered in the purity of your being, nothing now remaining that can shatter that inner unity, nothing from without clinging to the authentic man, when you find yourself wholly true to your essential nature, wholly that only veritable Light which is not measured by space, not narrowed to any circumscribed form nor again diffused as a thing void of term, but ever unmeasurable as something greater than all measure and more than all quantity – when you perceive that you have grown to this, you are now become very vision: now call up all your confidence, strike forward yet a step – you need a guide no longer – strain, and see.

This is the only eye that sees the mighty Beauty. If the eye that adventures the vision be dimmed by vice, impure, or weak, and unable in its cowardly blenching to see the uttermost brightness, then it sees nothing even though another point to what lies plain to sight before it. To any vision must be brought an eye adapted to what is to be seen, and having some likeness to it. Never did eye see the sun unless it had first become sun-like, and never can the soul have vision of the First Beauty unless itself be beautiful.

Therefore, first let each become godlike and each beautiful who cares to see God and Beauty. So, mounting, the Soul will come first to the Intellectual-Principle and survey all the beautiful Ideas in the Supreme and will avow that this is Beauty, that the Ideas are Beauty. For by their efficacy comes all Beauty else, by the offspring and essence of the Intellectual-Being. What is beyond the Intellectual-Principle we affirm to be the nature of Good radiating Beauty before it. So that, treating the Intellectual-Kosmos as one, the first is the Beautiful: if we make distinction there, the Realm of

Ideas constitutes the Beauty of the Intellectual Sphere; and The Good, which lies beyond, is the Fountain at once and Principle of Beauty: the Primal Good and the Primal Beauty have the one dwelling-place and, thus, always, Beauty's seat is There.

MAIMONIDES, *THE GUIDE FOR THE PERPLEXED*

From Moses Maimonides, *The Guide for the Perplexed*, translated by M. Friedlander, New York, Dover Publications, 1956

Maimonides (1135–1204), who was born in Spain and eventually emigrated to Egypt, was the most renowned Jewish philosopher of the Middle Ages. Besides his magnum opus, The Guide for the Perplexed, *he wrote treatises on medicine and law. Influenced strongly by Aristotle's thinking, he was interested in demonstrating that essential truth of the highest order is made available through philosophical study, and not through faith.*

Maimonides attempts to establish the existence of God, the highest level of reality, by a classical means: the use of deductive argument. (In the same manner, geometry proceeds from axioms and propositions to give proofs of, say, the Pythagorean theorem.) Beginning with simple, indisputable ideas, like motion and cause, Maimonides carefully constructs, with these building blocks, an edifice that demonstrates the necessity of a first cause. What brings all change into existence, and what is not caused to change by anything else, is, he believes, conclusively of the highest level of reality.

Introduction

Twenty-five of the propositions which are employed in the proof for the existence of God, or in the arguments demonstrating that

God is neither corporeal nor a force connected with a material being, or that He is One, have been fully established, and their correctness is beyond doubt. Aristotle and the Peripatetics who followed him have proved each of these propositions. There is, however, one proposition which we do not accept — namely, the proposition that affirms the Eternity of the Universe, but we will admit it for the present, because by doing so we shall be enabled clearly to demonstrate our own theory.

Proposition I

The existence of an infinite magnitude is impossible.

Proposition II

The coexistence of an infinite number of finite magnitudes is impossible.

Proposition III

The existence of an infinite number of causes and effects is impossible, even if these were not magnitudes; if, e.g., one Intelligence were the cause of a second, the second the cause of a third, the third the cause of a fourth, and so on, the series could not be continued *ad infinitum*.

Proposition IV

Four categories are subject to change:
(a) *Substance*. Changes which affect the substance of a thing are called genesis and destruction.

(b) *Quantity*. Changes in reference to quantity are increase and decrease.

(c) *Quality*. Changes in the qualities of things are transformations.

(d) *Place*. Change of place is called motion.

The term 'motion' is properly applied to change of place, but is also used in a general sense of all kinds of changes.

Proposition V

Motion implies change and transition from potentiality to actuality.

Proposition VI

The motion of a thing is either essential or accidental; or it is due to an external force, or to the participation of the thing in the motion of another thing. This latter kind of motion is similar to the accidental one. An instance of essential motion may be found in the translation of a thing from one place to another. The accident of a thing, as, e.g., its black colour, is said to move when the thing itself changes its place. The upward motion of a stone, owing to a force applied to it in that direction, is an instance of a motion due to an external force. The motion of a nail in a boat may serve to illustrate motion due to the participation of a thing in the motion of another thing; for when the boat moves, the nail is said to move likewise. The same is the case with everything composed of several parts: when the thing itself moves, every part of it is likewise said to move.

Proposition VII

Things which are changeable are, at the same time, divisible. Hence everything that moves is divisible, and consequently corporeal; but that which is indivisible cannot move, and cannot therefore be corporeal.

Proposition VIII

A thing that moves accidentally must come to rest, because it does not move of its own accord; hence accidental motion cannot continue for ever.

Proposition IX

A corporeal thing that sets another corporeal thing in motion can only effect this by setting itself in motion at the time it causes the other thing to move.

Proposition X

A thing which is said to be contained in a corporeal object must satisfy either of the two following conditions: it either exists through that object, as is the case with accidents, or it is the cause of the existence of that object; such is, e.g., its essential property. In both cases it is a force existing in a corporeal object.

Proposition XI

Among the things which exist through a material object, there are some which participate in the division of that object, and are therefore accidentally divisible, as, e.g., its colour, and all other qualities that spread throughout its parts. On the other hand, among the things which form the essential elements of an object, there are some which cannot be divided in any way, as, e.g., the soul and the intellect.

Proposition XII

A force which occupies all parts of a corporeal object is finite, that object itself being finite.

Proposition XIII

None of the several kinds of change can be continuous, except motion from place to place, provided it be circular.

Proposition XIV

Locomotion is in the natural order of the several kinds of motion the first and foremost. For genesis and corruption are preceded by transformation, which, in its turn, is preceded by the approach of the transforming agent to the object which is to be transformed. Also, increase and decrease are impossible without previous genesis and corruption.

Proposition XV

Time is an accident that is related and joined to motion in such a manner that the one is never found without the other. Motion is only possible in time, and the idea of time cannot be conceived otherwise than in connection with motion; things which do not move have no relation to time.

Proposition XVI

Incorporated bodies can only be numbered when they are forces situated in a body; the several forces must then be counted together with substances or objects in which they exist. Hence purely spiritual beings, which are neither corporeal nor forces situated in corporeal objects, cannot be counted, except when considered as causes and effects.

Proposition XVII

When an object moves, there must be some agent that moves it, from without, as, e.g., in the case of a stone set in motion by the hand; or from within, e.g., when the body of a living being moves. Living beings include in themselves, at the same time, the moving agent and the thing moved; when, therefore, a living being dies, and the moving agent, the soul, has left the body, i.e., the thing moved, the body remains for some time in the same condition as before, and yet cannot move in the manner it has moved previously. The moving agent, when included in the thing moved, is hidden from, and imperceptible to, the senses. This circumstance gave rise to the belief that the body of an animal moves without the aid of a moving agent. When we therefore affirm, concerning a thing in motion, that it is its own moving agent, or, as is generally said, that it moves of its own accord, we mean to say that the force which really set the body in motion exists in that body itself.

Proposition XVIII

Everything that passes over from a state of potentiality to that of actuality, is caused to do so by some external agent; because if that agent existed in the thing itself, and no obstacle prevented the transition, the thing would never be in a state of potentiality, but always in that of actuality. If, on the other hand, while the thing itself contained that agent, some obstacle existed, and at a certain time that obstacle was removed, the same cause which removed the obstacle would undoubtedly be described as the cause of the transition from potentiality to actuality, [and not the force situated within the body]. Note this.

Proposition XIX

A thing which owes its existence to certain causes has in itself merely the possibility of existence; for only if these causes exist, the thing likewise exists. It does not exist if the causes do not exist at all, or if they have ceased to exist, or if there has been a change in the relation which implies the existence of that being as a necessary consequence of those causes.

Proposition XX

A thing which has in itself the necessity of existence cannot have for its existence any cause whatever.

Proposition XXI

A thing composed of two elements has necessarily their composition as the cause of its present existence. Its existence is therefore not necessitated by its own essence; it depends on the existence of its two component parts and their combination.

Proposition XXII

Material objects are always composed of two elements [at least], and are without exception subject to accidents. The two component elements of all bodies are substance and form. The accidents attributed to material objects are quantity, geometrical form, and position.

Proposition XXIII

Everything that exists potentially, and whose essence includes a certain state of possibility, may at some time be without actual existence.

Proposition XXIV

That which is potentially a certain thing is necessarily material, for the state of possibility is always connected with matter.

Proposition XXV

Each compound substance consists of matter and form, and requires an agent for its existence, viz., a force which sets the substance in motion, and thereby enables it to receive a certain form. The force which thus prepares the substance of a certain individual being, is called the immediate motor.

Here the necessary arises of investigating into the properties of motion, the moving agent and the thing moved. But this has already been explained sufficiently; and the opinion of Aristotle may be expressed in the following proposition: Matter does not move of its own accord — an important proposition that led to the investigation of the Prime Motor (the first moving agent).

Of these foregoing twenty-five propositions some may be verified by means of a little reflection and the application of a few propositions capable of proof, or of axioms or theorems of almost the same force, such as have been explained by me. Others require many arguments and propositions, all of which, however, have been established by conclusive proofs partly in the Physics and its commentaries, and partly in the Metaphysics and its commentary. I have already stated that in this work it is not my intention to copy the books of the philosophers or to explain difficult problems, but simply to mention those propositions which are closely connected with our subject, and which we want for our purpose.

To the above propositions one must be added which enunciates that the universe is eternal, and which is held by Aristotle to be true, and even more acceptable than any other theory. For the present we admit it, as a hypothesis, only for the purpose of demonstrating our theory. It is the following proposition:

Proposition XXVI

Time and motion are eternal, constant, and in actual existence.

In accordance with this proposition, Aristotle is compelled to assume that there exists actually a body with constant motion, viz., the fifth element. He therefore says that the heavens are not subject to genesis or destruction, because motion cannot be generated nor destroyed. He also holds that every motion must necessarily be preceded by another motion, either of the same or of a different kind. The belief that the locomotion of an animal is not preceded by another motion, is not true; for the animal is caused to move, after it had been in rest, by the intention to obtain those very things which bring about that locomotion. A change in its state of health, or some image, or some new idea can produce a desire to seek that which is conducive to its welfare and to avoid that which is contrary. Each of these three causes sets the living being in motion, and each of them is produced by various kinds of motion. Aristotle likewise asserts that everything which is created must, before its actual creation, have existed *in potentia*. By inferences drawn from this assertion he seeks to establish his proposition, viz., The thing that moves is finite, and its path finite; but it repeats the motion in its path an infinite number of times. This can only take place when the motion is circular, as has been stated in Proposition XIII. Hence follows also the existence of an infinite number of things which do not coexist but follow one after the other.

Aristotle frequently attempts to establish this proposition; but I believe that he did not consider his proofs to be conclusive. It appeared to him to be the most probable and acceptable proposition. His followers, however, and the commentators of his books, contend that it contains not only a probable but a demonstrative proof, and that it has, in fact, been fully established. On the other hand, the Mutakallimun* try to prove that the proposition cannot be true, as, according to their opinion, it is impossible to conceive how an infinite number of things could even come into existence successively. They assume this impossibility as an axiom. I, however, think that this proposition is admissible, but neither demonstrative, as the commentators of Aristotle assert, nor, on the other hand, impossible, as the Mutakallimun say. We have no intention to explain here the proofs given by Aristotle, or to show our doubts concerning them, or to set forth our opinions on the creation of the universe. I here simply desire to mention those propositions which we shall require for

*Scholastic theologians of Islam.

the proof of the three principles stated above. Having thus quoted and admitted these propositions, I will now proceed to explain what may be inferred from them.

KANT, *RELIGION WITHIN THE LIMITS OF REASON ALONE*

From Immanuel Kant, *Religion within the Limits of Reason Alone*, translated by Greene and Hudson, La Salle (Illinois), Open Court Publishing Company, 1960

Immanuel Kant (1724–1804), a Prussian philosopher, stressed the role of empirical knowledge in setting the limits of thought. His desire to make room for faith left him to place moral thinking in a central position. He wrote on evolution and astronomy before turning to The Critique of Pure Reason, *in which he denied a place for mere speculative thought.*

In this selection, Kant notes two sides to our nature, one mechanical, the other moral. Ordinarily, the dominance of the first leaves us insensitive to our higher destiny, which grants us access to a reality vaster than our ordinary conceptions of things. Kant argues that by a revolution, a complete turn-about in our thinking, we can place ourselves under the moral law. In that case, our actions will bear testimony to our relation to what lies above.

But if a man is corrupt in the very ground of his maxims, how can he possibly bring about this revolution by his own powers and of himself become a good man? Yet duty bids us do this, and duty demands nothing of us which we cannot do. There is no reconciliation possible here except by saying that man is under the necessity of, and is therefore capable of, a revolution in his cast of mind, but only of a gradual reform in his sensuous nature (which places obstacles in the way of the former). That is, if a man reverses, by a single unchangeable decision, that highest ground of his maxims whereby he was an evil man (and thus puts on the new man), he is, so far as his principle and cast of mind are concerned, a subject susceptible of goodness, but only in continuous labour and growth is he a good man. That is, he can hope in the light of that purity of the principle which he has adopted as the supreme maxim of his will, and of its stability, to find himself upon the good (though strait) path of continual *progress* from bad to better. For Him who penetrates to the intelligible ground of the heart (the ground of all maxims of the will) and for whom this unending progress is a unity, i.e., for God, this amounts to his being actually a good man (pleasing to Him); and, thus viewed, this change can be regarded as a revolution. But in the judgement of men, who can appraise themselves and the strength of their maxims only by the ascendancy which they win over their sensuous nature in time, this change must be regarded as nothing but an ever-during struggle towards the better, hence as a gradual reformation of the propensity to evil, the perverted cast of mind.

From this it follows that man's moral growth of necessity begins not in the improvement of his practices but rather in the transforming of his cast of mind and in the grounding of a character: though customarily man goes about the matter otherwise and fights against vices one by one, leaving undisturbed their common root. And yet even the man of greatest limitations is capable of being impressed by respect for an action conforming to duty — a respect which is the greater the more he isolates it, in thought, from other incentives which, through self-love, might influence the maxim of conduct. Even children are capable of detecting the smallest trace of admixture of improper incentives; for an action thus motivated at once loses, in their eyes, all moral worth. This predisposition to goodness is cultivated in no better way than by adducing the actual *example* of good men (of that which concerns their conformity to law) and by allowing young students of morals to judge the impurity of various maxims on the basis of the actual incentives motivating the conduct of these good men. The predisposition is thus gradually transformed into a cast of mind, and *duty*, for its own sake, begins to have a noticeable importance in their hearts. But to teach a pupil to *admire* virtuous actions, however great the sacrifice these may have entailed, is not in harmony with preserving his feeling for moral goodness. For be a man never so virtuous, all the goodness he can ever perform is still his simple duty; and to do his duty is nothing more than to do what is in the common moral order and hence in no way deserving of wonder. Such wonder is rather a lowering of our feeling for duty, as if to act in obedience to it were something extraordinary and meritorious.

Yet there is one thing in our soul which we cannot cease from regarding with the highest wonder, when we view it properly, and for which admiration is not only legitimate but even exalting, and that is the original moral predisposition itself in us. What is it in us (we can ask ourselves) whereby we, beings ever dependent upon nature through so many needs, are at the same time raised so far above these needs by the idea of an original predisposition (in us) that we count them all as nothing, and ourselves as unworthy of existence, if we cater to their satisfaction (though this alone can make life worth desiring) in opposition to the law — a law by virtue of which our reason commands us potently, yet without making either promises or threats? The force of this question every man, even one of the meanest capacity, must feel more deeply — every man, that is, who previously has been taught the holiness which inheres in the idea of duty but who has not yet advanced to an inquiry into the concept of freedom, which first and foremost emerges from this law: and the very incomprehensibility of this predisposition, which announces a divine origin, acts perforce upon the spirit even to the point of exaltation, and strengthens it for whatever sacrifice a man's respect for his duty may demand of him. More frequently to excite in man this feeling of the sublimity of his moral destiny is especially commendable as a method of awakening moral sentiments. For to do so works directly against the innate propensity to invert the incentives in the maxims of our will and towards the re-establishment in the human heart, in the form of an unconditional respect for the law as the ultimate condition upon which maxims are to be adopted, of the original moral order among the incentives, and so of the predisposition to good in all its purity.

ATTAR, *THE CONFERENCE OF THE BIRDS*

From Farid ud-Din Attar, *The Conference of the Birds*, translated by C. S. Nott, London, Arkana, 1985

Farid ud-Din Attar (died c. 1230) turned to Sufi ideas when an itinerant dervish entered his father's perfume shop and asked, 'How can you ever turn your mind to death and renounce all these worldly goods?' Thereupon, the dervish lay down and died. Said to have the highest knowledge of Sufi thought of his time, Attar composed about 200,000 verses.

Attar's Conference of the Birds is a full-length poem expounding a pathway to higher reality. Different birds personify different aspects of a person's nature. Most present reasons why it is impossible to undertake the search for knowledge. In this selection, the Hoopoe, representing a clear vision of the way, admonishes a cowardly bird, arguing that it is in fact in one's self-interest to undertake the venture. One needs, Attar might say, to recognize the many distractions in order to strengthen one's resolve to this single-minded pursuit.

Mahmud and the Woodcutter

Another time when Sultan Mahmud was riding alone he met an

old woodcutter leading his donkey loaded with brambles. At that moment the donkey stumbled, and as he fell the thorns skinned the old man's head. The Sultan, seeing the brambles on the ground, the donkey upside down, and the man rubbing his head, asked: 'O unlucky man, do you need a friend?' 'Indeed I do,' replied the woodcutter. 'Good cavalier, if you will help me I shall reap the benefit and you will come to no harm. Your looks are a good omen for me. It is well known that one meets with goodwill from those who have a pleasing countenance.' So the kind-hearted Sultan got off his horse and, having pulled the donkey to its feet, lifted up the faggot of thorns and fastened it on its back. Then he rode off to rejoin the army. He said to the soldiers: 'An old woodcutter is coming along with a donkey loaded with brambles. Bar the way so that he will have to pass in front of me.' When the woodcutter came up to the soldiers he said to himself: 'How shall I get through with this feeble beast?' So he went by another way, but catching sight of the royal parasol in the distance began to tremble, for the road he was compelled to take would bring him face to face with the Sultan. As he got nearer he was overcome with confusion, for under the parasol he saw a familiar face. 'O God,' he said, 'what a state I'm in! Today I have had Mahmud for my porter.'

When he came up, Mahmud said to him: 'My poor friend, what do you do for a living?' The woodcutter replied: 'You know already. Be honest. You don't recognize me? I am a poor old man, a woodcutter by trade; day and night I gather brambles in the desert and sell them, yet my donkey dies of hunger. If you wish me well give me some bread.' 'You poor man,' said the Sultan, 'how much do you want for your faggot?' The woodcutter replied: 'Since you do not wish to take it for nothing and I do not wish to sell it, give me a purse of gold.' At this the soldiers cried out: 'Hold your tongue, fool! Your faggot is not worth a handful of barley. You should give it for nothing.' The old man said: 'That is all very well, but its value has changed. When a lucky man like the

Sultan puts his hands to my bundle of thorns they become bunches of roses. If he wishes to buy them he must pay a dinar at the very least for he has raised the value of my thorns a hundred times by touching them.'

The speech of the second bird

Another bird came up to the Hoopoe and said: 'O protectress of the army of Solomon! I have not the strength to undertake this journey. I am too weak to cross the valleys. The road is so difficult that I shall lie down and die at the first stage. There are volcanoes in the way. Also, it is not expedient for everyone to engage in such an enterprise. Thousands of heads have rolled like the balls in polo, for many have perished who went in quest of the Simurgh [the Supreme Ruler of All]. On such a road, where many sincere creatures have hidden their heads in fear, what shall become of me, who am only dust?'

The Hoopoe replied: 'O you of the doleful countenance! Why is your heart so oppressed? Since you are of so little value in the world it is all the same whether you be young and valiant or old and feeble. The world is truly ordure; creatures perish there at every door. Thousands turn yellow as silk, and perish in the midst of tears and affliction. It is better to lose your life in the quest than to languish miserably. If we should not succeed, but die of grief, ah well, so much the worse, but, since errors are numerous in this world, we may at least avoid acquiring new ones. Thousands of creatures are craftily occupied in the pursuit of the dead body of the world; so, if you give yourself up to this commerce, above all with guile, will you be able to make your heart an ocean of love? Some say that the wish for spiritual things is presumption, and that no mere upstart can attain them. But isn't it better to sacrifice one's life in pursuit of this desire than to be identified with a business? I have seen everything and done everything, and nothing will shake my resolve. For a long time I have had to do with men and have seen how few there be who are truly unattached to riches. So long as we do not die to ourselves, and so long as we are identified with someone or something, we shall never be free. The spiritual way is not for those wrapped up in exterior life. Set your foot in this Way if you are a man who can act, and do not indulge in feminine shifts. Know surely, that even if this quest were impious, it would still be necessary to undertake it. Certainly, it is not easy; the fruit is without leaves on the tree of love. Tell him who has leaves to renounce them.

'When love possesses a man it lifts his heart, it plunges him in blood, it throws him prostrate outside the curtain, it gives him no rest for a single instant; it kills him yet still demands the price of blood. He drinks the water of tears and eats bread leavened with mourning; but be he more feeble than an ant, love will lend him strength.'

Anecdote of a contemplative

A madman, a fool of God, went naked when other men went clothed. He said: 'O God, give me a beautiful garment, then I shall be content as other men.' A voice from the unseen world answered him: 'I have given you a warm sun, sit down and revel in it.' The madman said: 'Why punish me? Haven't you a better garment than the sun?' The voice said: 'Wait patiently for ten days, and without more ado I will give you another garment.' The sun scorched him for eight days; then a poor man came along and gave him a garment which had a thousand patches. The fool said to God: 'O you who have knowledge of hidden things, why have you given me this patched-up garment? Have you burnt all your garments and had to patch up this old one? You have sewn together a thousand garments. From whom have you learned this art?'

It is not easy to have dealings at the Court of God. A man must become as the dust in the road which leads there. After a long struggle he thinks he has reached the goal only to discover that it is still to be attained.

The story of Rabi'ah

Rabi'ah, although a woman, was the crown of men. She once spent eight years making a pilgrimage to the Ka'aba* by measuring her length on the ground. When at last she reached the door of the sacred temple she thought: 'Now at last, have I performed my task.' On the consecrated day, when she was to go in to the Ka'aba, her women deserted her. So Rabi'ah retraced her steps and said: 'O God, possessor of glory, for eight years I have measured the way with the length of my body, and now, when the longed-for day has come in answer to my prayers, you put thorns in my way!'

To understand the importance of such an incident it is necessary to discover a lover of God like Rabi'ah. So long as you float on the deep ocean of the world its waves will receive and repel you, turn by turn. At times you will be admitted into the Ka'aba, sometimes you will sigh in a pagoda. If you succeed in withdrawing from the attachments of the world you will enjoy felicity; but if you remain attached your head will turn like the grindstone of a mill. Not for a moment will you be tranquil; you will be upset by a single fly.

The fool of God

It was the custom of a poor man in love with God to stand in a

---

*The building at the centre of the Mosque at Mecca.

certain place; and one day a king of Egypt, who had often passed him with his courtiers, stopped, and said: 'I see in you a certain quality of tranquillity and relaxation.' The fool replied: 'How should I be tranquil, seeing that I am delivered up to the flies and the fleas? All day the flies torment me, and at night the fleas won't let me sleep. One tiny fly which entered the ear of Nimrod troubled the brain of that idiot for centuries. Perhaps I am the Nimrod of these times for I have had my share of my friends, the flies and the fleas.'

The speech of the third bird

The third bird said to the Hoopoe: 'I am full of faults, so how shall I set out on the road? Can a dirty fly be worthy of the Simurgh of the Caucasus? How can a sinner who turns away from the true path approach the King?'

The Hoopoe said: 'O despondent bird, do not be so hopeless, ask for grace and favour. If you so lightly throw away your shield you task truly will be difficult.'

Anecdote of a criminal

A man guilty of many sins repented bitterly and returned to the right path. But in time, his desire for the things of the world returned stronger than ever, and he again surrendered himself to evil thoughts and acts. Then sorrow wrung his heart and reduced him to a miserable state. Again he wished to change his attitude, but had not the strength to do so. Day and night, as a grain of wheat in a hot pan, his heart could not keep still, and his tears watered the dust. One morning, a mysterious voice spoke to him: 'Listen to the Lord of the World. When you repented the first time I accepted your penitence. Though I could have punished you I did not do so. A second time when you fell into sin I gave you a respite, and now even in my anger I have not caused you to die. And today, O fool, you acknowledge your perfidy and wish to return to me a third time. Return, then, to the Way. I open my door to you and wait. When you have truly changed your attitude your sins will be forgiven.'

TATANKA-OHITIKA

From Frances Densmore, 'Teton Sioux Music',
Bulletin, **Bureau of American Ethnology, Washington, DC, 1918, no. 61**

Tatanka-ohitika (1838–1911) was born a Sioux Indian in North Dakota, son of a prominent medicine man. The way to knowledge for him included a quest of a vision, or great dream, in which some communication with a higher being [Wakan tanka] is established. He gives a view of a world permeated by this mysterious higher force, Wakan tanka. In such a world, the objects which we encounter every day take on hidden meaning, as if surrounded by an invisible aura. By pursuing these thoughts, we arrive at the fundamental question concerning our place on earth.

When I was ten years of age I looked at the land and the rivers, the sky above, and the animals around me and could not fail to realize that they were made by some great power. I was so anxious to understand this power that I questioned the trees and the bushes. It seemed as though the flowers were staring at me, and I wanted to ask them, 'Who made you?' I looked at the moss-covered stones; some of them seemed to have the features of a man, but they could not answer me. Then I had a dream, and in my dream one of these small round stones appeared to me and told me that the maker of all was Wakan tanka, and that in order to honour him I must honour his works in nature. The stone said that by my search I had shown myself worthy of supernatural help. It said that if I were curing a sick person I might ask its assistance, and that all the forces of nature would help me work a cure.

It is significant that certain stones are not found buried in the earth, but are on the top of high buttes. They are round, like the sun and moon, and we know that all things which are round are related to each other. Things which are alike in their nature grow to look like each other, and these stones have lain there a long time, looking at the sun. Many pebbles and stones have been shaped in the current of a stream, but these stones were found far from the water and have been exposed only to the sun and the wind. The earth contains many thousand such stones hidden beneath its surface. The thunderbird is said to be related to these stones, and when a man or an animal is to be punished, the thunderbird strikes the person, and if it were possible to follow the course of the lightning, one of these stones would be found embedded in the earth. Some believe that these stones descend with the lightning, but I believe they are on the ground and are projected downwards by the bolt. In all my life I have been faithful to the sacred stones. I have lived according to their requirements, and they have helped me in all my troubles. I have tried to qualify myself as well as possible to handle these sacred stones, yet I know that I am not worthy to speak to Wakan tanka. I make my request of the stones and they are my intercessors.

MUNDAKA UPANISHAD

From *The Thirteen Principal Upanishads*, translated by R. E. Hume, Oxford University Press, 2nd ed., 1931

The Mundaka Upanishad is one of the principal Upanishads, the writings of a philosophical movement of ancient India, beginning around the sixth century BC. In these explorations, the great questions of the meaning of life and the relation of the individual to the cosmos are sounded with profound depth and originality. In toto, they must be ranked with the foremost discoveries in the realm of thought.

In the selection from the Mundaka Upanishad, all that exists is traced back to the supreme person, the Purusha. By a series of progressively lower manifestations, the known cosmos is called into being. In this way of thinking, one's inner self is mysteriously identical to the All. Holding that what separates us from perceiving the unity is partial vision, the Upanishad suggests a pathway to greater wholeness.

First Mundaka

Saunaka's quest for the clue to an understanding of the world

3. Saunaka, verily, indeed, a great householder, approached Angiras according to rule, and asked: 'Through understanding of what, pray, does all this world become understood, sir?'

Two kinds of knowledge: the traditions of religion, and the knowledge of the eternal

4. To him then he said: 'There are two knowledges to be known — as indeed the knowers of Brahma are wont to say: a higher [para] and also a lower [apara] . . .'

The imperishable source of all things

6. That which is invisible, ungraspable, without family,
    without caste [a-varna] —
   Without sight or hearing is It, without hand or foot,

Eternal, all-pervading, omnipresent, exceedingly
  subtile;
That is the Imperishable, which the wise perceive as
  the source of beings.

7. As a spider emits and draws in [its thread],
  As herbs arise on the earth,
  As the hairs of the head and body from a living person,
  So from the Imperishable arises everything here.

8. By austerity [tapas] Brahma becomes built up.
  From that, food is produced;
  From food — life-breath, mind, truth,
  The worlds, immortality too in works.

9. He who is all-knowing, all-wise,
  Whose austerity consists of knowledge —
  From Him are produced the Brahma here,
  [Namely] name and form,* and food . . .

The consequence of ignorance

8. Those abiding in the midst of ignorance,
  self-wise, thinking themselves learned,
  Hard smitten, go around deluded,
  Like blind men led by one who is himself blind.

9. Manifoldly living in ignorance,
  They think to themselves, childishly: 'We have
    accomplished our aim!'
  Since doers of deeds [karmin] do not understand,
    because of passion [rage],
  Therefore, when their worlds are exhausted, they
    sink down wretched.

*A Sanskrit idiom for the modern term 'individuality'.(Trans.)

10. Thinking sacrifice and merit is the chiefest thing,
    Naught better do they know – deluded!
    Having had enjoyment on the top of the heaven
        won by good works,
    They re-enter this world, or a lower.

But unstriving, retiring knowers, without sacrifice, reach the eternal Person

11. They who practise austerity [*tapas*] and faith [*sraddha*]
        in the forest,
    The peaceful [*santa*] knowers who live on alms,
    Depart passionless [*vi-raga*] through the door of the
        sun,
    To where is that immortal Person [Purusha], e'en the
        imperishable Spirit [Atman].

This knowledge of Brahma to be sought properly from a qualified teacher

12. Having scrutinized the worlds that are built up by
        work, a Brahman
    Should arrive at indifference. The [world] that was
        not made is not [won] by what is done.
    For the sake of this knowledge let him go, fuel in hand,*
    To a spiritual teacher [*guru*] who is learned in the
        scriptures and established on Brahma.
13. Such a knowing [teacher], unto one who has
        approached properly,

*The token of pupilship. (Trans.)

117

Whose thought is tranquillized, who has reached
  peace,
Teaches in its very truth that knowledge of Brahma
Whereby one knows the Imperishable, the Person,
  the True.

Second Mundaka

THE DOCTRINE OF BRAHMA-ATMAN

First Khanda

The Imperishable, the source and the goal of all beings

1. This is the truth:
    As, from a well-blazing fire, sparks
    By the thousand issue forth of like form,
    So from the Imperishable, my friend, beings manifold
    Are produced, and thither also go.

The supreme Person

2. Heavenly [*divya*], formless [*a-murtta*] is a Person
      [Purusha].
    He is without and within, unborn,
    Breathless [*a-prana*], mindless [*a-manas*], pure [*subhra*],
    Higher than the high Imperishable.

The source of the human person and of the cosmic elements

3. From Him is produced breath [*prana*],
   Mind [*manas*], and all the senses [*indriya*],
   Space [*kha*], wind, light, water,
   And earth, the supporter of all.

The macrocosmic Person

4. Fire in His head; His eyes, the moon and sun;
   The regions of space, His ears; His voice, the revealed Vedas;
   Wind, His breath [*prana*]; His heart, the whole world. Out of His feet,
   The earth. Truly, He is the Inner Soul [Atman] of all.

The source of the world and of the individual

5. From Him [proceeds] fire, whose fuel is the sun;
   From the moon [Soma], rain; herbs, on the earth.
   The male pours seed in the female.
   Many creatures are produced from the Person (Purusha) . . .

The source of the world – the immanent Soul of things

9. From Him, the seas and the mountains all.
   From Him roll rivers of every kind.

And from Him all herbs, the essence, too,
Whereby that Inner Soul [*antaratman*] dwells in beings.

The supreme Person found in the heart

10. The Person [Purusha] himself is everything here:
Work [*karman*] and austerity [*tapas*] and Brahma,
    beyond death.
He who knows That, set in the secret place [of the
    heart] —
He here on earth, my friend, rends asunder the knot
    of ignorance.

Second Khanda

The all-inclusive Brahma

1. Manifest, [yet] hidden; called 'Moving-in-secret';
The great abode! Therein is placed that
        Which moves and breathes and winks.
        What that is, know as Being [*sad*] and Non-being
        [*a-sad*],
        As the object of desire, higher than
        understanding,
        As what is the best of creatures!
2. That which is flaming, which is subtler than the subtle,
On which the worlds are set, and their inhabitants —
        That is the imperishable Brahma.
        It is life [*prana*], and It is speech and mind.
        That is the real. It is immortal.
        It is [a mark] to be penetrated. Penetrate It, my
        friend! . . .

The immortal Soul, the one warp of the world and of the individual

5. He on whom the sky, the earth, and the atmosphere
    Are woven, and the mind, together with all the life-
        breaths [*prana*],
    Him alone know as the one Soul [Atman]. Other
    Words dismiss. He is the bridge to immortality.

The great Soul to be found in the heart

6. Where the channels are brought together
    Like the spokes in the hub of a wheel —
    Therein he moves about,
    Becoming manifold.
    Om! — Thus meditate upon the Soul [Atman].
    Success to you in crossing to the farther shore beyond
        darkness!
7. He who is all-knowing, all wise,
    Whose is this greatness on the earth —
    He is in the divine Brahma city
    And in the heaven established! The Soul [Atman]!
    Consisting of mind, leader of the life-breaths and of
        the body,
    He is established on food, controlling the heart.
    By this knowledge the wise perceive
    The blissful Immortal that gleams forth.

Deliverance gained through vision of Him

8. The knot of the heart is loosened,
    All doubts are cut off,

And one's deeds (*karman*) cease
When He is seen — both the higher and the lower.

The self-luminous light of the world

9. In the highest golden sheath
   Is Brahma, without stain, without parts.
   Brilliant is It, the light of lights —
   That which knowers of the Soul [Atman] do know!
10. The sun shines not there, nor the moon and stars:
    These lightnings shine not, much less this [earthly]
       fire!
    After Him, as He shines, doth everything shine.
    This whole world is illumined with His light.

The omnipresent Brahma

11. Brahma, indeed, is this immortal. Brahma before,
    Brahma behind, to right and to left.
    Stretched forth below and above,
    Brahma, indeed, is this whole world, this widest
       extent.

PART FOUR

The Fact of Death

Undoubtedly the fact that all things come to an end makes us pause to think. Everything that happens comes to a close and so ceases to be subject to change.

Each experience, mental, emotional, or physical, lasts for a limited time only, and however intense it is while it lasts, when it is over the effect invariably fades. Some experiences are so vivid that we think we will never forget them, yet they too sink into the depths of the memory and are only recalled accidentally by the operation of some trigger. All endings point towards one particular ending; the passing of each moment parallels the passing of an entire life. The ending which undoubtedly provokes the deepest thought is our own ending – death.

Why is there death? What is the meaning of death for the living? What, if anything, happens after death? What attitude is appropriate to an awareness of the presence of death in life? Questions like these have called people to a fuller examination of human existence in the light of its inevitable end.

An unavoidable event (a difficult appointment, a job deadline) often gives rise to anxiety, dread, and fear. One may be so overwhelmed that one is temporarily brought to a halt, unable to do anything. Similarly, the universality of death stops us in our tracks and this gives us an opportunity to look at our own life more impartially. The universality of death gives us a sense of objectivity towards self. The danger is that the sense of doom may be overwhelming and cause everything else to seem meaningless by comparison. There is a danger that one may become immobilized, dispirited, paralysed. But this, according to Heidegger, presents a challenge. By means of what he calls an 'anticipatory resoluteness', we can be, moment by moment, more authentically *in* our lives. Death is then not so much a force that marks life's end as an agent of its new beginning. When we take on board the fact that we are going to die, we tend to renew our search for understanding. We cannot treat death as a mere statistic, an event that happens to others but not to ourselves. We cannot de-personalize death. The sense of our personal death, Heidegger argues, derives ultimately from the mystery of conscience — conscience conceived not as a moral faculty but as a source of knowing how to be fully what one is. To attend to this moment of awareness gives one a deep knowledge of how to live with one's own mortality. Death can be seen, as Heidegger suggests, as a creator, or at least a reminder of real possibilities. Death is not to be fought, but rather to be acknowledged and used to advantage, to be worked with and even consulted as an ally.

According to a different view, however, isn't death the des-troyer? Death takes our loved ones away from us; every day we hear of the depredations of death — of calamity, catastrophe, freak accident, or premeditated slaughter. For Sartre, death is a termina-tion, a door closing. In death, everything 'has slipped entirely into the past'. Since the past is a repository of frozen possibilities, of choices played out, the realm of death is, of necessity, one where nothing is to be done. Whatever death touches is impervious to human action. Death threatens to snare the very heart of meaning in life, the capacity to question. A person embued with a sense of death, for Sartre, is one chained to the past by a force that is non-human.

But whether it makes us aware of more possibilities or restricts our field of action, death is inexorably connected with suffering and the painful side of human existence. However, in an age when we are exposed to the suffering of others through the lens of public media, when technology has given us the means of extend-ing biological life in the face of unrelenting physical agony, death surely comes as a release. Even although, as Hamlet reminds us, we do not know what awaits us after death, the release given by death still seems preferable to the prolonging of unbearable pain. The difficulty of letting go of life is poignantly described in Tolstoy's story, 'The Death of Ivan Ilich'. Ivan Ilich suffers terribly from an incurable illness. Through a moving exploration of Ilich's inner life, Tolstoy suggests that Ilich's pain is the result of certain illusions he holds regarding himself and what others appear to think of him. When he is able to relinquish them, he experiences the comfort of a vast, new freedom as he confronts the reality of that which he had previously shunned, his own death.

That an understanding of one's death is a powerful agent of freedom is the theme of many ancient and traditional schools of thought. A person's existence, it is held, passes through a number of phases, forever returning to its beginning. To a primitive mind, nature seems to be rhythmic, impelled by fits of creation and destruction inseparably bound to one another: the alteration of night and day, the seasons, the phases of the moon, the tides, the migration of birds and animals. To this way of thinking, if death follows life, then life must follow death. Here the dominant idea is neither annihilation nor release, but rebirth, regeneration, and resurrection. Death is the door to a new round of existence.

The cyclical view of life can also be applied on the smallest scale: each moment has its own life, arising, maturing, ageing, and perishing as the next moment arrives. According to Buddhist ideas, the life that follows death is a continuation and elaboration of the automatic impulses and character traits formed before death. As one advances in understanding of life, one's identity tends to grow more or less independent from this kind of mech-anical rebirth. Since, in this view, becoming entangled in the unconscious drive to *do* things is the cause of suffering, only a death which is not followed by rebirth constitutes freedom: 'from the stopping of birth, ageing and dying, grief, sorrow, suffering, lamentation and despair are stopped'. Living wisely is the best preparation for dying well. We become free from the pain of mortality when we are finally no longer burdened by our lack of understanding. A good death can thus be compared to the extinguishing of a well-made candle: putting out such a candle leaves no trace, while putting out a poorly made candle leaves a trail of smoke and soot.

What does it mean to claim, as Plato does, that our living, when philosophically motivated, is a preparation for our dying? The idea is that each moment as we come to it contains the totality of our existence when we are ourselves present in it. Being born, ageing, dying: we can experience these phenomena in time present, not in the past or the future. The more we inhabit our living time, the more we are aware of the expectations, fears, and attachments with which we meet experience, and the more realistic is our approach to dying. At the last, facing our own mortality, the very same attitude persists, writ larger. 'Overcome your ignorance; become liberated,' the Buddhist exhorts us. At a fundamental level, the recommendation is simply to grow more attentive to the living process to avoid unthinking repetition. The idea of preparation is conveyed in Plato's myth of Er, who returns after death and gives an account of what he has seen. Plato suggests that the merit of a person's actions in this life determines the kind of life he or she will proceed to. Although choice is 'mostly governed by the habits of their former life', those who quest for understanding would have more favourable circumstances in the next life. The narrative is allegorical, of course, and does not necessarily suggest that we are literally reborn.

From the individual's standpoint, mortality represents either release and preparation for release or the brute fact of annihilation. But what of the cosmic view, where one's death represents the loss of one member of a species of some five billion, among a multitude of some four billion species? What is death on such a scale, where planets, suns, and even whole universes live and perish? Lewis Thomas reminds us that the recycling of the materials of life is a necessary principle of creation. 'Everything that comes alive seems to be in trade for something that dies, cell for cell.' Conservation of matter and energy means that the claim of any one entity to a particular assortment of particles is relative to a time and a place, for the same assortment ends up somewhere else at another time as quite another entity. The particles themselves have a relative immortality, but any single combination of them has a strictly limited lifetime.

While some exchange of material is necessary to maintain the universe, not all thinkers would agree that a person's identity can be equated with his or her biochemical composition. The question is, is the whole something more than the sum of the parts? Even a simple compound, such as water, has properties quite different from those of hydrogen and oxygen, the elements of which it is composed. What is called life is not just the sum of the constituents – organs, tissues, and so on – that make up the living body. 'Life' is not strictly identical to physical life, to the body's life. It comes into being in the form of an activity or process which relates, in a moment-to-moment way, the components to one another. Plato, in the *Phaedo*, a dialogue which describes Socrates' death, compares the process of regulation to the tuning of a musical instrument: 'our soul,' he says, 'is a temperament or adjustment of these same extremes, when they are combined in just the right proportion.' The intelligence, which resides in the body and which regulates the millions of delicate biochemical balances, could be considered the seat of life. This interpretation of it leaves open the question of whether any aspect of it survives the body's death.

Asking whether any part of ourselves is not destroyed in death does in fact clarify the meaning of 'life'. It is fair to ask, is the primary sense of 'death' found in the event or process corresponding to our biological termination? Plato's suggestion, and the Buddhist's, can be taken as speaking of life within our life which exists whenever we consciously participate in the balance of our components. This 'inner life' flickers out of existence whenever we

are preoccupied elsewhere. The life within is not given but a
potential, which we can cultivate if we choose to do so. The
power of thought is one of the most effective tools for realizing
our potential. In this sense, our dying is akin to a forgetting.
Whenever the project of creating an inner life passes into oblivion,
we too die. A life without a regard for life is a kind of living death
– within which the question of death does not meaningfully arise.

PLATO, 'THE MYTH OF ER'

**From Plato, *The Republic*, translated by B. Jowett,
Clarendon Press, 1892**

In the final section of his longest and most famous work, The Republic,
*Plato (see also p. 24) gives an allegorical account of one individual's
existence after death. For unknown reasons, Er, a soldier, returns to life
after being dead for twelve days, and recounts his vision of the other
world and the justice which is meted out there; according to the quality
of their deeds, a person's choice of the 'next life' is higher or lower. We
are left with the question of how to understand the soul, the bearer of
immortality, and its capacity to have a relatively permanent identity.
Glaucon, Socrates' interlocutor, was a political figure of contemporary
Athens.*

Well, I said, I will tell you a tale; not one of the tales which
Odysseus tells to the hero Alcinous, yet this too is a tale of a hero,
Er the son of Armenius, a Pamphylian by birth. He was slain in
battle, and ten days afterwards, when the bodies of the dead were
taken up already in a state of corruption, his body was found
unaffected by decay, and carried away home to be buried. And on
the twelfth day, as he was lying on the funeral pile, he returned to
life and told them what he had seen in the other world. He said

that when his soul left the body he went on a journey with a great company and that they came to a mysterious place at which there were two openings in the earth; they were near together, and over against them were two other openings in the heaven above. In the intermediate space there were judges seated, who commanded the just, after they had given judgement on them and had bound their sentences in front of them, to ascend by the heavenly way on the right hand; and in like manner the unjust were bidden by them to descend by the lower way on the left hand; these also bore the symbols of their deeds, but fastened on their backs. He drew near, and they told him that he was to be the messenger who would carry the report of the other world to men, and they bade him hear and see all that was to be heard and seen in that place. Then he beheld and saw on one side the souls departing at either opening of heaven and earth when sentence had been given on them; and at the two other openings other souls, some ascending out of the earth dusty and worn with travel, some descending out of heaven clean and bright. And arriving ever and anon they seemed to have come from a long journey, and they went forth with gladness into the meadow, where they encamped as at a festival; and those who knew one another embraced and conversed, the souls which came from earth curiously inquiring about the things above, and the souls which came from heaven about the things beneath. And they told one another of what had happened by the way, those from below weeping and sorrowing at the remembrance of the things which they had endured and seen in their journey beneath the earth (now the journey lasted a thousand years), while those from above were describing heavenly delights and visions of inconceivable beauty. The story, Glaucon, would take too long to tell; but the sum was this: – he said that for every wrong which they had done to any one they suffered tenfold; or once in a hundred years – such being reckoned to be the length of man's life and the penalty being thus paid ten times in a thousand years. If, for example, there were any who had been the cause of many deaths, or had betrayed or enslaved cities or armies, or been guilty of any other evil behaviour, for each and all of their offences they received punishment ten times over, and the rewards of beneficence and justice and holiness were in the same proportion. I need hardly repeat what he said concerning young children dying almost as soon as they were born. Of piety and impiety to gods and parents, and of murderers, there were retributions other and greater far which he described. He mentioned that he was present when one of the spirits asked another, 'Where is Ardiaeus the Great?' (Now this Ardiaeus lived a thousand years before the time of Er: he had been the tyrant of some city of Pamphylia, and had murdered his aged father and his elder brother, and was said to have committed many other abominable crimes.) The answer of the other spirit was: 'He comes not hither and will never come. And this,' said he, 'was one of the dreadful sights which we ourselves witnessed. We were at the mouth of the cavern, and, having completed all our experiences, were about to reascend, when all of a sudden Ardiaeus appeared and several others, most of whom were tyrants; and there were also besides the tyrants private individuals who had been great criminals; they were just, as they fancied, about to return into the upper world, but the mouth, instead of admitting them, gave a roar, whenever any of these incurable sinners or some one who had not been sufficiently punished tried to ascend; and then wild men of fiery aspect, who were standing by and heard the sound, seized and carried them off; and Ardiaeus and others they bound head and foot and hand, and threw them down and flayed them with scourges, and dragged them along the road at the side, carding them on thorns like wool, and declaring to the passers-by what were their crimes, and that they were being taken away to be cast into hell.' And of all the many terrors which they had endured, he said that there was none like the terror which each of them felt at that moment, lest they should hear the voice; and when there was silence, one by one they ascended with exceeding joy. These, said Er, were the penalties and retributions, and there were blessings as great.

Now when the spirits which were in the meadow had tarried seven days, on the eighth they were obliged to proceed on their journey, and, on the fourth day after, he said that they came to a place where they could see from above a line of light, straight as a column, extending right through the whole heaven and through the earth, in colour resembling the rainbow, only brighter and purer; another day's journey brought them to the place, and there, in the midst of the light, they saw the ends of the chains of heaven let down from above: for this light is the belt of heaven, and holds together the circle of the universe, like the under-girders of a trireme. From these ends is extended the spindle of Necessity, on which all the revolutions turn. The shaft and hook of this spindle are made of steel, and the whorl is made partly of steel and also partly of other materials. Now the whorl is in form like the whorl used on earth; and the description of it implied that there is one large hollow whorl which is quite scooped out, and into this is fitted another lesser one, and another, and another, and four others, making eight in all, like vessels which fit into one another; the whorls show their edges on the upper side, and on their lower side all together form one continuous whorl. This is pierced by the spindle, which is driven home through the centre of the eighth. The first and outermost whorl has the rim broadest, and the seven inner whorls are narrower, in the following proportions — the sixth is next to the first in size, the fourth next to the sixth; then comes the eighth; the seventh is fifth, the fifth is sixth, the third is seventh, last and eighth comes the second. The largest [or fixed stars] is spangled, and the seventh [or sun] is brightest; the eighth [or moon] coloured by reflected light of the seventh; the second and fifth [Saturn and Mercury] are in colour like one another, and yellower than the preceding; the third [Venus] has the whitest light; the fourth [Mars] is reddish; the sixth [Jupiter] is in whiteness second. Now the whole spindle has the same motion; but, as the whole revolves in one direction, the seven inner circles move slowly in the other, and of these the swiftest is the eighth; next in swiftness are the seventh, sixth, and fifth, which move together; third in swiftness appeared to move according to the law of this reversed motion the fourth; the third appeared fourth and the second fifth. The spindle turns on the knees of Necessity; and on the upper surface of each circle is a siren, who goes round with them, hymning a single tone or note. The eight together form one harmony; and round about, at equal intervals, there is another band, three in number, each sitting upon her throne; these are the Fates, daughters of Necessity, who are clothed in white robes and have chaplets upon their heads, Lachesis and Clotho and Atropos, who accompany with their voices the harmony of the sirens – Lachesis singing of the past, Clotho of the present, Atropos of the future; Clotho from time to time assisting with a touch of her right hand the revolution of the outer circle of the whorl or spindle, and Atropos with her left hand touching and guiding the inner ones, and Lachesis laying hold of either in turn, first with one hand and then with the other.

When Er and the spirits arrived, their duty was to go at once to Lachesis; but first of all there came a prophet who arranged them in order; then he took from the knees of Lachesis lots of samples of lives, and having mounted a high pulpit, spoke as follows: 'Hear the word of Lachesis, the daughter of Necessity. Mortal souls, behold a new cycle of life and mortality. Your genius will not be allotted to you, but you will choose your genius; and let him who draws the first lot have the first choice, and the life which he chooses shall be his destiny. Virtue is free, and as a man honours or dishonours her he will have more or less of her; the responsibility is with the chooser – God is justified.' When the Interpreter had thus spoken he scattered lots indifferently among them all, and each of them took up the lot which fell near him, all but Er himself (he was not allowed), and each as he took his lot perceived the number which he had obtained. Then the Interpreter placed on the ground before them the samples of lives; and there were many more lives than the souls present, and they were of all

THE FACT OF DEATH

sorts. There were lives of every animal and of man in every condition. And there were tyrannies among them, some lasting out the tyrant's life, others which broke off in the middle and came to an end in poverty and exile and beggary; and there were lives of famous men, some who were famous for their form and beauty as well as for their strength and success in games, or, again, for their birth and the qualities of their ancestors; and some who were the reverse of famous for the opposite qualities. And of women likewise; there was not, however, any definite character in them, because the soul, when choosing a new life, must of necessity become different. But there was every other quality, and they all mingled with one another, and also with elements of wealth and poverty, and disease and health; and there were mean states also. And here, my dear Glaucon, is the supreme peril of our human state; and therefore the utmost care should be taken. Let each one of us leave every other kind of knowledge and seek and follow one thing only, if peradventure he may be able to learn and may find some one who will make him able to learn and discern between good and evil, and so to choose always and everywhere the better life as he has opportunity. He should consider the bearing of all these things which have been mentioned severally and collectively upon virtue; he should know what the effect of beauty is when combined with poverty or wealth in a particular soul, and what are the good and evil consequences of noble and humble birth, of private and public station, of strength and weakness, of cleverness and dullness, and of all the natural and acquired gifts of the soul, and the operation of them when conjoined; he will then look at the nature of the soul, and from the consideration of all these qualities he will be able to determine which is the better and which is the worse; and so he will choose, giving the name of evil to the life which will make his soul more unjust, and good to the life which will make his soul more just; all else he will disregard. For we have seen and know that this is the best choice both in life and after death. A man must take with him into the

133

world below an adamantine faith in truth and right, that there too he may be undazzled by the desire of wealth or the other allurements of evil, lest, coming upon tyrannies and similar villainies, he do irremediable wrongs to others and suffer yet worse himself; but let him know how to choose the mean and avoid the extremes on either side, as far as possible, not only in this life but in all that which is to come. For this is the way of happiness.

And according to the report of the messenger from the other world this was what the prophet said at the time: 'Even for the last comer, if he chooses wisely and will live diligently, there is appointed a happy and not undesirable existence. Let not him who chooses first be careless, and let not the last despair.' And when he had spoken, he who had the first choice came forward and in a moment chose the greatest tyranny; his mind having been darkened by folly and sensuality, he had not thought out the whole matter before he chose, and did not at first sight perceive that he was fated, among the evils, to devour his own children. But when he had time to reflect, and saw what was in the lot, he began to beat his breast and lament over his choice, forgetting the proclamation of the prophet; for, instead of throwing the blame of his misfortune on himself, he accused chance and the gods, and everything rather than himself. Now he was one of those who came from heaven, and in a former life had dwelt in a well-ordered state, but his virtue was a matter of habit only, and he had no philosophy. And it was true of others who were similarly overtaken, that the greater number of them came from heaven and therefore they had never been schooled by trial, whereas the pilgrims who came from earth having themselves suffered and seen others suffer were not in a hurry to choose. And owing to this inexperience of theirs, and also because the lot was a chance, many of the souls exchanged a good destiny for an evil or an evil for a good. For if a man had always on his arrival in this world dedicated himself from the first to sound philosophy, and had been moderately fortunate in the number of the lot, he might, as

134

the messenger reported, be happy here, and also his journey to another life and return to this, instead of being rough and underground, would be smooth and heavenly. Most curious, he said, was the spectacle — sad and laughable and strange; for the choice of the souls was in the most cases based on their experience of a previous life. There he saw the soul which had once been Orpheus choosing the life of a swan out of enmity to the race of women, hating to be born of a woman because they had been his murderers; he beheld also the soul of Thamyris choosing the life of a nightingale; birds, on the other hand, like the swan and other musicians, wanting to be men. The soul which obtained the twentieth lot chose the life of a lion, and this was the soul of Ajax the son of Telamon, who would not be a man, remembering the injustice which was done him in the judgement about the arms. The next was Agamemnon, who took the life of an eagle, because, like Ajax, he hated human nature by reasons of his sufferings. About the middle came the lot of Atalanta: she, seeing the great fame of an athlete, was unable to resist the temptation; and after her there followed the soul of Epeius the son of Panopeus passing into the nature of a woman cunning in the arts; and far away among the last who chose, the soul of the jester Thersites was putting on the form of a monkey. There came also the soul of Odysseus having yet to make a choice, and his lot happened to be the last of them all. Now the recollection of former lots had disenchanted him of ambition, and he went about for a considerable time in search of the life of a private man who had no cares; he had some difficulty in finding this, which was lying about and had been neglected by everybody else; and when he saw it, he said that he would have done the same had his lot been first instead of last, and that he was delighted to have it. And not only did men pass into animals, but I must also mention that there were animals tame and wild who changed into one another and into corresponding human natures — the good into the gentle and the evil into the savage, in all sorts of combinations.

All the souls had now chosen their lives, and they went in the order of their choice to Lachesis, who sent with them the genius whom they had severally chosen, to be the guardian of their lives and the fulfiller of the choice: this genius led the souls first to Clotho, and drew them within the revolution of the spindle impelled by her hand, thus ratifying the destiny of each: and then, when they were fastened to this, carried them to Atropos, who spun the threads and made them irreversible, whence without turning round they passed beneath the throne of Necessity; and when they had all passed, they marched on in a scorching heat to the plain of Forgetfulness, which was a barren waste destitute of trees and verdure; and then towards evening they encamped by the river of Unmindfulness, whose water no vessel can hold; of this they were all obliged to drink a certain quantity, and those who were not saved by wisdom drank more than was necessary; and each one as he drank forgot all things. Now after they had gone to rest, about the middle of the night there was a thunderstorm and earthquake, and then in an instant they were driven upwards in all manner of ways to their birth, like stars shooting. He himself was hindered from drinking the water. But in what manner or by what means he returned to the body he could not say; only, in the morning, awakening suddenly, he found himself lying on the pyre.

And thus, Glaucon, the tale has been saved and has not perished, and will save us if we are obedient to the word spoken; and we shall pass safely over the river of Forgetfulness and our soul will not be defiled. Wherefore my counsel is that we hold fast ever to the heavenly way and follow after justice and virtue always, considering that the soul is immortal and able to endure every sort of good and every sort of evil. Thus shall we live dear to one another and to the gods, both while remaining here and when, like conquerors in the games who go round to gather gifts, we receive our reward. And it shall be well with us both in this life and in the pilgrimage of a thousand years which we have been describing.

SARTRE, *BEING AND NOTHINGNESS*

**From Jean-Paul Sartre, *Being and Nothingness*,
translated by H. Barnes, New York, Philosophical
Library, 1956, and London, Methuen, 1957**

*Jean-Paul Sartre (1905–80), French thinker, novelist, and Nobel Prize
winner. His primary concern, with human awareness and existence, can
be found throughout his diverse works, in* Nausea (*a novel*), The
Words (*an autobiography*), *and* Being and Nothingness (*his philosophical magnum opus*).

*Sartre views life as a process of diminishing a fund of possibilities,
and converting them into necessities. Each act, each choice, on his terms,
converts the for-itself (human possibility) into the in-itself (mechanical
necessity). Death is the final conversion. After death, there is nothing
more to be decided. A person is all past. Present and future are no more.
In this sense, death is also a conversion to absolute finality.*

I see first that the term 'was' is a mode of being. In this sense I am
my past. I do not have it; I am it. A remark made by someone
concerning an act which I performed yesterday or a mood which I
had does not leave me indifferent: I am hurt or flattered, I protest
or I let it pass; I am touched to the quick. I do not dissociate
myself from my past. Of course, in time I can attempt this
dissociation; I can declare that 'I am no longer what I was', argue
that there has been a change, progress. But this is a matter of a
secondary reaction which is given as such. To deny my solidarity
of being with my past at this or that particular point is to affirm it
for the whole of my life. At my limit, at that infinitesimal instant
of my death, I shall be no more than my past. It alone will define
me. This is what Sophocles wants to express in the *Trachiniae*
when he has Deianeira say, 'It is a proverb current for a long time
among men that one cannot pass judgement on the life of mortals
and say if it has been happy or unhappy, until their death.' This is

also the meaning of that sentence of Malraux's which we quoted earlier, 'Death changes life into Destiny.' Finally this is what strikes the Believer when he realizes with terror that at the moment of death the chips are down, there remains not a card to play. Death reunites us with ourselves. Eternity has changed us into ourselves. At the moment of death we are; that is, we are defenceless before the judgements of others. They can decide *in truth* what we are; ultimately we have no longer any chance of escape from what an all-knowing intelligence could do. A last-hour repentance is a desperate effort to crack all this being which has slowly congealed and solidified *around* us, a final leap to dissociate ourselves from what we are. In vain. Death fixes this leap along with the rest; it does no more than to enter into combination with what has preceded it, as one factor among others, as one particular determination which is understood only in terms of the totality. By death the for-itself is changed for ever into an in-itself in that it has slipped entirely into the past. Thus the past is the ever-growing totality of the in-itself which we are.

Nevertheless so long as we are not dead, we are not this in-itself in the mode of identity. We *have* to be it. Ordinarily a grudge against a man ceases with his death; this is because he has been reunited with his past; he *is it* without, however, being responsible for it. So long as he lives, he is the object of my grudge; that is, I reproach him for his past not only in so far as he *is it* but in so far as he reassumes it at each instant and sustains it in being, in so far as he is responsible for it. It is not true that the grudge fixes the man in what he was; otherwise it would survive death. It is addressed to the living man who in his being is freely what he was. I am my past and if I were not, my past would not exist any longer either *for me* or *for anybody*. It would no longer have any relation with the present. That certainly does not mean that it would not be but only that its being would be undiscoverable. I am the one by whom my past arrives in this world. But it must be understood that I do not give being to it. In other words it does not exist as 'my' representation. It is not because I 'represent' my past that it exists. But it is because I am my past that it enters into the world, and it is in terms of its being-in-the-world that I can by applying a particular psychological process represent it to myself.

The past is what I have to be, and yet its nature is different from that of my possibles. The possible, which also I have to be, remains as my concrete possible, that whose opposite is equally possible — although to a less degree. The past, on the contrary, is that which is without possibility of any sort: it is that which has consumed its possibilities. I have to be that which no longer depends on my being able to be, that which is already in itself all which it can be. The past which I am, I have to be with no possibility of not being it. I assume the total responsibility for it as if I could change it, and yet I can not be anything other than it. We shall see later that we continually preserve the possibility of changing the meaning of the past in so far as this is an ex-present which has a future. But from the content of the past as such I can remove nothing, and I can add nothing to it. In other words the past which I was is what it is; it is an in-itself like the things of the world. The relation of being which I have to sustain with the past is a relation of the type of the in-itself — that is, an identification with itself . . .

For-itself which has squeezed out all its nothingness and been reapprehended by the In-itself, a For-itself dissolving into the world — such is the Past, which I have to be, such is the avatar of the For-itself. But this avatar is produced in unity with the appearance of a For-itself which nihilates itself as Presence to the world and which has to be the Past which it transcends. What is the meaning of this upsurge? We must guard against seeing here the appearance of a new being. Everything happens as if the Present were a perpetual hole in being — immediately filled up and perpetually reborn — as if the Present were a perpetual flight away from the snare of the 'In-itself' which threatens it until that final victory of the In-itself which will drag it into a past which is no longer the past of any For-itself. It is death which is this victory, for death is the final arrest of Temporality by the making-past of the whole system, or, if you prefer, by the recapture of human Totality by the In-itself.

HEIDEGGER, *BEING AND TIME*

From Martin Heidegger, *Being and Time*, translated by J. Macquarrie and E. Robinson, New York, Harper & Row, 1962

Martin Heidegger (1889–1984), German philosopher, took as his major project the question of being. To remind us of the call to be, as opposed to doing of all kinds, he looked anew at the roots of thought, in pre-Socratic philosophy. His foremost book, Being and Time, is one of the most influential of the twentieth century.

Heidegger investigates a deepened level of being human (or Dasein, in his terminoloy), the level at which we are attentive to the call of conscience. Its language is silence. It calls us back to our essential position in the world, as beings who are forgetful, and are constantly on the verge of losing themselves in impersonal externals. In this call to return, we encounter, Heidegger believes, the fact of our death. That we are transient mortals enjoins us to be resolute in facing our existence. This new attitude in turn fosters an inner strength, so that we grow less prone to losing contact with the question of who we really are.

In the call to conscience, what is it that is talked about – in other words, to what is the appeal made? Manifestly *Dasein* itself. This answer is as incontestable as it is indefinite. If the call has so vague a target, then it might at most remain an occasion for *Dasein* to pay attention to itself. But it is essential to *Dasein* that along with the disclosedness of its world it has been disclosed to itself, so that

it always *understands itself*. The call reaches *Dasein* in this understanding of itself which it always has, and which is concerned in
an everyday, average manner. The call reaches the they-self of
concerned Being with Others.

And to what is one called when one is thus appealed to? To
one's *own Self*. Not to what *Dasein* counts for, can do, or concerns
itself with in being with one another publicly, nor to what it has
taken hold of, set about, or let itself be carried along with. The
sort of *Dasein* which is understood after the manner of the world
both for Others and for itself, gets *passed over* in this appeal; this is
something of which the call to the Self takes not the slightest
cognizance. And because only the *Self* of the they-self gets
appealed to and brought to hear, the 'they' and the manner in
which *Dasein* has been publicly interpreted does not by any means
signify that the 'they' is not *reached too*. Precisely *in passing over*
the 'they' (keen as it is for public repute) the call pushes it into
insignificance [*Bedeutungslosigkeit*]. But the Self, which the appeal
has robbed of this lodgement and hiding-place, gets brought to
itself by the call . . .

The call dispenses with any kind of utterance. It does not put
itself into words at all; yet it remains nothing less than obscure
and indefinite. *Experience discourses solely and constantly in the mode
of keeping silent*. In this way it not only loses none of its percepti-
bility, but forces the *Dasein* which has been appealed to and
summoned into the reticence of itself. The fact that what is called
in the call has not been formulated in words does not give this
phenomenon the indefiniteness of a mysterious voice, but merely
indicates that our understanding of what is 'called' is not to be tied
up with an expectation of anything like a communication.

Yet what the call discloses is unequivocal, even though it may
undergo a different interpretation in the individual *Dasein* in
accordance with its own possibilities of understanding. While the
content of the call is seemingly indefinite, the *direction it takes* is a
sure one and is not to be overlooked. The call does not require us

to search gropingly for him to whom it appeals, nor does it require any sign by which we can recognize that he is not the one who is meant. When 'delusions' arise in the conscience, they do so not because the call has committed some oversight (has miscalled), but only because the call gets *heard* in such a way that instead of becoming authentically understood, it gets drawn by the they-self into a soliloquy in which causes get pleaded, and it becomes perverted in its tendency to disclose . . .

The call does not report events; it calls without uttering anything. The call discourses in the uncanny mode of *keeping silent*. And it does this only because, in calling the one to whom the appeal is made, it does not call him into the public idle talk of the 'they', but *calls* him *back* from this *into the reticence of his existent* potentiality-for-Being. When the caller reaches him to whom the appeal is made, it does so with a cold assurance which is uncanny but by no means obvious. Wherein lies the basis for this assurance if not in the fact that when *Dasein* has been individualized down to itself in its uncanniness, it is for itself something that simply cannot be mistaken for anything else? What is it that so radically deprives *Dasein* of the possibility of misunderstanding itself by any sort of alibi and failing to recognize itself, if not the forsakenness [*Verlassenheit*] with which it has been abandoned [*Uberlassenheit*] to itself?

Uncanniness is the basic kind of Being-in-the-world, even though in an everyday way it has been covered up. Out of the depths of this kind of Being. *Dasein* itself, as conscience, calls. The 'it calls me' ['*es ruft mich*'] is a distinctive kind of discourse for *Dasein*. The call whose mood has been attuned by anxiety is what makes it possible first and foremost for *Dasein* to project itself upon its ownmost *potentiality-for-Being*. The call of conscience, existentially understood, makes known for the first time what we have hitherto merely contended: that uncanniness pursues *Dasein* and is a threat to the lostness in which it has forgotten itself.

The proposition that *Dasein* is at the same time both the caller and the one to whom the appeal is made, has now lost its empty formal character and its obviousness. *Conscience manifests itself as the call of care*: the caller is *Dasein*, which, in its thrownness (in its Being-already-in), is anxious about its potentiality-for-Being. The one to whom the appeal is made is this very same *Dasein*, summoned to its ownmost potentiality-for-Being (ahead of itself . . .). *Dasein* is falling into the 'they' (in Being-already-alongside the world of its concern), and it is summoned out of this falling by the appeal. The call of conscience – that is, conscience itself – has its ontological possibility in the fact that *Dasein*, in the very best of its Being, is care.

VINAYA-PITAKA, MAJJHIMA-NIKAYA, SAMYUTTA-NIKAYA

From E. Conze, ed., *Buddhist Texts through the Ages*, Oxford, Bruno Cassirer, 1954

Vinaya-pitaka, Samyutta-nikaya and Majjhima-nikaya are classical texts of the Hinayana tradition of Buddhism. The Vinaya-pitaka is a classical text for monastic life. Buddhism is a body of thought and practice which strives, through active study, to free the individual from all the impediments to full human expression. The study begins with suffering and impermanence and ends with realization that there is no self different from the cosmos as a whole. The Hinayana is the older and narrower interpretation of the Buddha's teachings, stressing an individual's self-realization over his relations with his fellow-creatures.

In summary form, these three brief texts from the Buddhist corpus embrace a distinctive view of death. Death is the end phase of a process stretching from birth through life and ageing. According to this idea, a lifetime simply repeats on a large scale what a moment enacts on a smaller scale. As soon as we try to hold on to some element of a passing moment, the frustration, negativity, and suffering that flavour our lives begin. To transform this basic condition, Buddhism suggests the relaxing of will, an opening of it to the benevolent powers which support it.

From *Vinaya-pitaka*, I, i

41. Conditioned by ignorance are the karma-formations;* conditioned by the karma-formations is consciousness; conditioned by consciousness is mind-and-body; conditioned by mind-and-body are the six sense-fields; conditioned by the six sense-fields is impression; conditioned by impression is feeling; conditioned by feeling is craving; conditioned by craving is grasping; conditioned by grasping is becoming; conditioned by becoming is birth; conditioned by birth there come into being ageing and dying, grief, sorrow, suffering, lamentation and despair. Thus is the origin of this whole mass of suffering.

But from the stopping of ignorance is the stopping of the karma-formations; from the stopping of the karma-formations is the stopping of consciousness; from the stopping of consciousness is the stopping of mind-and-body; from the stopping of mind-and-body is the stopping of the six sense-fields; from the stopping of the six sense-fields is the stopping of impression; from the stopping of impression is the stopping of becoming; from the stopping of becoming is the stopping of feeling; from the stopping of feeling is the stopping of craving; from the stopping of craving is the stopping of grasping; from the stopping of grasping is the stopping of birth; from the stopping of birth, ageing and dying, grief, sorrow, suffering, lamentation and despair are stopped. Thus is the stopping of this whole mass of suffering.

*The Samkhara are karma-formations or karmical formations, in the sense of 'forming', as opposed to 'formed'. As such they may be said to represent the volitional activity (*cetana*) of body (*kaya*), speech (*vaci*), and mind (*mano*). (Trans.)

From *Majjhima-nikaya*, I, 49–54

43. And what is ageing and dying? Whatever for this or that class of beings is ageing, decrepitude, breaking up, hoariness, wrinkling of the skin, dwindling of the life-span, over-ripeness of the sense-faculties: this is called ageing. Whatever for this or that being in this or that class of beings is the falling and decreasing, the breaking, the disappearance, the mortality and dying, the passing away, the breaking of the *khandhas*, the laying down of the body: this is called dying. This is called ageing and dying.

And what is birth? Whatever for this or that being in this or that class of beings is the conception, the birth, the descent, the production, the appearance of the *khandhas*, the acquiring of the sensory fields: this is called birth.

And what is becoming? There are these three becomings: sensuous becoming, fine-material becoming, immaterial becoming.

And what is grasping? There are four graspings: after sense-pleasures, after speculative view, after rite and custom, after the theory of self.

And what is craving? There are six classes of craving: for material shapes, sounds, smells, tastes, touches and mental objects.

And what is feeling? There are six classes of feeling: feeling due to visual, auditory, olfactory, gustatory, physical and mental impact.

And what is impression? There are six classes of impression: visual, auditory, olfactory, gustatory, physical and mental.

And what are the six sensory fields? The field of the eye, ear, nose, tongue, body, mind.

And what is mind-and-body? Feeling, perception, volition, impression, wise attention: this is called mind.* The four great

---

*... What is mind? The group of feeling, that of perception, that of the impulses, that of consciousness, and the uncompounded element: this is called mind. (Trans.)

elements* and the material shape derived from them: this is called body. Such is mind and such is body. This is called mind-and-body.

And what is consciousness? There are six classes of consciousness: visual, auditory, olfactory, gustatory, physical and mental consciousness.

And what are the karma-formations? There are three: karma-formations of body, of speech, of thought.

And what is ignorance? Whatever is the unknowing in regard to suffering, its arising, its stopping and the course leading to its stopping — this is called ignorance.

From *Samyutta-nikaya*, II, 65–6

48. That which we will and that which we intend to do and that with which we are occupied, this is an object for the support of consciousness. If there is an object there is a foothold for consciousness. With consciousness growing in this foothold there is rebirth and recurrent becoming in the future. If there is rebirth and recurrent becoming in the future, ageing and dying, grief, sorrow, suffering, lamentation and despair come into being in the future. Thus is the arising of this whole mass of suffering.

But if we neither will nor intend to do but are still occupied with something, the same sequence occurs.

But if we neither will nor intend to do and are not occupied with something, there is no object for the support of consciousness; hence no foothold for it; with consciousness having no foothold or growth, there is no rebirth or recurrent becoming in the future. In this absence birth, ageing and dying, grief, sorrow, suffering,

*Earth, water, fire and air. (Trans.)

lamentation and despair in the future are stopped. Thus is the stopping of this whole mass of suffering.

That which we will and that which we intend to do and that with which we are occupied is an object for the support of consciousness. If there is an object there is a foothold for consciousness. With consciousness growing in this foothold there is a descent of mind-and-body.

Conditioned by mind-and-body are the six sense-fields. Conditioned by these is impression . . . Thus is the origin of this whole mass of suffering.

But if we neither will nor intend to do nor are occupied with something, there is no object for the support of consciousness; hence there is no foothold for it. With consciousness having no foothold or growth, there is no descent of mind-and-body. From the stopping of mind-and-body is the stopping of the six sensory fields . . . Thus is the stopping of this whole mass of suffering.

LEWIS THOMAS, 'DEATH IN THE OPEN'

From Lewis Thomas, *The Lives of a Cell*, New York, Viking, 1974

Lewis Thomas (born 1913), American biologist and essayist, has consistently sought the deep meaning underlying various living phenomena. His studies have revealed new approaches to the great questions of survival, death, and evolution. His books include The Lives of a Cell *(1974) and* The Medusa and the Snail *(1979).*

Lewis Thomas approaches death as a natural event within an ecosystem. We never see a dead animal lying in the woods, he tells us, because the organic material is immediately recycled back to the living. In a sense, our planet is a living organism. From this cosmological perspective, its life depends on the reciprocal exchange between the living and the dead. Death is, on this view, depersonalized and granted a larger-than-life significance.

Most of the dead animals you see on highways near the cities are dogs, a few cats. Out in the countryside, the forms and colourings of the dead are strange; these are the wild creatures. Seen from a car window they appear as fragments, evoking memories of woodchucks, badgers, skunks, voles, snakes, sometimes the mysterious wreckage of a deer.

It is always a queer shock, part a sudden upwelling of grief, part unaccountable amazement. It is simply astounding to see an animal dead on a highway. The outrage is more than just the location; it is the impropriety of such visible death, anywhere. You do not expect to see dead animals in the open. It is the nature of animals to die alone, off somewhere, hidden. It is wrong to see them lying out on the highway; it is wrong to see them anywhere.

Everything in the world dies, but we only know about it as a kind of abstraction. If you stand in a meadow, at the edge of a hillside, and look around carefully, almost everything you can catch sight of is in the process of dying, and most things will be dead long before you are. If it were not for the constant renewal and replacement going on before your eyes, the whole place would turn to stone and sand under your feet.

There are some creatures that do not seem to die at all; they simply vanish totally into their own progeny. Single cells do this. The cell becomes two, then four, and so on, and after a while the last trace is gone. It cannot be seen as death; barring mutation, the descendants are simply the first cell, living all over again. The cycles of the slime mould have episodes that seem as conclusive as death, but the withered slug, with its stalk and fruiting body, is plainly the transient tissue of a developing animal; the free-swimming amoebocytes use this organ collectively in order to produce more of themselves.

There are said to be a billion billion insects on the earth at any moment, most of them with very short life expectancies by our standards. Someone has estimated that there are twenty-five million assorted insects hanging in the air over every temperate square mile, in a column extending upward for thousands of feet, drifting through the layers of the atmosphere like plankton. They are dying steadily, some by being eaten, some just dropping in their tracks, tons of them around the earth, disintegrating as they die, invisibly.

Who ever sees dead birds, in anything like the huge numbers stipulated by the certainty of the death of all birds? A dead bird is an incongruity, more startling than an unexpected live bird, sure evidence to the human mind that something has gone wrong. Birds do their dying off somewhere, behind things, under things, never on the wing.

Animals seem to have an instinct for performing death alone, hidden. Even the largest, most conspicuous ones find ways to conceal themselves in time. If an elephant missteps and dies in an open place, the herd will not leave him there; the others will pick him up and carry the body from place to place, finally putting it down in some inexplicably suitable location. When elephants encounter the skeleton of an elephant out in the open, they methodically take up each of the bones and distribute them, in a ponderous ceremony, over neighbouring acres.

It is a natural marvel. All of the life of the earth dies, all of the time, in the same volume as the new life that dazzles us each morning, each spring. All we see of this is the odd stump, the fly struggling on the porch floor of the summer house in October, the fragment on the highway. I have lived all my life with an embarrassment of squirrels in my backyard, they are all over the place, all year long, and I have never seen, anywhere, a dead squirrel.

I suppose it is just as well. If the earth were otherwise, and all the dying were done in the open, with the dead there to be looked at, we would never have it out of our minds. We can forget about it much of the time, or think of it as an accident to be avoided, somehow. But it does make the process of dying seem more exceptional than it really is, and harder to engage in at the times when we must ourselves engage.

In our way, we conform as best we can do the rest of nature. The obituary pages tell us of the news that we are dying away, while the birth announcements in finer print, off at the side of the page, inform us of our replacements, but we get no grasp from this of the enormity of scale. There are 3 billion of us on the earth, and all three billion must be dead, on a schedule, within this lifetime. The vast mortality, involving something over fifty million of us each year, takes place in relative secrecy. We can only really know of the deaths in our households, or among our friends. These, detached in our minds from all the rest, we take to be unnatural events, anomalies, outrages. We speak of our own dead in low voices; struck down, we say, as though visible death can only occur for cause, by disease or violence, avoidably. We send off for flowers, grieve, make ceremonies, scatter bones, unaware of the rest of the three billion on the same schedule. All of that immense mass of flesh and bone and consciousness will disappear by absorption into the earth, without recognition by the transient survivors.

Less than a half century from now, our replacements will have more than doubled the numbers. It is hard to see how we can continue to keep the secret, with such multitudes doing the dying. We will have to give up the notion that death is catastrophe, or detestable, or avoidable, or even strange. We will need to learn more about the cycling of life in the rest of the system, and about our connection to the process. Everything that comes alive seems to be in trade for something that dies, cell for cell. There might be some comfort in the recognition of synchrony, in the information that we all go down together, in the best of company.

TOLSTOY, *THE DEATH OF IVAN ILICH*

From Leo Tolstoy, *The Death of Ivan Ilich*, translated by Leo Wiener, Boston, Dana Estes & Co., 1904

Leo Nikolaevich Tolstoy (1828–1910), Russian-born novelist, story teller, and moral thinker and reformer. Before his great spiritual crisis of 1876–9, he wrote some of the world's finest fiction, including the two novels War and Peace *and* Anna Karenina. *Describing his experiences in* A Confession *(1879–82), he sought the formulation of a voluntary simplicity, based on the Gospel teachings, that included non-violence, manual labour, and communal property.*

In his novella, Tolstoy describes the advent of death in the life of a man, Ivan Ilich, who has been thoroughly egoistic. The character is afflicted with a terminal illness, and gradually confined to bed by pain and debility. The account shows Ivan Ilich's refusal of the fact of his dying. The terrible, unending suffering he undergoes finally allows him the opportunity of accepting death and gaining an understanding of what he has had to endure.

IX

His wife returned late in the night. She entered on tiptoe, but he heard her. He opened his eyes and hastened to shut them again. She wanted to send Gerasim away and to sit up with him. He opened his eyes, and said: 'No, go.'

'Do you suffer very much?'

'It makes no difference.'

'Take some opium.'

He consented, and took some. She went away.

Until about three o'clock he was in agonizing oblivion. It seemed to him that he with his pain was being shoved somewhere into a narrow, black, and deep bag, and shoved farther and farther, without coming out of it. And this terrible act was accompanied by suffering. And he was afraid, and wanted to go through the bag, and fought, and helped along. And suddenly he tore away, and fell, and woke up. The same Gerasim was sitting at his feet on the bed, drowsing calmly and patiently. But Ivan Ilich was lying, his emaciated, stockinged feet resting on Gerasim's shoulders, and there was the same candle with the shade, and the same uninterrupted pain.

'Go away, Gerasim,' he whispered.

'Never mind, sir, I will sit up.'

'No, go.'

He took his feet off Gerasim's shoulders, lay down sidewise on his arm and began to feel pity for himself. He just waited for Gerasim to go to the adjoining room, and no longer restrained himself, but burst out into tears, like a child. He wept on account of his helplessness, his terrible loneliness, the cruelty of men, the cruelty of God, the absence of God.

'Why has Thou done all this? Why didst Thou bring me to this? Why, why dost Thou torment me so terribly?'

He did not expect any answer, and was weeping because there was no answer and could be none. The pain rose again, but he did not stir, did not call. He said to himself:

'Go on, strike me! but for what? What have I done to Thee? For what?'

Then he grew silent and stopped not only weeping, but also breathing, and became all attention: it was as though he listened, not to the voice which spoke with sounds, but to the voice of his soul, to the train of thoughts which rose in him.

'What do you want?' was the first clear expression, capable of being uttered in words, which he heard.

'What do you want? What do you want?' he repeated to himself. 'What? Not to suffer. To live!' he answered.

And again he abandoned himself wholly to attention, to such tense listening, that his pain even did not distract him.

'To live? To live how?' asked the voice of his soul.

'To live as I used to live before – well, pleasantly.'

'As you lived before, well and pleasantly?' asked a voice. And he began in imagination to pass in review the best minutes of his pleasant life. But, strange to say, all these best minutes of his pleasant life now seemed to him to be different from what they had seemed to be before – all of them, except the first recollections of childhod. There, in childhood, there had been something really agreeable, with which it would be possible to live if life should return; but the man who had experienced those pleasant sensations was no more; it was like a recollection of somebody else.

As soon as there began that which resulted in the present man, in Ivan Ilich, everything which then had appeared as joys now melted in his sight and changed into something insignificant and even abominable.

And the farther away from childhood and nearer to the present, the more insignificant and doubtful were the joys. This began with the law school. There had been there something truly good; there had been there merriment, friendship, hopes. But in the upper classes these good minutes had happened more rarely; those were the recollections of the love of woman. Then all got mixed, and there was still less of what was good. Farther on there was still less of what was good, and the farther, the less.

'The marriage – so sudden, and the disenchantment, and the odour from my wife's mouth, and sensuality, and hypocrisy! And this dead service, and these cares about the money, and thus passed a year, and two, and ten, and twenty – all the time the same. The farther, the deader. It was as though I were going evenly downhill, imagining that I was going uphill. And so it was. In public opinion I went uphill, – and just in that proportion did my life vanish under me. – And now it is all done, – go and die!

'So what is this? Why? Impossible. It cannot be that life should be so senseless and so abominable! And if it has indeed been so abominable and meaningless, what sense is there in dying, and in dying with suffering? Something is wrong.

'Perhaps I did not live the proper way,' it suddenly occurred to him. 'But how can that be, since I did everything that was demanded of me?' he said to himself, and immediately, he repelled from himself this only solution of the whole enigma of life and of death, as something totally impossible.

'What do you want now? To live? To live how? To live as you live in the court, when the bailiff proclaims, "The court is coming!" The court is coming, the court is coming!' he repeated to himself. 'Here is the court! But I am not guilty!' he shouted in anger. 'For what?' And he stopped weeping and, turning his face to the wall, began to think of nothing but this one thing: 'Why, for what is all this terror?'

But, no matter how much he thought, he found no answer. And when the thought occurred to him, and it occurred to him often, that all this was due to the fact that he had not lived in the proper way, he immediately recalled all the regularity of his life, and dispelled this strange thought.

X

Two more weeks passed. Ivan Ilich no longer rose from his divan. He did not want to lie in his bed, and lay on the divan. Lying nearly all the time with his face to the wall, he suffered in loneliness the same insoluble sufferings, and in loneliness thought the same insoluble thought. 'What is this? Is this really death?' And an inner voice answered him: 'Yes, it is.' 'What are these torments for?' and the voice answered: 'For no special reason.' After that and outside of that there was nothing.

From the very beginning of his sickness, from the first time that he went to see the doctor, his life was divided into two opposite moods which gave way to one another: now it was despair and the expectancy of incredible and terrible death, and now hope and an absorbing observation of the activity of his body. Now there was before his eyes nothing but his kidney or gut, which had for the time being deflected from the fulfilment of its obligations, and now it was the one incomprehensible, terrible death, from which it was impossible to be freed in any way whatever.

These two moods alternated from the very beginning of his sickness; but the farther his disease proceeded, the more doubtful and fantastic did his imagination grow in respect to the kidney, and the more real came to be the consciousness of impending death.

He needed but to recall what he had been three months before and what he was now, to recall how evenly he had been going downhill, in order that every possibility of hope should be destroyed.

During the last stage of the loneliness in which he was, lying with his face turned to the back of the divan, of that loneliness amidst a populous city and his numerous acquaintances and his family — a loneliness fuller than which can nowhere be found, neither at the bottom of the sea, nor in the earth — during the last stages of this terrible loneliness Ivan Ilich lived in his imagination only in the past. One after another there arose before him pictures of his past. They always began with what was nearest in time and ran back to what was most remote, to childhood, and there they stopped. If Ivan Ilich thought of the stewed prunes which he was offered today to eat, he recalled the raw, wrinkled French prunes of his childhood, their particular taste, and the abundance of saliva when he reached the stone, and side by side with this recollection of the taste there arose a whole series of recollections from that time — the nurse, the brother, the toys.

'I must not think of this — it is too painful,' Ivan Ilich said to himself, and again transferred himself to the present. A button on the back of the divan and wrinkles in the morocco. 'The morocco is expensive — not durable — there was a quarrel on account of it. It was a different kind of morocco, and a different quarrel, when we tore father's portfolio, and were punished, and mother brought us patties.' And again his thoughts stopped at his childhood, and again he felt a pain, and tried to dispel it and to think of something else.

And again, together with this train of his recollections, another train of recollections passed through his soul as to how his disease increased and grew. Again it was the same: the farther back, the more there was of life. There was more good in life and more of life itself. Both blended.

'Just as my suffering is growing worse and worse, so my whole life has been getting worse and worse,' he thought. There was one bright point there behind, in the beginning of life, and then everything grows blacker and blacker, and goes faster and faster. 'In inverse proportion to the square of the distance from death,' thought Ivan Ilich. And this representation of a stone flying downward with increasing rapidity fell into his soul. Life, a series of increasing sufferings, flew more and more rapidly towards its end, a most terrible suffering. 'I fly —' He trembled, and shook, and wanted to resist; but he knew that it was useless to resist, and again he looked at the back of the divan with eyes weary from looking, which could not help but look at what was in front of him, and he waited and waited for that terrible fall, push, and destruction.

'It is impossible to resist,' he said to himself. 'But if I only understood what it is all for. And this is impossible. One might be able to explain it, if it could be said that I had not lived properly. But that can by no means be asserted,' he said to himself, as he recalled all the lawfulness, regularity, and decency of his life. 'It is impossible to admit this,' he said to himself, smiling with his lips, as though some one could see this smile of his and be deceived by it. 'There is no explanation! Torment, death — Why?'

XI

...

The doctor arrived at the usual hour. Ivan Ilich answered him, 'Yes, no,' without taking his glance of fury from him, and finally said:

'You know yourself that nothing will help me, so let it go.'

'We can alleviate your suffering,' said the doctor.

'You cannot do that, either — let it go.'

156

The doctor went into the drawing-room and informed Prask-ovya Fedorovna that he was in a very bad state, and that there was one means — opium — in order to alleviate the sufferings, which must be terrible.

The doctor said that his physical suffering was terrible, and that was true; but more terrible than his physical suffering was his moral suffering, and in this lay his chief agony.

His moral suffering consisted in this, that on that night, as he looked upon Gerasim's sleepy, good-natured face with its prominent cheek-bones, it suddenly occurred to him, 'What if indeed my whole life, my conscious life, was not the right thing?'

It occurred to him that what before had presented itself to him as an utter impossibility, namely, that he had passed all his life improperly, might after all be the truth. It occurred to him that those faint endeavours at struggling against that which was regarded as good by persons in superior positions, faint endeavours which he had immediately repelled from himself, might be real, while everything else might be the wrong thing. He tried to defend all this to himself. And suddenly he felt the weakness of everything which he was defending, and there was nothing to defend.

'And if this is so,' he said to himself, 'and I go away from life with the consciousness of having ruined everything which was given me, and that it is impossible to mend it, what then?'

He lay down on his back and began to pass his life in review in an entirely new fashion. When, in the morning, he saw the lackey, then his wife, then his daughter, then the doctor, every one of their motions, every word of theirs confirmed for him the terrible truth which had been revealed to him the night before. In them he saw himself, all that he had been living by, and saw clearly that all that was not the right thing, that it was all a terrible, huge deception, which concealed both life and death. This consciousness increased, multiplied tenfold his physical sufferings. He groaned and tossed about and picked at his clothes. It seemed to him that his clothes choked and suffocated him. And for this he hated them.

He was given a big dose of opium and he fell into oblivion, but at dinner the same began once more. He drove all away from himself, and tossed from one place to another.

His wife came to him, and said:

'*Jean*, my darling, do this for me.' ('For me?') 'It cannot hurt, and frequently it helps. Healthy people frequently do it.'

He opened his eyes wide.

'What? Communion? What for? It is not necessary! Still –'

She burst out weeping.

'Yes, my dear? I will send for our priest – he is such a nice man.'

'All right, very well,' he muttered.

When the priest came and took his confession, he softened, seemed to feel a relief from his doubts, and so from his suffering, and for a moment was assailed by hope. He began once more to think of his blind gut and the possibility of mending it. He took his communion with tears in his eyes.

When, after the communion, he was put down on the bed, he for a moment felt easier, and again there appeared hope of life. He began to think of the operation which had been proposed to him. 'I want to live, to live,' he said to himself. His wife came back to congratulate him; she said the customary words, and added:

'Truly, are you not feeling better?'

Without looking at her, he said, 'Yes.'

Her attire, her figure, the expression of her face, the sound of her voice – everything told him one and the same thing: 'It is not the right thing. Everything which you have lived by is a lie, a deception, which conceals from you life and death.' The moment he thought so, there arose his hatred, and with his hatred came physical, agonizing sufferings, and with the sufferings the consciousness of inevitable, near perdition. Something new had taken place: something began to screw up and shoot, and to choke him.

The expression of his face, when he uttered, 'Yes,' was terrible. Having said this 'Yes,' he looked straight into her face and with unusual rapidity for his weakness turned his face downward, and called out:

'Go away, go away, leave me alone!'

XII

From this moment there began that cry which lasted three days and was so terrible that it was not possible to hear it without horror through two doors. At the moment when he answered his wife, he understood that he was lost, that there was no return, that the end had come, the real end, and yet his doubt was not solved — it remained the doubt it had been.

'Oo! Oo! Oo!' he cried, in various intonations. He had begun to cry, 'I do not want to!' and continued to cry the sound 'oo'.

During the three days, in the course of which time did not exist for him, he fluttered about in that black bag whither an invisible, invincible force was shoving him. He struggled as a prisoner condemned to death struggles in the hands of the hangman, knowing that he cannot be saved; and with every minute he felt that, in spite of all the efforts of the struggle, he was coming nearer and nearer to what terrified him. He felt that his suffering consisted in his being shoved into that black hole, and still more in his not being able to get through it. What hindered him from crawling through was the consciousness of this, that his life was good. This justification of his life grappled him and did not allow him to get on and tormented him more than anything.

Suddenly a certain force pushed him in the chest and in the side, and still more compressed his throat, and he fell into the hole, and there, at the end of the hole, there was some light. What happened to him was what happens in a railway car, when a man thinks that he is riding forwards, while he is riding backwards, and suddenly discovers the real direction.

'Yes, it was all the wrong thing,' he said to himself, 'but that is nothing. It is possible, it is possible to do the right thing. What is the right thing?' he asked himself, and suddenly grew quiet.

This happened at the end of the third day, two hours before his death. At just this time the little gymnasiast stole quietly up to his father, and walked over to his bed. The dying man was crying pitifully and tossing about his hands. His hand fell on the head of the little gymnasiast. The little gymnasiast caught it and pressed it to his lips, and burst out weeping.

Just then Ivan Ilich tumbled in and saw the light, and it was revealed to him that his life had not been what it ought to have been, but that it was still possible to mend it. He asked himself: 'What is the right thing?' and he grew silent, and listened. Here he felt that some one was kissing his hand. He opened his eyes and glanced at his son. He was sorry for him. His wife came up to him. He glanced at her. She looked at him with a desperate expression, her mouth being wide open and the tears remaining unwiped on her nose. He was sorry for her.

'Yes, I am tormenting them,' he thought. 'They are sorry, but they will be better off when I am dead.' That was what he meant to say, but he did not have the strength to utter it. 'However, what is the use of talking? I must do,' he thought. He indicated his son to his wife with his glance, and said:

'Take him away — am sorry — and you, too —'

He wanted to add, 'Forgive,' but said, 'Forgivive,' and being unable to correct himself, he waved his hand, knowing that who needed would understand.

Suddenly it became clear to him that what had been vexing him and could not come out, now was coming out all at once, from two sides, from ten sides, from all sides. They were to be pitied; it was necessary to do something to save them pain, to free them and free himself from these sufferings.

'How good and how simple!' he thought. 'And the pain?' he asked himself. 'What of it? Well, pain, where are you?'

He began to listen.

'Yes, here it is. Well, let it pain.'

'And death? Where is it?'

And he sought his former customary fear of death, and could not find it.

'Where is it? What death?'

There was no fear, because there was also no death.

Instead of death there was a light.

'So this it is!' he suddenly spoke out in a loud voice. 'What joy!'

For him all this took place in one moment, and the significance of this moment no longer changed. But for those who were present the agony lasted two hours longer. Something palpitated in his heart, and his emaciated body jerked. Then the palpitation and the rale grew rarer and rarer.

'It is ended!' some one said over him.

He heard these words and repeated them in his soul.

'Death is ended,' he said to himself. 'It is no more.'

He inhaled the air, stopped in the middle of his breath, stretched himself, and died.

PART FIVE

The Unfinished Animal

Armed conflict, personal anguish, collective guilt, moral indecisiveness, self-doubt – all these are part of the human condition, but recognizing this need not imply a pessimistic view of the world: we can simply accept that certain human tendencies show how much we still need to change. The future evolution of men and women – not their dark predetermination – is the problem to be confronted. We must remember, as well as the mean, heartless and cruel aspects of human behaviour, the countless numbers of people who have gained a level of understanding or of being where they are no longer blighted by such negative traits. We have all experienced occasions when both sides of an issue ('Should I avoid injuring someone or should I allow it to happen?') are vividly present. Even if the less harmful choice is refused, one has at least had a glimpse of a better choice, a higher potential.

When we fail to measure up to our expectations, or betray our true selves, we become aware of a deficiency in ourselves. Two kinds of question immediately arise. First, can the deficiency be corrected, at least to some degree, or is it inherent – the price, the fatalist would add, of being human? Second, what is the nature of the deficiency? Does it belong to the active, willing side of our nature or to the reflective, knowing one? Can we rid ourselves of a weak, vacillating will or of the shackles of an ignorance that prevents us from seeing our situation clearly?

Among modern thinkers, Nietzsche offers one of the clearest answers. According to him, we have allowed ourselves to be burdened by an idea of morality which opposes what we ought to do to how we are. But reference to an ideal state puts us in contradiction to our active natures. The result, for Nietzsche, is that a person 'must have become not only calculating but himself calculable, regular even to his own perception'. We have grown over-analytic, ceaselessly weighing consequences, commenting on alternative possibilities, evaluating past decisions. The intellect has been stimulated in a single direction rather than in a balanced way, and we are caught in the overwhelming din of its ceaseless chatter. Just as a body can become muscle-bound, losing its natural balance and flexibility, so the mind can become constrained by categories and classifications, allowing no new lines of thought to develop. It is small wonder that one is aware of conflict in many aspects of one's life. Only a new way of thinking that cuts through the mind's habitual preoccupation with its own inventions can liberate the suppressed action-seeking side of human nature.

Is there anyone who is not handicapped in this way? No, according to Plato, who argues that whoever arrives at an age of questioning feels the same affliction, the same deficiency. The implication is that it is up to us to make ourselves complete — we are, to adapt one of Nietzsche's phrases, a matter of unfinished business. To *be* more than what we are born to, it is imperative to *know* more. The better kind of knowledge is surely not factual knowledge, gained from analysis, but wisdom arising from within ourselves. There, to use the thought-provoking image of Plato's allegory of the cave, 'the instrument whereby each of us apprehends is that of an eye that cannot be converted to the light from the darkness except by turning the whole body'. A 180° about-face is required, in order to re-educate the entire person — mind, body, and feeling. The first step towards acquiring inner vision involves relaxing our hold on habit; each subsequent step then actually draws power from overcoming the obstacles which stand in the way.

To do this, we need to take a quite different direction to that which the self-important ego desires to follow. 'Be not wise in thine own eyes,' the Book of Proverbs cautions, as if to say that the illusion of wisdom will have the effect of preventing us from achieving a higher state. So-called knowledge only feeds our competitiveness, our hunger for more territory to conquer, our thirst for supremacy. For wisdom to enter the heart, however, the centre of one's being, one must turn away from self-love and vanity. One will then realize that the new-found knowledge, since it originates from beyond oneself, brings with it a responsibility to communicate it to others. As Plato says, the philosopher, after leaving the cave and making his discoveries, turns towards the task of sharing them with the world. In this work — which the ego continually threatens — there is also well-being. 'Happy is the man that findeth wisdom,' the Book of Proverbs says, 'and the man that getteth understanding.'

Our not being all that we can be is due to a lack of balance or a disproportion in our attributes. We are just like a mechanical device, a gear system for example, which does not function properly when the parts are out of adjustment. Our thought veers towards the familiar and established, our feelings often seem stale, and our physical existence stressful. Chuang Tzu incorporates the idea of a habitual state of imbalance into his reflections on what is lacking in the human condition. For him, the natural state is harmony, in which opposites — good and bad, high and low, simple and complex, still and moving — are subtly blended. As soon as the mind attaches itself to a single element ('this is good'), so implicitly or explicitly rejecting the opposing one ('this is bad'), we lose our finely poised integrity. The greater our reliance on such partial judgement, the more isolated we become from our own nature and the more we allow ourselves to exploit the rest of the natural world. If, however, we cultivate an attitude of fundamental relaxation, in which opposing ideas can coexist, we allow our natural balance to reassert itself. 'Therefore, the sage harmonizes right with wrong and rests in the balance of nature. This is called taking both sides at once,' Chuang Tzu tells us.

The danger of alienation from one's own nature is discussed by Heraclitus, whose viewpoint parallels that of Chuang Tzu in many aspects. The tendency to live a life according to a 'private intelligence' which fantasizes, schemes, and forms designs based on partial evidence accounts for disharmonies in our behaviour. 'We should let ourselves be guided by what is common to all,' he asserts. The common element, the Logos, is difficult to discern: 'men are unable to understand it – not only before hearing it, but even after they have heard it for the first time'. Our thinking has grown passive, like the dreamlike state we drift into just before dropping off to sleep. By opening our ears and eyes, it is possible, Heraclitus believes, to develop an awareness of how relative our thought and perception really is. Experiencing this relativity is itself not relative. It is a step towards realizing how our subjectivity obstructs our reception of data from the real world.

The first step is the awareness that something is lacking. But what then? Some would advocate a new, empirical approach, since too much respect for past authority clouds the mind to current reality and leads us to form conclusions which relate only approximately to present circumstances. We must therefore encourage the evolution of an attitude which is flexible and sensitive to change, and we must prune away all subjective bias.

This still does not answer the question of whether what we lack is knowledge or will, however. It may be that neither on its own can supply our need, but only something from that depth of our nature where both are in unison. Call this the centre or, as Rumi does, the heart. Unless the impulse to know or to do arises from close to this centre, an essential ingredient will always be lacking. This centre has to do with man's place in the scheme of things, and serves to integrate a person inwardly, and also with the universe at large. If we could achieve this integration we would no longer be at odds with nature, exploiting the world's resources, destroying other forms of life, and disregarding the ecological balance. 'The knowledge of men of heart bears them up,' Rumi says. Such knowledge is great knowledge. It is knowledge both of the nature of our personal powers and of their limits. The knowledge of one's real place in a cosmic sense brings an authority not known to ordinary ways of thinking.

In this lies the 'cure' for our condition. We can now see that our state is that of a seed awaiting germination. Our frequent experiences of some deficiency in ourselves serve to remind us of our task, which is to nurture the unknown within us so that it can bear fruit.

PLATO, 'THE ALLEGORY OF THE CAVE'

From Plato, *The Republic*, translated by B. Jowett, Clarendon Press, 1892

In this well-known allegory, given in the form of a dialogue, Plato (see also pp. 24 and 128) describes our ordinary condition in terms of imprisonment in a darkened cave. Our lack of vision is such that we have no recognition of our state. We are unaware that the forms we see are simply shadows of things or, as it were, slide projections cast by a light source behind us. In the account, one person is able to break his bonds and move into the direct light. For a while he sees things as they are. But on his return none of his companions will believe him when he speaks of their delusions. From this analogy, Plato draws some powerful conclusions concerning education and the right government of a state.

'And now,' I said, 'let me show in a figure how far our nature is enlightened or unenlightened: behold human beings living in an underground den, which has a mouth open towards the light and reaching all along the den; here they have been from their childhood, and have their legs and necks chained so that they cannot move, and can only see before them, being prevented by the chains from turning round their heads. Above and behind them a fire is blazing at a distance, and between the fire and the prisoners there is a raised way; and you will see, if you look, a low wall built along the way, like the screen which marionette players put in front of them, over which they show the puppets.'

'I see.'

'And do you see,' I said, 'men passing along the wall carrying all sorts of vessels, and statues and figures of animals made of wood and stone and various materials, which appear over the wall? Some of them are talking, others silent.'

'You have shown me a strange thing, and they are strange prisoners.'

'Like ourselves,' I replied; 'and they see only their own shadows, or the shadows of one another, which the fire throws on the opposite wall of the cave?'

'True,' he said; 'how could they see anything but the shadows if they were never allowed to move their heads?'

'And of the objects which are being carried in like manner they would see only the shadows?'

'Yes,' he said.

'And if they were able to converse with one another, would they not suppose that they were naming what was actually before them?'

'Very true.'

'And suppose further that the prison had an echo which came from the other side, would they not be sure to fancy when one of the passers-by spoke that the voice which they heard came from the passing shadow?'

'No question,' he replied.

'To them,' I said, 'the truth would be literally nothing but the shadows of the images.'

'That is certain.'

'And now look again, and see what will naturally follow if the prisoners are released and disabused of their error. At first, when any of them is liberated and compelled suddenly to stand up and turn his neck round and walk and look towards the light, he will suffer sharp pains; the glare will distress him, and he will be unable to see the realities of which in his former state he had seen the shadows; and then conceive some one saying to him, that what he saw before was an illusion, but that now, when he is approaching nearer to being and his eye is turned towards more real existence, he has a clearer vision, — what will be his reply? And you may further imagine that his instructor is pointing to the objects as they pass and requiring him to name them, — will he not be perplexed? Will he not fancy that the shadows which he formerly saw are truer than the objects which are now shown to him?'

'Far truer.'

'And if he is compelled to look straight at the light, will he not have a pain in his eyes which will make him turn away to take refuge in the objects of vision which he can see, and which he will now conceive to be in reality clearer than the things which are now being shown to him?'

'True,' he said.

'And suppose once more, that he is reluctantly dragged up a steep and rugged ascent, and held fast until he is forced into the presence of the sun itself, is he not likely to be pained and irritated? When he approaches the light his eyes will be dazzled, and he will not be able to see anything at all of what are now called realities.'

'Not in a moment,' he said.

'He will require to grow accustomed to the sight of the upper world. And first he will see the shadows best, next the reflections of men and other objects in the water, and then the objects themselves; then he will gaze upon the light of the moon and the stars and the spangled heaven; and he will see the sky and the stars by night better than the sun or the light of the sun by day?'

'Certainly.'

'Last of all he will be able to see the sun, and not mere reflections of it in the water, but he will see it in its own proper place, and not in another; and he will contemplate it as it is.'

'Certainly.'

'He will then proceed to argue that this is he who gives the season and the years, and is the guardian of all that is in the visible world, and in a certain way the cause of all things which he and his fellows have been accustomed to behold?'

'Clearly,' he said, 'he would first see the sun and then reason about it.'

'And when he remembered his old habitation, and the wisdom of the den and his fellow prisoners, do you not suppose that he would felicitate himself on the change, and pity them?'

'Certainly, he would.'

'And if they were in the habit of conferring honours among themselves on those who were quickest to observe the passing shadows and to remark which of them went before, and which followed after, and which were together; and who were therefore best able to draw conclusions as to the future, do you think that he would care for such honours and glories, or envy the possessors of them? Would he not say with Homer, "Better to be the poor servant of a poor master," and to endure anything, rather than think as they do and live after their manner?'

'Yes,' he said, 'I think that he would rather suffer anything than entertain these false notions and live in this miserable manner.'

'Imagine once more,' I said, 'such a one coming suddenly out of the sun to be replaced in his old situation; would he not be certain to have his eyes full of darkness?'

'To be sure,' he said.

'And if there were a contest, and he had to compete in measuring the shadows with the prisoners who had never moved out of the den, while his sight was still weak, and before his eyes had become steady (and the time which would be needed to acquire this new habit of sight might be very considerable), would he not be ridiculous? Men would say of him that up he went and down he came without his eyes; and that it was better not even to think of ascending; and if any one tried to loose another and lead him up to the light, let them only catch the offender, and they would put him to death.'

'No question,' he said.

'This entire allegory,' I said, 'you may now append, dear Glaucon, to the previous argument; the prison-house is the world of sight, the light of the fire is the sun, and you will not misapprehend me if you interpret the journey upwards to be the ascent of the soul into the intellectual world according to my poor belief, which, at your desire, I have expressed – whether rightly or wrongly God knows. But, whether true or false, my opinion is that in the world of knowledge the idea of good appears last of all, and is seen only with an effort; and, when seen, is also inferred to be the universal author of all things beautiful and right, parent of light and of the lord of light in this visible world, and the immediate source of reason and truth in the intellectual; and that this is the power upon which he who would act rationally either in public or private life must have his eye fixed.'

'I agree,' he said, 'as far as I am able to understand you.'

'Moreover,' I said, 'you must not wonder that those who attain to this beatific vision are unwilling to descend to human affairs; for their souls are ever hastening into the upper world where they desire to dwell; which desire of theirs is very natural, if our allegory may be trusted.'

'Yes, very natural.'

'And is there anything surprising in one who passes from divine contemplations to the evil state of man, misbehaving himself in a ridiculous manner; if, while his eyes are blinking and before he has become accustomed to the surrounding darkness, he is compelled to fight in courts of law, or in other places, about the images or the shadows of images of justice, and is endeavouring to meet the conceptions of those who have never yet seen absolute justice?'

'Anything but surprising,' he replied.

'Anyone who has common sense will remember that the bewilderments of the eyes are of two kinds, and arise from two causes, either from coming out of the light or from going

into the light, which is true of the mind's eye, quite as much
as of the bodily eye; and he who remembers this when he sees
any one whose vision is perplexed and weak, will not be too
ready to laugh; he will first ask whether that soul of man has
come out of the brighter life, and is unable to see because
unaccustomed to the dark, or having turned from darkness to
the day is dazzled by excess of light. And he will count the
one happy in his condition and state of being, and he will pity
the other; or, if he have a mind to laugh at the soul which
comes from below into the light, there will be more reason in
this than in the laugh which greets him who returns from above
out of the light into the den . . .'

HERACLITUS, *THE COSMIC FRAGMENTS*

From Philip Wheelwright, *Heraclitus*, Princeton University Press, 1959

*Heraclitus of Ephesus, fifth and sixth centuries BC, pre-Socratic philo-
sopher and sage, was nicknamed 'the enigmatic', and very little is known
about his life. His style turns on a poetic vocabulary which makes little
use of technical or abstract terms. His views were important enough to
receive mention and critical review by Plato and Aristotle.*

*Heraclitus left no writings, but after his death, pupils collected
fragments of his teachings. In this selection, we have a sense of a broad,
deep vision of reality. Because what is real is also hidden, Heraclitus
holds that we must approach it indirectly. We first confront our dreams
and private intelligences. Only after struggle do we perceive what is
common to all, real understanding, or the Logos, as he calls it. In this
effort, we are asked to realize that we live in a universe which also lives
and changes continually, where one element is soon replaced by its
opposite, and then back again, and that we too need to find this perfect
fluidity in ourselves.*

1. Although this Logos is eternally valid, yet men are unable to understand it — not only before hearing it, but even after they have heard it for the first time. That is to say, although all things come to pass in accordance with this Logos, men seem to be quite without any experience of it — at least if they are judged in the light of such words and deeds as I am here setting forth. My own method is to distinguish each thing according to its nature, and to specify how it behaves; other men, on the contrary, are as forgetful and heedless in their waking moments of what is going on around and within them as they are during sleep.

2. We should let ourselves be guided by what is common to all. Yet, although the Logos is common to all, most men live as if each of them has a private intelligence of his own.

3. Men who love wisdom should acquaint themselves with a great many particulars.

4. Seekers after gold dig up much earth and find little.

5. Let us not make arbitrary conjectures about the greatest matters.

6. Much learning does not teach understanding.

7. Of those whose discourses I have heard, there is not one who attains to the realization that wisdom stands apart from all else.

8. I have searched myself.

9. It pertains to all men to know themselves and to be temperate.

10. To be temperate is the greatest virtue. Wisdom consists in speaking and acting the truth, giving heed to the nature of things.

11. The things of which there can be sight, hearing, and learning — these are what I especially prize.

12. Eyes are more accurate witnesses than ears.

13. Eyes and ears are bad witnesses to men having barbarian souls.

14. One should not act or speak as if he were asleep.

15. The waking have one world in common; sleepers have each a private world of his own.

16. Whatever we see when awake is death; when asleep, dreams.

17. Nature loves to hide.

18. The Lord whose oracle is at Delphi neither speaks nor conceals, but gives signs.

19. Unless you expect the unexpected you will never find [truth], for it is hard to discover and hard to attain.

20. Everything flows and nothing abides; everything gives way and nothing stays fixed.

21. You cannot step twice into the same river, for other waters are continually flowing on.

22. Cool things become warm, the warm grows cool; the moist dries, the parched becomes moist.

23. It is in changing that things find repose.

24. Time is a child moving counters in a game; the royal power is a child's.

25. War is both father and king of all; some he has sown forth as gods and others as men, some he has made slaves and others free.

26. It should be understood that war is the common condition, that strife is justice, and that all things come to pass through the compulsion of strife.

27. Homer was wrong in saying, 'Would that strife might perish from amongst gods and men.' For if that were to occur, then all things would cease to exist.

28. There is exchange of all things for fire and of fire for all things, as there is of wares for gold and of gold for wares.

29. This universe, which is the same for all, has not been made by any god or man, but it always has been, is, and will be — an ever-living fire, kindling itself by regular measures and going out by regular measures.

30. [The phases of fire are] craving and satiety.

31. It throws apart and then brings together again; it advances and retires.

32. The transformations of fire are: first, sea; and of sea, half becomes earth; and half the lightning-flash.

33. When earth has melted into sea, the resultant amount is the same as there had been before the sea became hardened into earth.

34. Fire lives in the death of earth, air in the death of fire, water in the death of air, and earth in the death of water.

35. The thunderbolt pilots all things.

36. The sun is new each day.

37. The sun is the breadth of a man's foot.

38. If there were no sun, the other stars would not suffice to prevent its being night.

39. The boundary line of evening and morning is the Bear; and opposite the Bear is the boundary of bright Zeus.

40. The fairest universe is but a heap of rubbish piled up at random.

41. Every beast is driven to pasture by a blow.

42. You could not discover the limits of soul, even if you travelled every road to do so; such is the depth of its meaning.

43. [Soul] is the vaporization out of which everything else is derived; moreover it is the least corporeal of things and is in ceaseless flux, for the moving world can only be known by what is in motion.

44. Souls are vaporized from what is moist.

45. Soul has its own principle of growth.

46. A dry soul is wisest and best.

47. Souls take pleasure in becoming moist.

. . .

57. Most people do not take heed of the things they encounter, nor do they grasp them even when they have learned about them, although they suppose they do.

58. If all existing things were smoke, it is by smell that we would distinguish them.

59. In Hades souls perceive by smelling.

60. Corpses are more fit to be thrown out than dung.

61. Human nature has no real understanding; only the divine nature has it.

62. Man is not rational; only what encompasses him is intelligent.

63. What is divine escapes men's notice because of their incredulity.

64. Although intimately connected with the Logos, men keep setting themselves against it.

65. As in the night-time a man kindles for himself a light, so when a living man lies down in death with his vision extinguished he attaches himself to the state of death; even as one who has been awake lies down with his vision extinguished and attaches himself to the state of sleep.

66. Immortals become mortals, mortals become immortals; they live in each other's death and die in each other's life.

67. There await men after death such things as they neither expect nor have any conception of.

68. They arise into wakefulness and become guardians of the living and the dead.

69. A man's character is his guardian divinity.

70. Greater dooms win greater destinies.

71. Justice will overtake fabricators of lies and false witnesses.

72. Fire in its advance will judge and overtake all things.

73. How can anyone hide from that which never sets?

. . .

98. Opposition brings concord. Out of discord comes the fairest harmony.

99. It is by disease that health is pleasant; by evil that good is pleasant; by hunger, satiety; by weariness, rest.

100. Men would not have known the name of justice if these things had not occurred.

101. Sea water is at once very pure and very foul; it is drinkable and healthful for fishes, but undrinkable and deadly for men.

102. Donkeys would prefer straw to gold.

103. Pigs wash in mud, and domestic fowls in dust or ashes.

104. The handsomest ape is ugly compared with humankind; the wisest man appears as an ape when compared with a god – in wisdom, in beauty, and in all other ways.

105. A man is regarded as childish by spirit, just as a boy is by a man.

106. To God all things are beautiful, good, and right; men, on the other hand, deem some things right and others wrong.

107. Doctors cut, burn, and torture the sick, and then demand of them an undeserved fee for such services.

108. The way up and the way down are one and the same.

109. In the circle the beginning and the end are the same.

110. Into the same rivers we step and we do not step.

111. For wool-carders the straight way and the winding way are one and the same.

112. The bones connected by joints are at once a unitary whole and not a unitary whole. To be in agreement is to differ; the concordant is the discordant. From out of all the many particulars comes oneness, and out of oneness come all the many particulars.

113. It is one and the same thing to be living or dead, awake or asleep, young or old. The former aspect in each case becomes the latter, and the latter again the former, by sudden unexpected reversal.

114. Hesiod, whom so many accept as their wise teacher, did not even understand the nature of day and night; for they are one.

115. The name of the bow is life, but its work is death.

116. The hidden harmony is better than the obvious.

117. People do not understand how that which is at variance with itself agrees with itself. There is a harmony in the bending back, as in the case of the bow and the lyre.

118. Listening not to me but to the Logos, it is wise to acknowledge that all things are one.

119. Wisdom is one and unique; it is unwilling and yet willing to be called by the name of Zeus.

120. Wisdom is one – to know the intelligence by which all things are steered through all things.

. . .

123. All things come in their due seasons.

124. Even sleepers are workers and collaborators in what goes on in the universe.

CHUANG TZU, *INNER CHAPTERS*

From *A Source Book in Chinese Philosophy*, translated by Wing-Tsit Chan, Princeton University Press, 1963

Chuang Tzu (born c. 369 BC), Chinese thinker and follower of Lao Tzu. His interpretation of the way (Tao) gives it the sense of unceasing transformation, hence bringing movement to all relations. The comprehension of an essential oneness was, for him, the path to freedom and peace.

Like Heraclitus, Chuang Tzu speaks of a hidden principle of truth, the Tao. Why does it remain hidden, and yet seem so obvious when we are able to open to it? Chuang Tzu suggests that we are misled by partial understanding. We do not think, feel, or look with the whole of ourselves. We tend to base judgements on distinctions which we have not held up to examination. Chuang Tzu recommends us to relax, try to do nothing, let understanding come, rather than trying so hard to grasp it.

'If you do not know what is beneficial and what is harmful,' said Nieh Ch'ueh, 'does it mean that the perfect man does not know them also?'

'The perfect man is a spiritual being,' said Wang I. 'Even if great oceans burned up, he would not feel hot. Even if the great rivers are frozen, he would not feel cold. And even if terrific thunder were to break up mountains and the wind were to upset the sea, he would not be afraid. Being such, he mounts upon the clouds and forces of heaven, rides on the sun and the moon, and roams beyond the four seas. Neither life nor death affects him. How much less can such matters as benefit and harm?'

Ch'u-ch'iao Tzu asked Ch'ang-wu Tzu, 'I have heard from my grand master [Confucius] that the sage does not devote himself to worldly affairs. He does not go after gain nor avoid injury. He does not like to seek anything and does not purposely adhere to Tao. He speaks without speaking, and he does not speak when he speaks. Thus he roams beyond this dusty world. My grand master regarded this as a rough description of the sage, but I regard this to be the way the wonderful Tao operates. What do you think, sir?'

'What you have said would have perplexed even the Yellow Emperor,' replied Ch'ang-wu Tzu. 'How could Confucius be competent enough to know? Moreover, you have drawn a conclusion too early. You see an egg and you immediately want a cock to crow, and you see a sling and you immediately want to roast a dove. Suppose I say a few words to you for what they are worth and you listen to them for what they are worth. How about it? . . .

'The sage has the sun and moon by his side. He grasps the universe under the arm. He blends everything into a harmonious whole, casts aside whatever is confused or obscured, and regards the humble as honourable. While the multitude toil, he seems to be stupid and non-discriminative. He blends the disparities of ten thousand years into one complete purity. All things are blended like this and mutually involve each other.

'How do I know that the love of life is not a delusion? And how do I know the hate of death is not like a man who lost his home when young and does not know where his home is to return to? Li Chi was the daughter of the border warden of Ai. When the Duke of Chin first got her, she wept until the bosom of her dress was drenched with tears. But when she came to the royal residence, shared with the duke his luxurious couch and ate delicate food, she regretted that she had wept. How do I know that the dead will not repent having previously craved for life?

'Those who dream of the banquet may weep the next morning, and those who dream of weeping may go out to hunt after dawn. When we dream we do not know that we are dreaming. In our dreams we may even interpret our dreams. Only after we are awake do we know we have dreamed. Finally there comes a great awakening, and then we know life is a great dream. But the stupid think they are awake all the time, and believe they know it distinctly. Are we [honourable] rulers? Are we [humble] shepherds? How vulgar! Both Confucius and you were dreaming. When I say you were dreaming, I am also dreaming. This way of talking may be called perfectly strange. If after ten thousand generations we could meet one great sage who can explain this, it would be like meeting him in as short a time as in a single morning or evening.

'Suppose you and I argue. If you beat me instead of my beating you, are you really right and am I really wrong? If I beat you instead of your beating me, am I really right and are you really wrong? Or are we both partly right and partly wrong? Or are we both wholly right and wholly wrong? Since between us neither you nor I know which is right, others are naturally in the dark. Whom shall we ask to arbitrate? If we ask someone who agrees with you, since he has already agreed with you, how can he arbitrate? If we ask someone who agrees with me, since he has already agreed with me, how can he arbitrate? If we ask someone who disagrees with both you and me to arbitrate, since he has already disagreed with you and me, how can he arbitrate? If we ask someone who agrees with both you and me to arbitrate, since he has already agreed with you and me, how can he arbitrate? Thus among you, me, and others, none knows which is right. Shall we wait for still others? The great variety of sounds are relative to each other just as much as they are not relative to each other. To harmonize them in the functioning of Nature and leave them in the process of infinite evolution is the way to complete our lifetime.'

'What is meant by harmonizing them with the functioning of Nature?'

'We say this is right or wrong, and is so or is not so. If the right is really right, then the fact that it is different from the wrong leaves no room for argument. If what is so is really so, then the fact that it is different from what is not so leaves no room for argument. Forget the passage of time (life and death) and forget the distinction of right and wrong. Relax in the realm of the infinite and thus abide in the realm of the infinite.'

The Shade asks the Shadow, 'A little while ago you moved, and now you stop. A little while ago you sat down and now you stand up. Why this instability of purpose?'

'Do I depend on something else to be this way?' answered the Shadow. 'Does that something on which I depend also depend on something else? Do I depend on anything any more than a snake depends on its discarded scale or a cicada on its new wings? How can I tell why I am so or why I am not so?'

Once I, Chuang Tzu, dreamed that I was a butterfly and was happy as a butterfly. I was conscious that I was quite pleased with myself, but I did not know that I was Tzu. Suddenly I awoke, and there I was, visibly Tzu. I do not know whether it was Tzu dreaming that he was a butterfly or the butterfly dreaming that it was Tzu. Between Tzu and the butterfly there must be some distinction. [But one may be the other.] This is called the transformation of things.

NIETZSCHE, *GENEALOGY OF MORALS*

From Friedrich Nietzsche, *The Birth of Tragedy and the Genealogy of Morals*, translated by F. Golffing, New York, Doubleday, 1956

Friedrich Nietzsche (1844–1900), German philosopher and poet, is one of the most influential thinkers in the twentieth century. Lack of recognition of his genius, from his earliest writing, Birth of Tragedy (1872), to The Antichrist (1895), forced his thinking into a shriller, more vehement form. None the less, he was able to study great questions in metaphysics and morals, aesthetics and religion, before he suffered a complete mental collapse (1889), perhaps from syphilis.

Nietzsche writes of the loss of a certain presence with which we enter the world. This presence allows us to live in the present moment. As soon as we begin to develop other mental functions, particularly memory, our capacity to live in present time is sacrificed. This moment is now obscured behind our associations and past experiences. In an interesting aside, Nietzsche suggests that what we ordinarily call morality derives from this enslavement to memory and serves to perpetuate it.

I

To breed an animal with the right to make promises – is not this the paradoxical problem nature has set itself with regard to man? And is it not man's true problem? That the problem has in fact been solved to a remarkable degree will seem all the more surprising if we do full justice to the strong opposing force, the faculty of oblivion. Oblivion is not merely a *vis inertiae*, as is often claimed, but an active screening device, responsible for the fact that what we experience and digest psychologically does not, in the stage of digestion, emerge into consciousness any more than what we ingest physically does. The role of this active oblivion is that of a concierge: to shut temporarily the doors and windows of consciousness; to protect us from the noise and agitation with which our lower organs work for or against one another; to introduce a little quiet into our consciousness so as to make room for the nobler functions and functionaries of our organism which do the governing and planning. This concierge maintains order and etiquette in the household of the psyche; which immediately suggests that there can be no happiness, no serenity, no hope, no pride, no *present*, without oblivion. A man in whom this screen is damaged and inoperative is like a dyspeptic (and not merely *like* one): he can't be done with anything ... Now this naturally forgetful animal, for whom oblivion represents a power, a form of strong health, has created for itself an opposite power, that of remembering, by whose aid, in certain cases, oblivion may be suspended — specifically in cases where it is a question of promises. By this I do not mean a purely passive succumbing to past impressions, the indigestion of being unable to be done with a pledge once made, but rather an active not wishing to be done with it, a continuing to will what has once been willed, a veritable 'memory of the will'; so that, between the original determination and the actual performance of the thing willed, a whole world of new things, conditions, even volitional acts, can be interposed without snapping the long chain of the will. But how much all this presupposes! A man who wishes to dispose of his future in this manner must first have learned to separate necessity from accidental acts; to think causally; to see distant things as though they were near at hand; to distinguish means from ends. In short, he must have become not only calculating but himself calculable, regular even to his own perception, if he is to stand judge for his own future as a guarantor does.

II

This brings us to the long story of the origin or genesis of responsibility. The task of breeding an animal entitled to make promises involves, as we have already seen, the preparatory task of rendering man up to a certain point regular, uniform, equal among equals, calculable. The tremendous achievement which I have referred to in *Daybreak* as 'the custom character of morals', that labour man accomplished upon himself over a vast period of time, receives its meaning and justification here — even despite the brutality, tyranny, and stupidity associated with the process. With the help of custom and the social strait-jacket, man was, in fact, made calculable. However, if we place ourselves at the terminal point of this great process, where society and custom finally reveal their true aim, we shall find the ripest fruit of that tree to be the sovereign individual, equal only to himself, all moral custom left far behind. This autonomous, more than moral, individual (the terms *autonomous* and *moral* are mutually exclusive) has developed his own, independent, long-range will, which dares to make promises; he has a proud and vigorous consciousness of what he has achieved, a sense of power and freedom, of absolute accomplishment. This fully emancipated man, master of his will, who dares make promises — how should he not be aware of his superiority over those who are unable to stand security for themselves? Think how much trust, fear, reverence he inspires (all three fully *deserved*), and how, having that sovereign rule over himself, he has mastery too over all weaker-willed and less reliable creatures! Being truly free and possessor of a long-range, pertinacious will, he also possesses a scale of values. Viewing others from the centre of his own being, he either honours or disdains them. It is natural to him to honour his strong and reliable peers, all those who promise like sovereigns, rarely and reluctantly; who are chary of their trust; whose trust is a mark of distinction; whose promises are binding because they know that they will make them good in spite of all accidents, in spite of destiny itself. Yet he will inevitably reserve a kick for those paltry windbags who promise irresponsibly and a rod for those liars who break their word even in uttering it. His proud awareness of the extraordinary privilege responsibility confers has penetrated deeply and become a dominant instinct. What shall he call that dominant instinct, provided he ever feels impelled to give it a name? Surely he will call it his *conscience*.

RUMI, *THE MASNAWI*

From Jalalu'l-Din, *The Masnawi*, translated by R. Nicholson, Cambridge University Press, 1926

Jalalu'l-Din Rumi (1207–73), great mystical poet of Persia, found a teacher in a wandering dervish, Shams al-Din, in 1244. From that time on, his monumental literary output reflected his learning. Besides the Masnawi, of about 25,000 rhymed couplets, he composed the Rubaiyat, some 1,600 quatrains, and the Divan-i Shams-i Tabriz, a collection of 2,500 mysterical odes.

Rumi composed the Masnawi on the basis of his own personal experience. It is not strange, then, that he advocates a turning towards one's own experience as the sole means of knowing reality. Along this way, returning to one's centre, or heart, is much to be preferred to gathering information from external sources.

A certain man came and knocked at a friend's door: his friend asked him, 'Who art thou, O trusty one?'

He answered, 'I.' The friend said, 'Begone, 'tis not the time [for thee to come in]: at a table like this there is no place for the raw.'

Save the fire of absence and separation, who [what] will cook the raw one? Who [what] will deliver him from hypocrisy?

The wretched man went away, and for a year in travel [and] in separation from his friend he was burned with sparks of fire.

That burned one was cooked: then he returned and again paced to and fro beside the house of his comrade.

He knocked at the door with a hundred fears and respects, lest any disrespectful word might escape from his lips.

His friend called to him, 'Who is at the door?' He answered, ' 'Tis thou art at the door, O charmer of hearts.'

'Now,' said the friend, 'since thou art I, come in, O myself: there is not room in the house for two Is.'

THE BOOK OF PROVERBS

This extract is taken from Proverbs, one of the books of the Old Testament

In the Book of Proverbs, a collection of sayings traditionally attributed to King Solomon, is found a moving statement of the way of wisdom. That way begins and ends with the need to acquire great knowledge. All the distractions of ordinary life are held to be pointless, since such short-lived pleasures cannot be compared to the real confidence that knowledge can bring.

Chapter III

. . .

13. Happy the man that hath found wisdom, and the man that acquireth understanding.

14. For the obtaining of her is better than the obtaining of silver, and better than fine gold is her product.

15. She is more precious than pearls; and all the things thou valuest are not equal unto her.

16. Length of days is in her right hand: in her left are riches and honour.

17. Her ways are ways of pleasantness, and all her paths are peace.

18. A tree of life is she to those that lay hold on her: and every one that firmly graspeth her will be made happy.

19. The Lord hath through wisdom founded the earth: he hath established the heavens through understanding.

20. By his knowledge were the depths split open, and the skies drop down the dew.

21. My son, let them not be removed from thy eyes; keep [before thee] sound wisdom and discretion:

22. And they will be life unto thy soul, and grace to thy throat.

23. Then wilt thou walk in safety on thy way, and thy foot will not strike [against aught].

24. When thou layest thyself down, thou shalt feel no dread; and as thou liest down, thy sleep shall be pleasant.

25. Thou needest not to be afraid of sudden dread, neither of the [unlooked-for] tempest over the wicked, when it cometh.

26. For the Lord will be thy confidence, and he will guard thy foot from being caught.

27. Withhold not a benefit from him who is deserving it, when it is in the power of thy hand to do it.

28. Say not unto thy neighbour, Go, and return, and tomorrow will I give: when thou hast it by thee.

29. Contrive not against thy neighbour any evil, when he dwelleth in safety with thee.

30. Quarrel not with a man without cause, if he have done thee no harm.

31. Envy not the man of violence, and choose none of his ways.

32. For the froward is an abomination to the Lord; but with the upright is his goodwill.

33. The curse of the Lord is in the house of the wicked; but the habitation of the righteous will he bless.

34. If [it concern] the scornful, he will himself render these a scorn; but unto the lowly doth he give grace.

35. The wise shall inherit glory; but fools shall obtain disgrace as their portion.

Chapter IV

1. Hear, ye children, the correction of a father, and attend to know understanding.

2. For good information do I give you: my touching must you not forsake.

3. For I was a son unto my father, a tender and an only child before my mother.

4. And he instructed me, and said unto me, Let thy heart grasp firmly my words: observe my commandments and live.

5. Acquire wisdom, acquire understanding: forget not, and depart not from the sayings of my mouth.

6. Forsake her not, and she will watch over thee: love her, and she will keep thee.

7. The beginning of wisdom is, Acquire wisdom: and with all the acquisition acquire understanding.

8. Hold her in high esteem, and she will exalt thee: she will bring thee to honour, when thou embracest her.

9. She will give to thy head a wreath of grace: a crown of ornament will she deliver to thee . . .

Chapter V

. . .

12. And thou sayest 'How have I hated correction, and how hath my heart rejected reproof;

13. While I hearkened not to the voice of my instructions, and to my teachers I inclined not my ear;

14. But little more was wanting, and I had been in all [kinds of] unhappiness in the midst of the congregation and assembly.'

15. Drink water out of thy own cistern, and running waters out of thy own well:

16. So will thy springs overflow abroad; and in the open streets will be thy rivulets of water;

17. They will be thy own only, and not those of strangers with thee.

18. Thy fountain will be blessed; and rejoice with the wife of thy youth . . .

PART SIX

The Spectrum of Love

We live in an age in which conventional ideas of human relationships are increasingly under question; we are confronted daily with the problems of divorce and separation, the break-up of the nuclear family, domestic crime, lying and deceit in friendship, betrayal in all walks of life. Insecurity in our personal relationships can rob us of the fruits of being with another person and make us vulnerable to the forces of disintegration. We tend towards pessimism in matters of caring, truth-telling, respect, love, and communication with others. We overlook the value of intimate relationships for advancing our own understanding.

Are relationships actually necessary to us? Or is man by nature a solitary creature who turns towards others only out of weakness? To claim that people are not social animals but, like certain predatory mammals, bond together only for purposes of defence or procreation is to argue that all relationships are a matter of expedience. Aristotle rejects this point of view. In studying the needs of the individual he says, 'without friends no one would choose to live, though he had all other goods'. For him, living is a matter of following the dictates of 'the most authoritative element' in one's character. Only when one's many different qualities and competing desires are given the right priority can one live as one should. Furthermore, it is, Aristotle says, our nature 'to live with others', not out of fear nor from the thirst to dominate, but on terms of equality, with no conflict between friendship and self-love. One loves one's friends for the same reason that one loves oneself – in order to cultivate what we believe to be most worthy of admiration. Aristotle brings the question of relationships back to a person's own internal make-up: someone who is not guided by good ruling principles himself will be unable to appreciate the good qualities of others.

How then does our 'inner distribution' affect how we relate to those around us? For Plato, the answer is straightforward. A society is organized according to the same laws which create order within a person. Both are tripartite, consisting of intellect, appetite and emotion; both have a potential for strife and disharmony, or alternatively, concord and harmony; both, to function properly, require careful education, taking into account the differences between the three parts. To function properly a person must therefore have integrated responses — of mind, body, and feeling — which are appropriate to the situation at hand. A state, to function properly, must have full communication and non-aggressive relations between its members, with everyone playing their appropriate part in maintaining the whole. In his account of an ideally just society Plato emphasizes, not the natural equality of people, but the differences in natural aptitudes. He argues that relationships really work only when each person is 'in place'. To use a favourite metaphor of his, unless each instrument of an orchestra is properly tuned and plays its special part, the music will be off-key and displeasing to the ear.

It is Plato's view that people, when they form relationships, do so in accordance with their true nature, once they have discovered what this is. As well as becoming involved with other people, we also relate to animals, works of art, objects, nature itself. At times it seems to us as if we have actually become united with the other; for a moment the interconnectedness of all things seems possible and the ego shrinks to vanishing point. One is supported by a sense of belonging. But then, as the moment dissolves and one's ordinary identity returns, the experience (of a sunset, a symphony, a loved one) becomes subject to analysis, classification, and evaluation. One stands outside it again. This is a darkening of our vision. As Tagore puts it, 'Fear assumes unlimited dimensions in the dark, because it is the shadow of the self which has lost its foothold in the all . . .'

To the question, is relationship a real possibility for people, we give qualified assent. We oscillate between open, silent communion with our milieu and cognitive moments of appropriating an experience for our own ends. We are both part of a seamless fabric, and, because of the way we interpose our thinking between reality and ourselves, apart from it. To value a relationship more deeply is also to cultivate it, much as one can cultivate a love for great art. This duality in man is portrayed in another way by Gabriel Marcel. At one extreme, for him, is the experience of self-consciousness as, say, on entering a room in which one knows no one. The situation induces a physical and intellectual tension which prevents the formation of any relationship. We see ourselves as defined by a past to which the other person poses an imagined threat. Contrast this situation to that where there is a real 'intersubjectivity', as Marcel calls it, and shared images, presuppositions, fantasized histories, or anticipated futures occupy the middle ground. The struggle to find a meeting-place, against the ego's denial of the other's reality, is the 'struggle for existence', the struggle to enlarge a sense of self to include in it others' claims to being. We have to embrace the experience of the other person, whether pleasant or unpleasant.

This brings up another question: what role does pleasure play in the field of relationships? Ordinarily it is easy to see the predominance we give it. We seek to establish bonds with those we find pleasant to be with and avoid those that make us feel uncomfortable. We regard a certain emotion ('good feeling') as a positive sign of relationship and as its purpose, and we tend to forget that a relationship can also arise from opposition and resistance. But the growth of understanding can, in the short run, part ways with the pursuit of happiness; the precept, 'Love thy enemies,' propounded by Jesus of Nazareth, may mean that one should try to find in one's adversary what he has in common with oneself. Pleasure is not unimportant, but to make it central to one's life is to diminish rather than to enlarge one's existence. In the moving fable of Esarhaddon, King of Assyria, Tolstoy observes, 'You can make life better within yourself only by destroying the barriers that divide your life from that of other beings, and by regarding others as yourself and loving them.' Bent on a policy of revenge, Esarhaddon comes to see that executing his enemy would mean destroying himself as well.

We rarely have a vivid sense of oneness with those we find annoying, revolting, dangerous, or unattractive, but there are nevertheless conditions under which understanding can coexist with negative emotions. This points a way towards bonding in spite of opposition. The fact that intimacy *can* be approached through antagonism suggests that we need to be more attentive to whatever it is in us that resists forming relationships with others.

A basic ingredient in any relationship – whether with child, teacher, business partner, adversary, animal, or idea – is that of attention. Awareness is necessary before a relationship can arise. Conversely, inattention, not taking the other seriously, forms a barrier. When our attention flags, we fail to take account of all aspects of whatever we are engaged in. We fail, for instance, to see what the other person is really trying to communicate to us, and react instead in accordance with our own preconceived notions. Giving attention is not necessarily a question of making the other person 'feel good', however – as every parent and teacher knows, there are times when an abrupt, uncomfortable shock to the sensibilities is of more real value. Concern for the welfare of another requires us to know a great deal both about that person and about people in general. That we are rarely adequate to the task underlines the extent of the responsibility that caring implies. Could it be that our general casualness frequently gets in the way of deeper, more penetrating relationships?

A close exploration of the inner demands of relationships is given in the Sermon on the Mount. Jesus stresses the need for being empty oneself ('poor in spirit') so that one may be filled with the substance of a relationship, and for being equable ('peace-making') so as to avoid aggression. A subtle judgemental attitude lies at the core of the closed state; in all our attempts to form relationships with others we have to learn to overcome this limitation and move beyond it.

PLATO, 'THREE PARTS OF THE SOUL'

From Plato, *The Republic*, translated by B. Jowett

In this selection from The Republic, *Plato (see also p. 24) draws a comparison between the qualities we need in order to form good social relations, and the qualities we need for living harmoniously within ourselves. Of the life within, the soul, he distinguishes three distinct elements. There is the thinking part (reason), the appetitive part (the body), and the feeling part (the emotions). Ordinarily we find one in conflict with the other. This makes relations with others imbalanced and difficult. Hence, for Plato, a study of how to equilibrate our own parts must go hand in hand with the question of how to produce stable and just relations in the state.*

As before, Plato puts his argument in the form of a dialogue.

'We will not,' I said, 'be over-positive as yet; but if, on trial, this conception of justice be verified in the individual as well as in the State, there will be no longer any room for doubt; if it be not verified, we must have a fresh inquiry. First let us complete the old investigation, which we began, as you remember, under the impression that, if we could previously examine justice on the larger scale, there would be less difficulty in discerning her in the individual. That larger example appeared to be the State, and accordingly we constructed as good a one as we could, knowing well that in the good State justice would be found. Let the discovery which we made be now applied to the individual – if they agree, we shall be satisfied; or, if there be a difference in the individual, we will come back to the State and have another trial of the theory. The friction of the two when rubbed together may possibly strike a light in which justice will shine forth, and the vision which is then revealed we will fix in our souls.'

'That will be in regular course; let us do as you say.'

I proceeded to ask: 'When two things, a greater and less, are called by the same name, are they like or unlike in so far as they are called the same?'

'Like,' he replied.

'The just man then, if we regard the idea of justice only, will be like the just State?'

'He will.'

'And a State was thought by us to be just when the three classes in the State severally did their own business; and also thought to be temperate and valiant and wise by reason of certain other affections and qualities of these same classes?'

'True,' he said.

'And so of the individual; we may assume that he has the same three principles in his own soul which are found in the State; and he may be rightly described in the same terms, because he is affected in the right manner?'

'Certainly,' he said.

'Once more then, O my friend, we have alighted upon an easy question – whether the soul has these three principles or not?'

'An easy question! Nay, rather, Socrates, the proverb holds that hard is the good.'

'Very true,' I said; 'and I do not think that the method which we are employing is at all adequate to the accurate solution of this question; the true method is another and a longer one. Still we may arrive at a solution not below the level of the previous inquiry.'

'May we not be satisfied with that?' he said; 'under the circumstances, I am quite content.'

'I too,' I replied, 'shall be extremely well satisfied.'

'Then faint not in pursuing the speculation,' he said.

'Must we not acknowledge,' I said, 'that in each of us there are the same principles and habits which there are in the State; and that from the individual they pass into the State – how else can they come there? Take the quality of passion or spirit – it would be ridiculous to imagine that this quality, when found in States, is not derived from the individuals who are supposed to possess it, e.g., the Thracians, Scythians, and in general the northern nations; and the same may be said of the love of knowledge, which is the special characteristic of our part of the world, or of the love of money, which may, with equal truth, be attributed to the Phoenicians and Egyptians.'

'Exactly so,' he said.

'There is no difficulty in understanding this.'

'None whatever.'

'But the question is not quite so easy when we proceed to ask whether these principles are three or one; whether, that is to say, we learn with one part of our nature, are angry with another, and with a third part desire the satisfaction of our natural appetites; or whether the whole soul comes into play in each sort of action – to determine that is the difficulty.'

'Yes,' he said; 'there lies the difficulty.'

'Then let us now try and determine whether they are the same or different.'

'How can we?' he asked.

I replied as follows: 'The same thing clearly cannot act or be acted upon in the same part or in relation to the same thing at the same time, in contrary ways; and therefore whenever this contradiction occurs in things apparently the same, we know that they are really not the same, but different.'

'Good.'

'For example,' I said, 'can the same thing be at rest and in motion at the same time in the same part?'

'Impossible.'

'Still,' I said, 'let us have a more precise statement of terms, lest we should hereafter fall out by the way. Imagine the case of a man who is standing and also moving his hands and his head, and suppose a person to say that one and the same person is in motion and at rest at the same moment — to such a mode of speech we should object, and should rather say that one part of him is in motion while another is at rest.'

'Very true.'

'And suppose the objector to refine still further, and to draw the nice distinction that not only parts of tops, but whole tops, when they spin round with their pegs fixed on the spot, are at rest and in motion at the same time (and he may say the same of anything which revolves in the same spot), his objection would not be admitted to us, because in such cases things are not at rest and in motion in the same parts of themselves; we should rather say that they have both an axis and a circumference; and that the axis stands still, for there is no deviation from the perpendicular; and that the circumference goes round. But if, while revolving, the axis inclines either to the right or left, forwards or backwards, then in no point of view can they be at rest.'

'That is the correct mode of describing them,' he replied.

'Then none of these objections will confuse us, or incline us to believe that the same thing at the same time, in the same part or in relation to the same thing, can act or be acted upon in contrary ways.'

'Certainly not, according to my way of thinking.'

'Yet,' I said, 'that we may not be compelled to examine all such objections, and prove at length that they are untrue, let us assume their absurdity, and go forward on the understanding that hereafter, if this assumption turn out to be untrue, all the consequences which follow shall be withdrawn.'

'Yes,' he said, 'that will be the best way.'

'Well,' I said, 'would you not allow that assent and dissent, desire and aversion, attraction and repulsion, are all of them opposites, whether they are regarded as active or passive (for that makes no difference in the fact of their opposition)?'

'Yes,' he said, 'they are opposites.'

'Well,' I said, 'hunger and thirst, and the desires in general, and again willing and wishing, all these you would refer to the classes already mentioned. You would say, would you not, that the soul of him who desires is seeking after the object of his desires; or that he is drawing to himself the thing which he wishes to possess; or again, when a person wants anything to be given him, his mind, longing for the realization of his desires, intimates his wish to have it by a nod of assent, as if he had been asked a question?'

'Very true.'

'And what would you say of unwillingness and dislike and absence of desire; should not these be referred to the opposite class of repulsion and rejection?'

'Certainly.'

'Admitting this to be true of desire generally, let us suppose a particular class of desires, and out of these we will select hunger and thirst, as they are termed, which are the most obvious of them?'

'Let us take that class,' he said.

'The object of one is food, and of the other drink?'

'Yes.'

'And here comes the point: is not thirst the desire which the soul has of drink, and of drink only; not of drink qualified by anything else; for example, warm or cold, or much or little, or, in a word, drink of any particular sort: but if the thirst be accompanied by heat, then the desire is of cold drink; or, if accompanied by cold, then of warm drink; or, if the thirst be excessive, then the drink which is desired will be excessive; or, if not great, the quantity of drink will also be small: but thirst pure and simple will desire drink pure and simple, which is the natural satisfaction of thirst, as food is of hunger?'

'Yes,' he said; 'the simple desire is, as you say, in every case of the simple object, and the qualified desire of the qualified object.'

'But here a confusion may arise; and I should wish to guard against an opponent starting up and saying that no man desires drink only, but good drink, or food only, but good food; for good is the universal object of desire, and thirst being a desire, will necessarily be thirst after good drink; and the same is true of every other desire.'

'Yes,' he replied, 'the opponent might have something to say.'

'Nevertheless I should still maintain, that of relatives some have a quality attached to either term of the relation; others are simple and have their correlatives simple.'

'I do not know what you mean.'

'Well, you know of course that the greater is relative to the less?'

'Certainly.'

'And the much greater to the much less?'

'Yes.'

'And the sometime greater to the sometime less, and the greater that is to be to the less that is to be?'

'Certainly,' he said.

'And so of more and less, and of other correlative terms, such as the double and the half, or again, the heavier and the lighter, the swifter and the slower; and of hot and cold, and of any other relatives — is not this true of all of them?'

'Yes.'

'And does not the same principle hold in the sciences? The object of science is knowledge (assuming that to be the true definition), but the object of a particular science is a particular kind of knowledge; I mean, for example, that the science of house-building is a kind of knowledge which is defined and distinguished from other kinds and is therefore termed architecture.'

'Certainly.'

'Because it has a particular quality which no other has?'

'Yes.'

'And it has this particular quality because it has an object of a particular kind; and this is true of the other arts and sciences?'

'Yes.'

'Now, then, if I have made myself clear, you will understand my original meaning in what I said about relatives. My meaning was, that if one term of a relation is taken alone, the other is taken alone; if one term is qualified, the other is also qualified. I do not mean to say that the relatives may not be disparate, or that the science of health is healthy, or of disease necessarily diseased, or that the sciences of good and evil are therefore good and evil; but only that, when the term science is no longer used absolutely, but has a qualified object which in this case is the nature of health and disease, it becomes qualified, and is hence called not merely science, but the science of medicine.'

'I quite understand, and I think as you do.'

'Would you not say that thirst is one of these essentially relative terms, having clearly a relation —'

'Yes, thirst is relative to drink.'

'And a certain kind of thirst is relative to a certain kind of drink; but thirst taken alone is neither of much nor little, nor of good nor bad, nor of any particular kind of drink, but of drink only?'

'Certainly.'

'Then the soul of the thirsty one, in so far as he is thirsty, desires only drink; for this he yearns and tries to obtain it?'

'That is plain.'

'And if you suppose something which pulls a thirsty soul away from drink, that must be different from the thirsty principle which draws him like a beast to drink; for, as we were saying, the same thing cannot at the same time with the same part of itself act in contrary ways about the same.'

'Impossible.'

'No more than you can say that the hands of the archer push and pull the bow at the same time, but what you say is that one hand pushes and the other pulls.'

'Exactly so,' he replied.

'And might a man be thirsty, and yet unwilling to drink?'

'Yes,' he said, 'it constantly happens.'

'And in such a case what is one to say? Would you not say that there was something in the soul bidding a man to drink, and something else forbidding him, which is other and stronger than the principle which bids him?'

'I should say so.'

'And the forbidding principle is derived from reason, and that which bids and attracts proceeds from passion and disease?'

'Clearly.'

'Then we may fairly assume that they are two, and that they differ from one another; the one with which a man reasons, we may call the rational principle of the soul, the other, with which he loves and hungers and thirsts and feels the flutterings of any other desire, may be termed the irrational or appetitive, the ally of sundry pleasures and satisfactions?'

'Yes,' he said, 'we may fairly assume them to be different.'

'Then let us finally determine that there are two principles existing in the soul. And what of passion, or spirit? Is it a third, or akin to one of the preceding?'

'I should be inclined to say – akin to desire.'

'Well,' I said, 'there is a story which I remember to have heard, and in which I put faith. The story is, that Leontius, the son of Aglaion, coming up one day from the Piraeus, under the north wall on the outside, observed some dead bodies lying on the ground at the place of execution. He felt a desire to see them, and also a dread and abhorrence of them; for a time he struggled and covered his eyes, but at length the desire got the better of him; and forcing them open, he ran up to the dead bodies, saying, "Look, ye wretches, take your fill of the fair sight."'

'I have heard the story myself,' he said.

'The moral of the tale is, that anger at times goes to war with desire, as though they were two distinct things.'

'Yes; that is the meaning,' he said.

'And are there not many other cases in which we observe that when a man's desires violently prevail over his reason, he reviles. himself, and is angry at the violence within him, and that in this struggle, which is like the struggle of factions in a State, his spirit is on the side of his reason; – but for the passionate or spirited element to take part with the desires when reason decides that she should not be opposed, is a sort of thing which I believe that you never observed occurring in yourself, nor, as I should imagine, in any one else?'

'Certainly not.'

'Suppose that a man thinks he has done a wrong to another, the nobler he is the less able he is to feel indignant at any suffering, such as hunger, or cold, or any other pain which the injured person may inflict upon him – these he deems to be just, and, as I said, his anger refuses to be excited by them.'

'True,' he said.

'But when he thinks that he is the sufferer of wrong, then he boils and chafes, and is on the side of what he believes to be justice; and because he suffers hunger or cold or other pain he is only the more determined to persevere and conquer. His noble spirit will not be quelled until he either slays or is slain; or until he hears the voice of the shepherd, that is, reason, bidding his dog bark no more.'

'The illustration is perfect,' he replied; 'and in our State, as we were saying, the auxiliaries were to be dogs, and to hear the voice of the rulers, who are their shepherds.'

'I perceive,' I said, 'that you quite understand me; there is, however, a further point which I wish you to consider.'

'What point?'

'You remember that passion or spirit appeared at first sight to be a kind of desire, but now we should say quite the contrary; for in the conflict of the soul spirit is arrayed on the side of the rational principle.'

'Most assuredly.'

'But a further question arises: Is passion different from reason also, or only a kind of reason; in which latter case, instead of three principles in the soul, there will be only two, the rational and the concupiscent; or rather, as the State was composed of three classes, traders, auxiliaries, counsellors, so may there not be in the individual soul a third element which is passion, or spirit, and, when not corrupted by bad education, is the natural auxiliary of reason?'

MARCEL, *THE MYSTERY OF BEING*

From Gabriel Marcel, *The Mystery of Being*, vol. 1, translated by G. S. Fraser, Chicago, Regnery Gateway, 1950

Gabriel Marcel (1889–1972), French philosopher and dramatist, was deeply concerned with an approach to experiential thought. His method was devised with the intention of keeping in close touch with reality; his work centres on existence — its dimensions of knowing and being. His most notable books include The Mystery of Being, *his Metaphysical Journal, and* Creative Fidelity.

In his close-grained investigation of our everyday life, Marcel raises the question of the ego. To what extent does our tendency to protect, to possess, to divide ourselves from ourselves and others, obstruct real relationship? Only when we are able to relax our hold on preoccupation with ourselves does the opening to the other person appear. Only then, in Marcel's words, can we be with him, not against him. To the extent that we remain attached to this self-concept, to that extent will we be isolated, alienated, dehumanized. That thought in turn can lead us to feel out a way to be less tense, less fearful, in the face of other persons.

We should notice, to start with, that the ego, as such, shows up in an extraordinarily vivid and aggressive fashion in the mental world of the child; and one might add that this vividness and aggressiveness persist, in later years, to the degree to which that mental world survives in the adult. The child, let us say, runs up to his mother and offers her a flower. 'Look,' he says, 'that was me, I picked it.' His tone and his gestures are very significant; he is pointing himself out as somebody who deserves the admiration and gratitude of grown-ups. Look, it is I, I in person, I, all present and correct here, who have plucked this flower! Above all, don't believe for a moment that it was Jim or Lucy who picked it. The child's 'I did it,' in fact, excludes in the most definite fashion the deplorable misunderstanding by which my exploit could be attributed to others. But we find adults standing up in the same way for the ego's rights. Let us take the example of the amateur composer who has just been singing, in a throaty voice, a song for which he has written the tune. Some artless listener asks, was that by Debussy? 'Oh, no,' says the composer, bridling and smirking, 'that was a little thing of my own.' Here again the ego is trying to attract to itself the praise, the surprised and admiring comments, of a something other than itself, that it uses as a sounding-board. In every case of this sort one may say that the ego is present in the flesh, appealing or protesting, in various tones of voice, that nobody should infringe on its rights, or, if you like, tread on its toes. Notice, too, that in all such cases one essential factor is what I shall call, a little pedantically, ecceity: that is, a hereness and a nowness, or rather a here-and-nowness; we can think of the ego in this sense, in fact, as a sort of personified here-and-now that has to defend itself actively against other personified heres-and-nows, the latter appearing to it essentially as just so many threats to what I have called its rights. These rights, however, have essentially a prejuridical character, they are from the beginning inseparably linked to the very fact of existing and thus are exposed continually to all sorts of more or less mortifying infringements.

In so far as I feel myself in danger of being passively overlooked or actively slighted in a hundred different ways that all cut me to the quick, one might say, in fact, that I have no protective skin at all, that the quick is exposed already.

The obvious example to take at this point is, of course, that of the shy young man who is making his first appearance at some fashionable dance or cocktail party. Such a young man is, as you so admirably express it in English, to the highest degree self-conscious. He feels himself the cynosure, and the extremely vulnerable cynosure, of neighbouring eyes. It seems to him that all the other people in the party, none of whom he knows, are looking at him, and looking at him, too, with what meaning glances! Obviously they are making fun of him, perhaps of his new dinner-jacket, which does not fit him as well as it should, perhaps of his black bow tie, which was all right when he last looked in the mirror, but now, he feels quite sure, has gone lopsided. And then, of course, he cut himself when he was shaving. And everybody must have noticed how clumsily he held his glass just a moment ago, so that some of the sherry slopped over. And so on, and so on ... To such a young man it seems that he has been literally thrown (as Christians were thrown to the lions) to the malevolent lucidity of other people's glances. Thus he is at once preoccupied with himself to the highest possible degree and hypnotized at the same time to a quite supreme degree by others, by what he imagines other people may think of him. It is this paradoxical tension which your excellent word self-consciousness so compactly expresses.

But on the other hand this tension is quite at the opposite pole from what I have at various times called, and shall here call again, intersubjectivity. And the opposite nature of the two things cannot be too heavily underlined. Let us suppose that some unknown person comes up at our party to say a word or two to the shy young man and put him at his ease. The latter, to begin with, does not find himself entering into the direct relation with his new acquaintance that is expressed by the pronoun *you* but instead thinks of him as *him*. Why is he talking to me? What is he after? Is he trying to satisfy some sinister and mocking curiosity? Let us be on our guard anyway. Let us be extremely non-committal in our answers to his questions. Thus, because he is on the defensive with this other guest, our young man has to the least possible degree what can be described as a genuine encounter or conversation with him. He is not really with the other any more than he can help being. But in a very general fashion, indeed, one might say that it is the relationship expressed by the preposition *with* that is eminently intersubjective. The relationship that *with* expresses here, does not for instance really apply to the world of objects, which, taken as a whole, is a world merely of juxtaposition. A chair is alongside a table, or beside it, or we put the chair by the table, but the chair is never really *with* the table in this sense.

But let us get back to our example and let us suppose that the ice is after all broken, and that the conversation takes on a more intimate character. 'I am glad to meet you,' says the stranger, 'I once knew your parents,' and all at once a bond is created and, what specially matters, there is a relaxation of tension. The attention of the young man ceases to be concentrated on himself, it is as if something gripped tight together inside him were able to loosen up. He is lifted out of that stifling here-and-nowness in which, if I may be allowed a homely comparison, his ego was sticking to him as an adhesive plaster sticks to a small cut. He is lifted right out of the here and now, and, what is very strange surely, this unknown person whom he has just met accompanies him on this sort of magic voyage. They are together in what we must call an elsewhere, an elsewhere, however, which has a mysteriously intimate character. Let us say, if you like, that they are linked to each other by a shared secret. I shall have to come back, no doubt, to the notion of the secret as a mainspring of intersubjectivity, but let us notice, before we leave our example, that ties of quite a different nature might have grown up between the stranger and the shy young man. A man whom I run into quite casually learns that I am very fond of coffee, coffee is desperately scarce in France at the time, so he gives me a hint about how to get some on the black market. One cannot say that this incident is enough in itself to create a bond between me and him; all we have in common is a taste, and that is not enough to draw us together at the ontological level, that is *qua* beings. And neither, on the other hand, is a taste for coffee, even combined with a certain broadmindedness about means of getting hold of coffee, enough in itself to create the sense of complicity and freemasonry in vice that might arise from the avowal, to somebody who shared it, of some much more dubious inclination. But such a sense of complicity is not really what we have in mind, either; rather it is in the sort of case where I discover that a stranger has recognized the deep, individual quality of somebody whom I myself have tenderly loved and who retains a place in my heart, that true inter-subjectivity arises.

We could also take examples of intersubjectivity from artistic and religious experience. But it is clear that there would be no absolute discontinuity between the examples taken from ordinary life and those from the higher reaches of the spirit; on the contrary there would be a kind of graduated scale, with something like the mystical communion of souls in worship at the top end, and with something like an *ad hoc* association for some strictly practical and rigidly defined purpose at the bottom. But it would be possible to show that a single human relationship can work its way all the way up and down this scale; this, for instance, is quite obviously true of marriage. There may be moments of drought in marriage when the wife becomes for her husband merely that 'silly creature who should have been busy darning socks, but there she was clucking round the tea table with a lot of old hens', and there may be almost mystical moments when the wife is acknowledged and loved as the bearer of a unique value to which eternal bliss has been promised. One might therefore say that there is a hierarchy of choices, or rather of invocations, ranging from the call upon another which is like ringing a bell for a servant to the quite other sort of call which is really like a kind of prayer. But, as I tried to show in my first *Metaphysical Journal*, in invocations of the first sort — where we press a bell or make some other sort of signal to show that we want service — the Thou we are invoking is really a He or a She or even an It treated pragmatically as a Thou. When I stop somebody in the street to ask my way, I do say to him, it is true, 'Can you tell me how to get to such-and-such a Square?', but all the same I am making a convenience of him, I am treating him as if he were a signpost. No doubt, even in this limiting case, a touch of genuine intersubjectivity can break through, thanks to the magical powers of the tone of voice and the glance. If I have really lost my bearings, if it is late, if I fear that I may have to grope my way for hours through some labyrinthine and perhaps even dangerous warren of streets, I may have a fleeting but irresistible impression that the stranger I am appealing to is a brother eager to come to my aid. What happens is, in a word, that the stranger has started off by putting himself, as it were, ideally in my shoes. He has come within my reach as a person. It is no longer a mere matter of his showing me the way as a guidebook or a map might, but of his really giving a helping hand to somebody who is alone and in a bewildered state. This is nothing more than a sort of spark of spirituality, out as soon as it is in; the stranger and I part almost certainly never to see each other again, yet for a few minutes, as I trudge homewards, this man's unexpected cordiality makes me feel as if I had stepped out of a wintry day into a warm room . . .

It seems to me that we can never apply ourselves too strictly to the following problem: to what degree, and within what limits, can my relationship with my own past be brought before my mind? When, for instance, I see strange faces around me on a bus or in the tube, I am often haunted by the notion that each of them is carrying around with him his own past. But what does it mean to carry around something intangible, of this sort? There, as it seems to me, our whole problem lies. Of course, we might stop in our inquiry where the police stop. Each of my fellow passengers could be arrested, taken to a police-station, asked to state his identity, place of residence, and so on ... This means merely that each of them, unless suffering from loss of memory, has the data to hand that are required for the compilation of his or her dossier. There is a whole range of headings that might be relevant: illnesses, successive changes of residence, of job, religious affiliations, party membership, and so on. One might say perhaps that our imaginary detainee has a gramophone record inside that can reel off the answers to such questions. But just what we mean by that is still obscure. It will not do to say that he or she is a gramophone record; but only that he or she can become so if subjected, as so often happens in our contemporary world, to persistent questioning, and will become so only to the degree to which dehumanizing treatment brings about a state of self-estrangement. All we can say is that from the very start there was something that could become, or rather could be degraded into, a gramophone record. This means that we must take it as a basic assumption that each of us has it in his power to submit his own experience considered as a whole to the kind of treatment that inevitably distorts its nature. However, this experience as a whole, which can be distorted in this fashion, is just what we have in mind when we talk about somebody or other's past.

It is obvious, of course, that the more a man is detached from his experience, the more easily it will lend itself to this distorting treatment; the more his total experience is something which he is still actively living, the less easy it will be for him to extract from it the depersonalized data required as answers to the police questionnaire. This is the very reason why we assume that a child, the least detached kind of human being we can conceive of, will be incapable of filling in such questionnaires. All this forces us to recognize that we cling to our past in a very uneven way, that we are our past in a very uneven way, and it must be added that this unevenness is related to a similar unevenness in our present situation. Here, as several times before, it is Marcel Proust who can set us on our way. In other words, we must not believe that we can at some given moment make a distinction that will be valid for all the rest of our lives between what I am now, on the one hand, and what, on the other hand, I am now so detached from that I can speak of it in an abstract fashion, that I can reduce it merely to the state of some external object to which such distinctions are made, or are not made, varying with the fluctuation of our present experience itself. This is enough to show how unreal it is to represent the past to oneself as in some sense preserved or pickled, as if it were last year's blackberries or walnuts. At any moment in my life, a magic shutter may snap back and I am once more the small boy of eight who is in a state of deadly anxiety because his mother is so late in coming home and who is running over in his fancy all the accidents that may have befallen her. Ought I to conclude from this that I have never really ceased to be that small boy?

Here again we are up against the apparently self-contradictory answer, the yes and no, which seems to be inseparable from the fact of existing as a human being. It would be false to claim that the little boy has been continuing to exist all these years, just as a table or chair continues to exist even when I am not looking at it. The little boy of eight years old – who, in some sense, nevertheless, I still am – cannot by any means be conceived to have persisted after the fashion of a physical object. But on the other hand my assertion that I have never ceased to be this small boy is correct if we are ready to admit, like the fairy stories, which are the perfect symbolical expressions of this kind of truth, that there are modes of existence that are not objectifiable, but that have infinite possibilities of resurrection. Yet, strange as the symbol may be, it is only the extremely simplified expression of a much stranger reality. Between this latent mode of existence and the active, waking state in which I go out to post a letter and have to pause a moment at the pavement's edge to let the traffic pass, and so on, there lies an innumerable multiplicity of mental presences, that get in each other's way, and that enter into relations with me of such various sorts that it would be extremely useful to classify them even in the roughest and most approximate fashion. We might express this state of affairs by the simple formula that I am not merely myself: more strictly, is there any point in saying I am myself, since I am also somebody else? I am, for instance, the man I have been until quite recently, the man I was yesterday: there is a point of view, and a deep one, for which 'have been' and 'was' in such sentences lose all precise significance. There can be a real struggle for existence between the man I was yesterday, the man I have been until recently, and the man I have a tendency to be, a yearning to be, today.

ARISTOTLE, 'FRIENDSHIP'

From Aristotle, *Nichomachean Ethics*, translated by W. D. Ross, Oxford University Press, 1954

In this very interesting selection from his Nicomachean Ethics, *Aristotle (see also p. 77) discusses the nature of friendship. Although we often think of friendship as being the opposite of self-love, Aristotle argues that this is not the case. Properly understood, when we are able to extend a loving relation to ourselves, we put ourselves in a position to be open to relations with others. By the same token, although we sometimes feel that being happy means that we have passed beyond the need for being with others, Aristotle shows that this view also is mistaken. The happy person is one with an expanded vision, who sees the essential part that others play in maintaining his own well-being.*

The nature of true self-love

8. The question is also debated, whether a man should love himself most, or someone else. People criticize those who love themselves most, and call them self-lovers, using this as an epithet of disgrace, and a bad man seems to do everything for his own sake, and the more so the more wicked he is – and so men reproach him, for instance, with doing nothing of his own accord – while the good man acts for honour's sake, and the more so the better he is, and acts for his friend's sake, and sacrifices his own interest.

But the facts clash with these arguments, and this is not surprising. For men say that one ought to love best one's best friend, and a man's best friend is one who wishes well to the object of his wish for his sake, even if no one is to know of it; and these attributes are found most of all in a man's attitude towards himself, and so are all the other attributes by which a friend is defined; for, as we have said, it is from this relation that all the characteristics of friendship have extended to our neighbours. All the proverbs, too, agree with this, e.g., 'A single soul,' and 'What friends have is common property,' and 'Friendship is equality,' and 'Charity begins at home';* for all these marks will be found most in a man's relation to himself; he is his own best friend and therefore ought to love himself best. It is therefore a reasonable question, which of the two views we should follow; for both are plausible.

Perhaps we ought to mark off such arguments from each other and determine how far and in what respects each view is right. Now if we grasp the sense in which each school uses the phrase 'lover of self', the truth may become evident. Those who use the term as one of reproach ascribe self-love to people who assign to themselves the greater share of wealth, honours, and bodily

---

*Lit. 'the knee is nearer than the shin'. (Trans.)

210

pleasures; for these are what most people desire, and busy themselves about as though they were the best of all things, which is
the reason, too, why they become objects of competition. So
those who are grasping with regard to these things gratify their
appetites and in general their feelings and their irrational element
of the soul; and most men are of this nature (which is the reason
why the epithet has come to be used as it is — it takes its meaning
from the prevailing type of self-love, which is a bad one); justly,
therefore, are men who are lovers of self in this way reproached
for being so. That it is those who give themselves the preference
in regard to objects of this sort that most people usually call
lovers of self is plain; for if a man were always anxious that he
himself, above all things, should act justly, temperately, or in
accordance with any other of the virtues, and in general were
always to try to secure for himself the honourable course, no one
would call such a man a lover of self or blame him.

But such a man would seem more than the other a lover of self;
at all events he assigns to himself the things that are noblest and
best, and gratifies the most authoritative element in himself and in
all things obeys this; and just as a city or any other systematic
whole is most properly identified with the most authoritative
element in it, so is a man; and therefore the man who loves this
and gratifies it is most of all a lover of self. Besides, a man is said
to have or not to have self-control according to the assumption
that this is the man himself; and the things men have done on a
rational principle are thought most properly their own acts and
voluntary acts. That this is the man himself, then, or is so more
than anything else, is plain, and also that the good man loves most
this part of him. Whence it follows that he is most truly a lover of
self, of another type than that which is a matter of reproach, and
as different from that as living according to a rational principle is
from living as passion dictates, and desiring what is noble from
desiring what seems advantageous. Those, then, who busy themselves in an exceptional degree with noble actions all men approve

and praise, and if all were to strive towards what is noble and strain every nerve to do the noblest deeds, everything would be as it should be for the common weal, and everyone would secure for himself the goods that are greatest, since virtue is the greatest of goods.

Therefore the good man should be a lover of self (for he will both himself profit by doing noble acts, and will benefit his fellows), but the wicked man should not; for he will hurt both himself and his neighbours, following as he does evil passions. For the wicked man, what he does clashes with what he ought to do, but what the good man ought to do he does; for reason in each of its possessors chooses what is best for itself, and the good man obeys his reason. It is true of the good man too that he does many acts for the sake of his friends and his country, and if necessary dies for them; for he will throw away both wealth and honours and in general the goods that are objects of competition, gaining for himself nobility; since he would prefer a short period of intense pleasure to a long one of mild enjoyment, a twelvemonth of noble life to many years of humdrum existence, and one great and noble action to many trivial ones. Now those who die for others doubtless attain this result; it is therefore a great prize that they choose for themselves. They will throw away wealth too on condition that their friends will gain more; for while a man's friend gains wealth he himself achieves nobility; he is therefore assigning the greater good to himself. The same too is true of honour and office; all these things he will sacrifice to his friend; for this is noble and laudable for himself. Rightly then is he thought to be good, since he chooses nobility before all else. But he may even give up actions to his friend; it may be nobler to become the cause of his friend's acting than to act himself. In all the actions, therefore, that men are praised for, the good man is seen to assign to himself the greater share in what is noble. In this sense, then, as has been said, a man should be a lover of self; but in the sense in which most men are so, he ought not.

Why does the happy man need friends?

9. It is also disputed whether the happy man will need friends or
not. It is said that those who are supremely happy and self-
sufficient have no need of friends; for they have the things that are
good, and therefore being self-sufficient they need nothing further,
while a friend, being another self, furnishes what a man cannot
provide by his own effort; whence the saying, 'When fortune is
kind, what need of friends?' But it seems strange, when one
assigns all good things to the happy man, not to assign friends,
who are thought the greatest of external goods. And if it is more
characteristic of a friend to do well by another than to be well
done by, and to confer benefits is characteristic of the good man
and of virtue, and it is nobler to do well by friends than by
strangers, the good man will need people to do well by. This is
why the question is asked whether we need friends more in
prosperity or in adversity, on the assumption that not only does a
man in adversity need people to confer benefits on him, but also
those who are prospering need people to do well by. Surely it is
strange, too, to make the supremely happy man a solitary; for no
one would choose the whole world on condition of being alone,
since man is a political creature and one whose nature is to live
with others. Therefore even the happy man lives with others; for
he has the things that are by nature good. And plainly it is better
to spend his days with friends and good men than with strangers
or any chance persons. Therefore the happy man needs friends.

What then do holders of the first view mean, and in what respect
are they right? Is it that most men identify friends with useful
people? Of such friends indeed the supremely happy man will have
no need, since he already has the things that are good; nor will he
need those whom one makes one's friends because of their pleasantness, or he will need them only to a small extent (for his life,
being pleasant, has no need of adventitious pleasure); and because
he does not need such friends he is thought not to need friends.

But that is surely not true. For we have said at the outset that happiness is an activity; and activity plainly comes into being and is not present at the start like a piece of property. If (1) happiness lies in living and being active, and the good man's activity is virtuous and pleasant in itself, as we have said at the outset, and (2) a thing's being one's own is one of the attributes that make it pleasant, and (3) we can contemplate our neighbours better than ourselves and their actions better than our own, and if the actions of virtuous men who are their friends are pleasant to good men (since these have both the attributes that are naturally pleasant),* if this be so, the supremely happy man will need friends of this sort, since his purpose is to contemplate worthy actions and actions that are his own, and the actions of a good man who is his friend have both these qualities.

Further, men think that the happy man ought to live pleasantly. Now if he were a solitary, life would be hard for him; for by oneself it is not easy to be continuously active; but with others and towards others it is easier. With others therefore his activity will be more continuous, and it is in itself pleasant, as it ought to be for the man who is supremely happy; for a good man *qua* good delights in virtuous actions and is vexed at vicious ones, as a musical man enjoys beautiful tunes but is pained at bad ones. A certain training in virtue arises also from the company of the good, as Theognis has said before us.

If we look deeper into the nature of things, a virtuous friend seems to be naturally desirable for a virtuous man. For that which is good by nature, we have said, is for the virtuous man good and pleasant in itself. Now life is defined in the case of animals by the power of perception, in that of man by the power of perception or thought; and a power is defined by reference to the corresponding activity, which is the essential thing; therefore life seems to be

---

*i.e., the attribute of goodness and that of being their own. (Trans.)

essentially the act of perceiving or thinking. And life is among the things that are good and pleasant in themselves, since it is determinate and the determinate is of the nature of the good; and that which is good by nature is also good for the virtuous man (which is the reason why life seems pleasant to all men); but we must not apply this to a wicked and corrupt life or to a life spent in pain; for such a life is indeterminate, as are its attributes. The nature of pain will become plainer in what follows. But if life itself is good and pleasant (which it seems to be, from the very fact that all men desire it, and particularly those who are good and supremely happy; for to such men life is most desirable, and their existence is the most supremely happy); and if he who sees perceives that he sees, and he who hears, that he hears, and he who walks, that he walks, and in the case of all other activities similarly there is something which perceives that we are active, so that if we perceive, we perceive that we perceive, and if we think, that we think; and if to perceive that we perceive or think is to perceive that we exist (for existence was defined as perceiving or thinking); and if perceiving that one lives is in itself one of the things that are pleasant (for life is by nature good, and to perceive what is good present in oneself is pleasant); and if life is desirable, and particularly so for good men, because to them existence is good and pleasant (for they are pleased at the consciousness of the presence in them of what is in itself good); and if as the virtuous man is to himself, he is to his friend also (for his friend is another self) — if all this be true, as his own being is desirable for each man, so, or almost so, is that of his friend. Now his being was seen to be desirable because he perceived his own goodness, and such perception is pleasant in itself. He needs, therefore, to be conscious of the existence of his friend as well, and this will be realized in their living together and sharing in discussion and thought; for this is what living together would seem to mean in the case of man, and not, as in the case of cattle, feeding in the same place.

If, then, being is in itself desirable for the supremely happy man (since it is by its nature good and pleasant), and that of his friend is very much the same, a friend will be one of the things that are desirable. Now that which is desirable for him he must have, or he will be deficient in this respect. The man who is to be happy will therefore need virtuous friends.

TOLSTOY, 'ESARHADDON, KING OF ASSYRIA'

From Leo Tolstoy, *Twenty-three Tales*, translated by L. and A. Maude, Frowde, 1906

Tolstoy (see also p. 151) creates the fable for us of a king, Esarhaddon, who is motivated by ordinary feelings of hatred and revenge. However, through an extraordinary event, he is able to live and experience what his enemy, King Lailie, suffers as a result of his vengeance. This opportunity opens him to a vision of unity which transforms his entire being, a vision which appears across the distance from his conscience.

The Assyrian King, Esarhaddon, had conquered the kingdom of King Lailie, had destroyed and burnt the towns, taken all the inhabitants captive to his own country, slaughtered the warriors, beheaded some chieftains and impaled or flayed others, and had confined King Lailie himself in a cage.

As he lay on his bed one night, King Esarhaddon was thinking how he should execute Lailie, when suddenly he heard a rustling near his bed, and opening his eyes saw an old man with a long grey beard and mild eyes.

'You wish to execute Lailie?' asked the old man.

'Yes,' answered the King. 'But I cannot make up my mind how to do it.'

'But you are Lailie,' said the old man.

'That's not true,' replied the King. 'Lailie is Lailie, and I am I.'

'You and Lailie are one,' said the old man. 'You only imagine you are not Lailie, and that Lailie is not you.'

'What do you mean by that?' said the King. 'Here am I, lying on a soft bed; around me are obedient men-slaves and women-slaves, and tomorrow I shall feast with my friends as I did today; whereas Lailie is sitting like a bird in a cage, and tomorrow he will be impaled, and with his tongue hanging out will struggle till he dies, and his body will be torn in pieces by dogs.'

'You cannot destroy his life,' said the old man.

'And how about the fourteen thousand warriors I killed, with whose bodies I built a mound?' said the King. 'I am alive, but they no longer exist. Does not that prove that I can destroy life?'

'How do you know they no longer exist?'

'Because I no longer see them. And, above all, they were tormented, but I was not. It was ill for them, but well for me.'

'That, also, only seems so to you. You tortured yourself, but not them.'

'I do not understand,' said the King.

'Do you wish to understand?'

'Yes, I do.'

'Then come here,' said the old man, pointing to a large font full of water.

The King rose and approached the font.

'Strip, and enter the font.'

Esarhaddon did as the old man bade him.

'As soon as I begin to pour this water over you,' said the old man, filling a pitcher with the water, 'dip down your head.'

The old man tilted the pitcher over the King's head, and the King bent his head till it was under water.

And as soon as King Esarhaddon was under the water, he felt that he was no longer Esarhaddon, but some one else. And, feeling himself to be that other man, he saw himself lying on a rich bed, beside a beautiful woman. He had never seen her before, but he knew she was his wife. The woman raised herself and said to him:

217

'Dear husband, Lailie! You were wearied by yesterday's work and have slept longer than usual, and I have guarded your rest, and have not roused you. But now the Princes await you in the Great Hall. Dress and go out to them.'

And Esarhaddon — understanding from these words that he was Lailie, and not feeling at all surprised at this, but only wondering that he did not know it before — rose, dressed, and went into the Great Hall where the Princes awaited him.

The Princes greeted Lailie, their King, bowing to the ground, and then they rose, and at his word sat down before him; and the eldest of the Princes began to speak, saying that it was impossible longer to endure the insults of the wicked King Esarhaddon, and that they must make war on him. But Lailie disagreed, and gave orders that envoys should be sent to remonstrate with King Esarhaddon; and he dismissed the Princes from his audience. Afterwards he appointed men of note to act as ambassadors, and impressed on them what they were to say to King Esarhaddon. Having finished this business, Esarhaddon — feeling himself to be Lailie — rode out to hunt wild asses. The hunt was successful. He killed two wild asses himself, and, having returned home, feasted with his friends, and witnessed a dance of slave girls. The next day he went to the Court, where he was awaited by petitioners, suitors, and prisoners brought for trial; and there as usual he decided the cases submitted to him. Having finished this business, he again rode out to his favourite amusement: the hunt. And again he was successful: this time killing with his own hand an old lioness, and capturing her two cubs. After the hunt he again feasted with his friends, and was entertained with music and dances, and the night he spent with his wife, whom he loved.

So, dividing his time between kingly duties and pleasures, he lived for days and weeks, awaiting the return of the ambassadors he had sent to that King Esarhaddon who used to be himself. Not till a month had passed did the ambassadors return, and they returned with their noses and ears cut off.

King Esarhaddon had ordered them to tell Lailie that what had been done to them – the ambassadors – would be done to King Lailie himself also, unless he sent immediately a tribute of silver, gold, and cypress-wood, and came himself to pay homage to King Esarhaddon.

Lailie, formerly Esarhaddon, again assembled the Princes, and took counsel with them as to what he should do. Then all with one accord said that war must be made against Esarhaddon, without waiting for him to attack them. The King agreed; and taking his place at the head of the army, started on the campaign. The campaign lasts seven days. Each day the King rode round the army to rouse the courage of his warriors. On the eighth day his army met that of Esarhaddon in a broad valley through which a river flowed. Lailie's army fought bravely, but Lailie, formerly Esarhaddon, saw the enemy swarming down from the mountains like ants, overrunning the valley and overwhelming his army; and, in his chariot, he flung himself into the midst of the battle, hewing and felling the enemy. But the warriors of Lailie were but as hundreds, while those of Esarhaddon were as thousands; and Lailie felt himself wounded and taken prisoner. Nine days he journeyed with other captives, bound, and guarded by the warriors of Esarhaddon. On the tenth day he reached Nineveh, and was placed in a cage. Lailie suffered not so much from hunger and from his wound as from shame and impotent rage. He felt how powerless he was to avenge himself on his enemy for all he was suffering. All he could do was to deprive his enemies of the pleasure of seeing his sufferings; and he firmly resolved to endure courageously, without a murmur, all they could do to him. For twenty days he sat in his cage, awaiting execution. He saw his relatives and friends led out to death; he heard the groans of those who were executed: some had their hands and feet cut off, others were flayed alive, but he showed neither disquietude, nor pity, nor fear. He saw the wife he loved, bound, and led by two black eunuchs. He knew she was being taken as a slave to Esarhaddon.

That, too, he bore without a murmur. But one of the guards placed to watch him said, 'I pity you, Lailie; you were a king, but who are you now?' And hearing these words, Lailie remembered all he had lost. He clutched the bars of his cage, and, wishing to kill himself, beat his head against them. But he had not the strength to do so, and, groaning in despair, he fell upon the floor of his cage.

At last two executioners opened his cage door, and, having strapped his arms tight behind him, led him to the place of execution, which was soaked with blood. Lailie saw a sharp stake dripping with blood, from which the corpse of one of his friends had just been torn, and he understood that this had been done that the stake might serve for his own execution. They stripped Lailie of his clothes. He was startled at the leanness of his once strong, handsome body. The two executioners seized that body by its lean thighs; they lifted him up and were about to let him fall upon the stake.

'This is death, destruction!' thought Lailie, and, forgetful of his resolve to remain bravely calm to that end, he sobbed and prayed for mercy. But no one listened to him.

'But this cannot be,' thought he. 'Surely I am asleep. It is a dream.' And he made an effort to rouse himself, and he did indeed awake, to find himself neither Esarhaddon nor Lailie – but some kind of an animal. He was astonished that he was an animal, and astonished, also, at not having known this before.

He was grazing in a valley, tearing the tender grass with his teeth, and brushing away flies with his long tail. Around him was frolicking a long-legged, dark-grey ass-colt, striped down its back. Kicking up its hind legs, the colt galloped at full speed to Esarhaddon, and poking him under the stomach with its smooth little muzzle, searched for the teat, and, finding it, quieted down, swallowing regularly. Esarhaddon understood that he was a she-ass, the colt's mother, and this neither surprised nor grieved him, but rather gave him pleasure. He experienced a glad feeling of simultaneous life in himself and in his offspring.

But suddenly something flew near with a whistling sound and hit him in the side, and with its sharp point entered his skin and flesh. Feeling a burning pain, Esarhaddon – who was at the same time the ass – tore the udder from the colt's teeth, and laying back his ears galloped to the herd from which he had strayed. The colt kept up with him, galloping by his side. They had already nearly reached the herd, which had started off, when another arrow in full flight struck the colt's neck. It pierced the skin and quivered in its flesh. The colt sobbed piteously and fell upon its knees. Esarhaddon could not abandon it, and remained standing over it. The colt rose, tottered on its long, thin legs, and again fell. A fearful two-legged being – a man – ran up and cut its throat.

'This cannot be; it is still a dream!' thought Esarhaddon, and made a last effort to awake. 'Surely I am not Lailie, nor the ass, but Esarhaddon!'

He cried out, and at the same instant lifted his head out of the font . . . The old man was standing by him, pouring over his head the last drops from the pitcher.

'Oh, how terribly I have suffered! And for how long!' said Esarhaddon.

'Long?' replied the old man, 'you have only dipped your head under water and lifted it again; see, the water is not yet all out of the pitcher. Do you now understand?'

Esarhaddon did not reply, but only looked at the old man with terror.

'Do you now understand,' continued the old man, 'that Lailie is you, and the warriors you put to death were you also? And not the warriors only, but the animals which you slew when hunting and ate at your feasts were also you. You thought life dwelt in you alone, but I have drawn aside the veil of delusion, and have let you see that by doing evil to others you have done it to yourself also. Life is one in them all, and yours is but a portion of this same common life. And only in that one part of life that is yours, can you make life better or worse – increasing or decreasing

221

it. You can only improve life in yourself by destroying the barriers that divide your life from that of others, and by considering others as yourself, and loving them. By so doing you increase your share of life. You injure your life when you think of it as the only life, and try to add to its welfare at the expense of other lives. By so doing you only lessen it. To destroy the life that dwells in others is beyond your power. The life of those you have slain has vanished from your eyes, but is not destroyed. You thought to lengthen your own life and to shorten theirs, but you cannot do this. Life knows neither time nor space. The life of a moment, and the life of a thousand years: your life, and the life of all the visible and invisible beings in the world, are equal. To destroy life, or to alter it, is impossible; for life is the one thing that exists. All else but seems to us to be.'

Having said this the old man vanished.

Next morning King Esarhaddon gave orders that Lailie and all the prisoners should be set at liberty and that the executions should cease.

On the third day he called his son Assur-bani-pal, and gave the kingdom over into his hands; and he himself went into the desert to think over all he had learnt. Afterwards he went about as a wanderer through the towns and villages, preaching to the people that all life is one, and that when men wish to harm others, they really do evil to themselves.

THE SERMON ON THE MOUNT

From the Gospel of St Matthew, Authorized Version

In the Sermon on the Mount, Jesus speaks of living in contact with the ever-present demands of love. The ideas expressed here are important not only for our relations with others, but, more centrally, for our relationship with ourselves.

Chapter V

1. And seeing the multitudes, he went up into a mountain: and when he was set, his disciples came unto him:

2. And he opened his mouth and taught them, saying,

3. Blessed are the poor in spirit: for theirs is the kingdom of heaven.

4. Blessed are they that mourn: for they shall be comforted.

5. Blessed are the meek: for they shall inherit the earth.

6. Blessed are they which hunger and thirst after righteousness: for they shall be filled.

7. Blessed are the merciful: for they shall obtain mercy.

8. Blessed are the pure in heart: for they shall see God.

9. Blessed are the peacemakers: for they shall be called the children of God.

10. Blessed are they which are persecuted for righteousness' sake: for theirs is the kingdom of heaven.

11. Blessed are ye, when men shall revile you, and persecute you, and shall say all manner of evil against you falsely, for my sake.

12. Rejoice, and be exceeding glad: for great is your reward in heaven: for so persecuted they the prophets which were before you.

13. Ye are the salt of the earth: but if the salt have lost his savour, wherewith shall it be salted? it is thenceforth good for nothing, but to be cast out, and to be trodden under foot of men.

14. Ye are the light of the world. A city that is set on an hill cannot be hid.

15. Neither do men light a candle, and put it under a bushel, but on a candlestick; and it giveth light unto all that are in the house.

16. Let your light so shine before men, that they may see your good works, and glorify your Father which is in heaven.

17. Think not that I am come to destroy the law, or the prophets: I am not come to destroy, but to fulfil.

18. For verily I say unto you, Till heaven and earth pass, one jot or one tittle shall in no wise pass from the law, till all be fulfilled.

19. Whosoever therefore shall break one of these least commandments, and shall teach men so, he shall be called the least in the kingdom of heaven: but whosoever shall do and teach them, the same shall be called great in the kingdom of heaven.

20. For I say unto you, That except your righteousness shall exceed the righteousness of the scribes and Pharisees, ye shall in no case enter into the kingdom of heaven.

21. Ye have heard that it was said by them of old time, Thou shalt not kill; and whosoever shall kill shall be in danger of the judgement:

22. But I say unto you, That whosoever is angry with his brother without a cause shall be in danger of the judgement: and whosoever shall say to his brother, Raca, shall be in danger of the council: but whosoever shall say, Thou fool, shall be in danger of hell fire.

23. Therefore if thou bring thy gift to the altar, and there rememberest that thy brother hath aught against thee;

24. Leave there thy gift before the altar, and go thy way; first be reconciled to thy brother, and then come and offer thy gift.

25. Agree with thine adversary quickly, whiles thou art in the way with him; lest at any time the adversary deliver thee to the judge, and the judge deliver thee to the officer, and thou be cast into prison.

26. Verily I say unto thee, Thou shalt by no means come out thence, till thou has paid the uttermost farthing.

27. Ye have heard that it was said by them of old time, Thou shalt not commit adultery:

28. But I say unto you, That whosoever looketh on a woman to lust after her hath committed adultery with her already in his heart.

29. And if thy right eye offend thee, pluck it out, and cast it

from thee: for it is profitable for thee that one of thy members should perish, and not that thy whole body should be cast into hell.

30. And if thy right hand offend thee, cut it off, and cast it from thee: for it is profitable for thee that one of thy members should perish, and not that thy whole body should be cast into hell.

31. It hath been said, Whosoever shall put away his wife, let him give her a writing of divorcement:

32. But I say unto you, That whosoever shall put away his wife, saving for the cause of fornication, causeth her to commit adultery: and whosoever shall marry her that is divorced committeth adultery.

33. Again, ye have heard that it hath been said by them of old time, Thou shalt not forswear thyself, but shalt perform unto the Lord thine oaths:

34. But I say unto you, Swear not at all; neither by heaven; for it is God's throne:

35. Nor by the earth; for it is his footstool: neither by Jerusalem; for it is the city of the great King.

36. Neither shalt thou swear by thy head, because thou canst not make one hair white or black.

37. But let your communication be, Yea, yea; Nay, nay: for whatsoever is more than these cometh of evil.

38. Ye have heard that it hath been said, An eye for an eye, and a tooth for a tooth:

39. But I say unto you, That ye resist not evil: but whosoever shall smite thee on thy right cheek, turn to him the other also.

40. And if any man will sue thee at the law, and take away thy coat, let him have thy cloak also.

41. And whosoever shall compel thee to go a mile, go with him twain.

42. Give to him that asketh thee, and from him that would borrow of thee turn not thou away.

43. Ye have heard that it hath been said, Thou shalt love thy neighbour, and hate thine enemy.

44. But I say unto you, Love your enemies, bless them that curse you, do good to them that hate you, and pray for them which despitefully use you, and persecute you;

45. That ye may be the children of your Father which is in heaven: for he maketh his sun to rise on the evil and on the good, and sendeth rain on the just and on the unjust.

46. For if ye love them which love you, what reward have ye? do not even the publicans the same?

47. And if ye salute your brethren only, what do ye more than others? do not even the publicans so?

48. Be ye therefore perfect, even as your Father which is in heaven is perfect.

TAGORE, 'THOUGHT RELICS'

From Rabindranath Tagore, *Sadhana*, New York and London, Macmillan, 1913

Rabindranath Tagore (1861–1942), Indian philosopher and poet, winner of the Nobel Prize (1913). Writing over one hundred books of poetry, fifty plays, and some fifteen books of philosophy, his most important books are The Realization of Life *(1913),* The Religion of Man *(1931), and* Man *(1937). His interest throughout lies in demonstrating the transcendent purpose to our lives, bringing the disparate elements of which we are composed into a balanced unity.*

In a series of moving comparisons, Tagore describes the open and accepting attitude which is what he means by love. The startling newness of experience may make us hesitant, fearful, or doubting; but if we are free and loving, that attitude brings us to a sense of oneness with ourselves and with life. In this sense of unity, on all levels, Tagore locates the force of love at work.

We are like a stray line of a poem, which ever feels that it rhymes with another line and must find it, or miss its own fulfilment. This quest of the unattained is the great impulse in man which brings forth all his best creations. Man seems deeply to be aware of a separation at the root of his being; he cries to be led across it to a union, and somehow he knows that it is love which can lead him to a love which is final.

The horse harnessed to a carriage is only a part of it; the master is he who drives it unattached. We are enjoined to work with vigour and yet retain our detachment of mind. For our deeds must express our freedom above all, otherwise we become like wheels revolving because compelled. There is a harmony between doing and not doing, between gaining and renouncing, which we must attain.

Our daily flow of prayer carries our self into the supreme Self, it makes us feel the reality of that fullness which we gain by utterly giving ourselves up, makes our consciousness expand in a large world of peace, where movements are beauty and all relations are truth because of their inner freedom, which is disinterestedness.

Love is not a mere impulse, it must contain truth, which is law. It accepts limitations from truth because of its own inner wealth. The child willingly exercises restraint to correct its bodily balance, because it has true pleasure in the freedom of its movements; and love also counts no cost as too great to realize its truth. Poetry is much more strict in its form of expression than prose, because poetry has the freedom of joy in its origin and end. Our love of God is accurately careful of its responsibilities. It is austere in its probity and it must have intellect for its ally. Since what it deals with is immense in value, it has to be cautious about the purity of its coins. Therefore, when our soul cries for the gift of immortality, its first prayer is, 'Lead me from the unreal to truth.'

We criticize nature from outside when we separate it in our mind from human nature, and blame it for being devoid of pity and justice. Let the wick burn with indignation at the want of light in the rest of the candle, but the truth is that the wick represents the whole candle in its illumination. Obstacles are necessary companions to expression, and we know that the positive element in language is not in its obstructiveness. Exclusively viewed from the side of the obstacle, nature appears inimical to the idea of morality. But if that were absolutely true, moral life could never come to exist. Life, moral or physical, is not a completed fact, but a continual process, depending for its movement upon two contrary forces, the force of resistance and that of expression. Dividing these forces into two mutually opposing principles does not help us, for the truth dwells not in the opposition but in its continual reconciliation.

Fear assumes unlimited dimensions in the dark, because it is the shadow of the self which has lost its foothold in the all, the self which is a doubter, an unbeliever, which puts its emphasis upon negation, exaggerating detached facts into fearful distortions. In the light we find the harmony of things and know that our world is great and therefore we are great; we know that with more and more extensive realization of truth, conflicts will vanish, for existence itself is harmony.

An acquaintance of mine has suddenly died and once again I come to know death, the tritest of all truisms in this world.

The moralist teaches us to know the world as unreal through the contemplation of death. But to make renunciation easy by calling the world names is neither true, nor brave. For that renunciation is no renunciation at all in which things have lost their value.

On the contrary, the world is so true, that death's wheel leaves no mark upon it. The untruth is in the belief that this self of ours for its own permanent use can rob this world of even a particle of its things. Death has its concern only with our self and not with this world. The world never loses an atom; it is our self which suffers.

There are men whose idea of life is static, who long for its continuation after death only because of their wish for permanence and not perfection; they love to imagine that the things to which they are accustomed will persist for ever. They completely identify themselves in their minds with their fixed surroundings and with whatever they have gathered, and to have to leave these is death for them. They forget that the true meaning of living is outliving, it is ever growing out of itself. The fruit clings to its stem, its skin clings to the pulp, and the pulp to the seed so long as the fruit is immature, so long as it is not ready for its course of further life. Its outer covering and its inner core are not yet differentiated and it only proves its life by its strength of tenacity. But when the seed is ripe its hold upon its surrounding is loosened, its pulp attains fragrance, sweetness and detachment, and is dedicated to all who need it. Birds peck at it and it is not hurt, the storm plucks it and flings it to the dust and it is not destroyed. It proves its immortality by its renunciation.

The life of the seed within the fruit is absolutely different from its life of growth as a tree. The life which is bound on all sides within the environment of our self, within the limited range of our senses, must be so fundamentally different from the life of an emancipated soul that it is impossible to imagine the latter while we are immured in the sheath of self. And therefore, in our desire for eternal life we pray for an eternity of our habit and comfort, forgetting that immortality is in repeatedly transcending the definite forms of life in order to pursue the infinite truth of life. Those who think that life's true meaning is in the persistence of its particular forms which are familiar to us are like misers who have not the power to know that the meaning of money can only be found by spending it, by changing the symbol into truth.

The world of sleep is fundamental; it is the world of the mother's womb. It is the world where the grass and the trees live and find their beauty of reposefulness. Our consciousness has freed itself from its embrace, asserting its independence. It is the freedom of the fountain which must come over and over again to its origin to renew its play. The whole depth and spread of the still water finds its own play in the play of this little fountain. In like manner, it is in our own consciousness that the universe knows itself. Therefore this consciousness has to be great in order to be true. Our consciousness is the music of the world, its dance, its poem. It has its pauses in the bosom of the original sleep, to be fed with immortality at her breast.

But we cannot afford to fritter away our solitude where lies the throne of the infinite. We cannot truly live for one another if we never claim the freedom to live alone, if our social duties consist in helping one another to forget that we have souls. To exhaust ourselves completely in mere efforts to give company to each other is to cheat the world of our best, the best which is the product of the amplitude of our inner atmosphere of leisure. Society poisons the air it breathes, where it hems in the individual with a revolving crowd of distractions.

Some part of the earth's water becomes rarefied and ascends to the skies. With the movement and the music it acquires in those pure heights it then showers down, back to the water of the earth, making it wholesome and fresh. Similarly, part of the mind of humanity rises up out of the world and flies skyward; but this sky-soaring mind attains completeness only when it has returned to mingle with the earth-bound mind. This is the ventilation of religion, the circulation of man's ideals between heaven and earth.

Our greatest men have shown immense respect for mankind in their expectations. We come to believe in ourselves because of what is asked of us. Practical men base their arrangements upon their estimates of man's limitations. Therefore the great creations of history, the creations that have their foundations upon the faith in the infinite in man, have not their origin in the common sense of practical men. When Buddha said to men, 'Spread thy thoughts of love beyond limits,' when Christ said, 'Love thine enemies,' their words transcended the average standard of ideals belonging to the ordinary world. But they ever remind us that our true love is not the life of the ordinary world, and we have a fund of resources in us which is inexhaustible. It is not for us to despair, because the highest hope for mankind has been uttered by the great words of great men.

To fledgling birds, flight in the sky may appear incredible. They may with apparent reason measure the highest limit of their possibilities by the limited standard of their nests. But in the meanwhile they find that their food is not grown inside those nests; it is brought to them across the measureless blue. There is a silent voice that speaks to them, that they are more than what they are, and that they must not laugh at the message of soaring wings and glad songs of freedom.

The old is prudent but is not wise. Wisdom is that freshness of mind which enables one to realize that truth is not hoarded in caskets of maxims, it is free and living. Great sufferings lead us to wisdom because these are the birth-throes through which our mind is freed from its habit-environment, and comes naked into the arms of reality. Wisdom has the character of the child perfected through knowledge and feeling.

To alleviate pain, to try to remove its causes, is worthy of man. All the same, we must know that a great part of our sufferings should be ascribed to the beginning of our entrance into a new plane of existence to which our vital nature has not been completely adapted nor our mind thoroughly accustomed. From a narrow perfection of animality man has arrived in the imperfectness of spiritual life, where the civil war between the forces of our primitive past and those belonging to our future has robbed us of peace. Not having reached its normal stage, humanity is enveloped in the incandescent vapour of suffering.

We must know that to be provided with an exact apportionment of what we deserve and need is like travelling in a world whose flatness is ideally perfect, and therefore where the fluid forces of nature are held in suspense. We require ups and downs, however unpleasant they may be, in our life's geography, in order to make our thoughts and energies fluently active. Our life's journey is a journey in an unknown country, where hills and hollows come in our way unawares, keeping our minds ever active in dealing with them. They do not come according to our deserts, but our deserts are judged according to our treatment of them.

In a lyrical poem, the metre and the idea are blended in one. Treated separately, they reveal themselves as two contrary forces; and instances are common in which their natural antagonism has not been overcome, thus resulting in the production of bad poems.

We are the artists, before whom lie materials which are mutually obstructive. They continually clash, until they develop into a creation perfect in unity. Very often, in order to shirk trouble and secure peace, we sacrifice one of the contending parties. This makes the fight impossible, but also the creation. The restless spirit of nature divorced from the soul's repose drives us to the madness of work which piles up towers of things. On the other hand the spiritual being deprived of its world of reality lives only in the exile of abstraction, creating phantoms in which exaggerations, unchecked by the strict necessities of forms, run riot.

Our nature being complex, it is unsafe to generalize about things that are human, and it is an incomplete statement of truth to say that habits have the sole effect of deadening our mind. The habits that are helped are like a channel, which helps the current to flow. It is open where the water runs onward, guarding it only where it has the danger of deviation. The bee's life in its channel of habit has no opening, it revolves within a narrow circle of perfection. Man's life has its institutions, which are its organized habits. When these act as enclosures, then the result may be perfect, like a beehive of wonderful precision of form, but unsuitable for the mind which has unlimited possibilities of growth.

For the current of our spiritual life creeds, rituals are channels which may thwart or help, according to their fixity or openness. When a symbol or spiritual idea becomes rigidly elaborate in its construction, it supplants the idea which it should support. In art and literature metaphors which are the symbol of our emotional perceptions excite our imagination but do not arrest it. For they never claim a monopoly of our attention; they leave open the way for the endless possibility of other metaphors. They lose their artistic value if they degenerate into fixed habits of expression. Shelley, in his poem on the skylark, pours out images which we value because they are only a few suggestions of the immeasurableness of our enjoyment. But if, because of their fitness and beauty, a law were passed that while thinking about a skylark these images should be treated as final and no others admitted, then Shelley's poem would at once become false; for its truth is in its fluidity, in its modesty, which tacitly admits that it has not the last word.

The question is asked, if life's journey be endless where is its goal? The answer is, it is everywhere. We are in a palace which has no end, but which we have reached. By exploring it and extending our relationship with it we are ever making it more and more our own. The infant is born in the same universe where lives the adult of ripe mind. But its position is not like a schoolboy who has yet to learn his alphabet, finding himself in a college class. The infant has its own joy of life because the world is not a mere road, but a home, of which it will have more and more as it grows up in wisdom. With our road the gain is at every step, for it is the road and the home in one; it leads us on yet gives us shelter.

A block of stone is unplastic, insensitive, inert; it offers resistance to the creative idea of the artist. But for a sculptor its very obstacles are an advantage and he carves his image out of it. Our physical existence is an obstacle to our spirit, it has every aspect of a bondage, and to all appearance it is a perpetual humiliation to our soul. And therefore it is the best material for our soul to manifest herself through it, to proclaim her freedom by fashioning ornaments out of her fetters. The limitations of our outer circumstances are only to give opportunities to our soul, and by being able to defy them she realizes her truth.

When I was a child, God also became a child with me to be my playmate. Otherwise my imperfections would have weighed me down, and every moment it would have been a misery to be and yet not fully to be. The things that kept me occupied were trifling and the things I played with were made of dust and sticks. But nevertheless my occupations were made precious to me and the importance that was given to my toys made them of equal value with the playthings of the adult. The majesty of childhood won for me the world's homage, because there was revealed the infinite in its aspect of the small.

And the reason is the same, which gives the youth the right to claim his full due and not be despised. The divinity which is ever young has crowned him with his own wreath, whispering to his ears that he is the rightful inheritor of all the world's wealth.

The infinite is with us in the beauty of our childhood, in the strength of our youth, in the wisdom of our age, in play, in earning, and in spending.

The world of senses in which animals live is limited. Our reason has opened the gate for our mind into the heart of the infinite. Yet this freedom of reason is but a freedom in the outer court-yard of existence. Objects of knowledge maintain an infinite distance from us who are the knowers. For knowledge is not union. Therefore the further world of freedom awaits us there where we reach truth, not through feeling it by senses or knowing it by reason, but through union or perfect sympathy. This is an emancipation difficult fully to imagine; we have but glimpses of its character. We perceive the fact of a picture by seeing it, we know about it by measuring its lines, analysing its colours and studying the laws of harmony in its composition. But even then it is no realization of the picture, for which we want an intimate union with it immediate to ourselves.

The picture of a flower in a botanical book is information; its mission ends with our knowledge. But in pure art it is a personal communication. And therefore until it finds its harmony in the depth of our personality it misses its mark. We can treat existence solely as a textbook furnishing us lessons, and we shall not be disappointed, but we know that its mission does not end there. For in our joy in it, which is an end in itself, we feel that it is a communication, the final response to which is not the response to our knowing but the response of our being.

KRISHNAMURTI, *FREEDOM FROM THE KNOWN*

**From Jiddu Krishnamurti, *Freedom from the Known*,
New York, Harper & Row, 1969**

Jiddu Krishnamurti (1895–1986), born in India, was educated in England and Paris, as well as being an early student of theosophy. His teachings centre on self-knowledge and the capacity of each person to be self-reliant. Amongst his many books are The Flight of the Eagle, The Urgency of Change, *and* Freedom from the Known.

Krishnamurti takes a radical and active approach towards violence, the root of war. The expression of violence, in personal anger or in mass destruction, stems, he argues, from our ignorance about it. About it and ourselves we know very little — because we have failed to take an objective look at the question. Instead, our labours are spent on self-justification or condemnation. What we need instead, he believes, is a 'total perception' of the experience. Only then does the real possibility of stopping violence at its heart arise.

Violence – anger – justification and condemnation – the ideal and the actual

Fear, pleasure, sorrow, thought and violence are all interrelated. Most of us take pleasure in violence, in disliking somebody, hating a particular race or group of people, having antagonistic feelings towards others. But in a state of mind in which all violence has come to an end there is a joy which is very different from the pleasure of violence with its conflicts, hatreds and fears.

Can we go to the very root of violence and be free from it? Otherwise we shall live everlastingly in battle with each other. If that is the way you want to live – and apparently most people do – then carry on; if you say, 'Well, I'm sorry, violence can never end,' then you and I have no means of communication, you have blocked yourself; but if you say there might be a different way of living, then we shall be able to communicate with each other.

So let us consider together, those of us who can communicate, whether it is at all possible totally to end every form of violence in ourselves and still live in this monstrously brutal world. I think it is possible. I don't want to have a breath of hate, jealousy, anxiety or fear in me. I want to live completely at peace. Which doesn't mean that I want to die. I want to live on this marvellous earth, so full, so rich, so beautiful. I want to look at the trees, flowers, rivers, meadows, women, boys and girls, and at the same time live completely at peace with myself and with the world. What can I do?

If we know how to look at violence, not only outwardly in society — the wars, the riots, the national antagonisms and class conflicts — but also in ourselves, then perhaps we shall be able to go beyond it.

Here is a very complex problem. For centuries upon centuries man has been violent; religions have tried to tame him throughout the world and none of them have succeeded. So if we are going into the question we must, it seems to me, be at least very serious about it because it will lead us into quite a different domain, but if we want merely to play with the problem for intellectual entertainment we shall not get very far.

You may feel that you yourself are very serious about the problem but that as long as so many other people in the world are not serious and are not prepared to do anything about it, what is the good of your doing anything? I don't care whether they take it seriously or not. I take it seriously, that is enough. I am not my brother's keeper. I myself, as a human being, feel very strongly about this question of violence and I will see to it that in myself I am not violent — but I cannot tell you or anybody else, 'Don't be violent.' It has no meaning — unless you yourself want it. So if you yourself really want to understand this problem of violence let us continue on our journey of exploration together.

Is this problem of violence out there or here? Do you want to solve the problem in the outside world or are you questioning violence itself as it is in you? If you are free of violence in yourself the question arises, 'How am I to live in a world full of violence, acquisitiveness, greed, envy, brutality? Will I not be destroyed?' That is the inevitable question which is invariably asked. When you ask such a question it seems to me you are not actually living peacefully. If you live peacefully you will have no problem at all. You may be imprisoned because you refuse to join the army or shot because you refuse to fight — but that is not a problem; you will be shot. It is extraordinarily important to understand this.

We are trying to understand violence as a fact, not as an idea, as a fact which exists in the human being, and the human being is myself. And to go into the problem I must be *completely* vulnerable, open, to it. I must expose myself to myself — not necessarily expose myself to you because you may not be interested — but I must be in a state of mind that demands to see this thing right to the end and at no point stops and says I will go no further.

Now it must be obvious to me that I am a violent human being. I have experienced violence in anger, violence in my sexual demands, violence in hatred, creating enmity, violence in jealousy and so on — I have experienced it, I have known it, and I say to myself, 'I want to understand this whole problem, not just one fragment of it expressed in war, but this aggression in man which also exists in the animals and of which I am a part.'

Violence is not merely killing another. It is violence when we use a sharp word, when we make a gesture to brush away a person, when we obey because there is fear. So violence isn't merely organized butchery in the name of God, in the name of society or country. Violence is much more subtle, much deeper, and we are inquiring into the very depths of violence.

When you call yourself an Indian or a Muslim or a Christian or a European, or anything else, you are being violent. Do you see why it is violent? Because you are separating yourself from the rest of mankind. When you separate yourself by belief, by nationality, by tradition, it breeds violence. So a man who is seeking to understand violence does not belong to any country, to any religion, to any political party or partial system; he is concerned with the total understanding of mankind.

Now there are two primary schools of thought with regard to violence, one which says, 'Violence is innate in man,' and the other which says, 'Violence is the result of the social and cultural heritage in which man lives.' We are not concerned with which school we belong to – it is of no importance. What is important is the *fact* that we are violent, not the reason for it.

One of the most common expressions of violence is anger. When my wife or sister is attacked I say I am righteously angry; when my country is attacked, my ideas, my principles, my way of life, I am righteously angry. I am also angry when my habits are attacked or my petty little opinions. When you tread on my toes or insult me I get angry, or if you run away with my wife and I get jealous, that jealousy is called righteous because she is my property. And all this anger is morally justified. But to kill for my country is also justified. So when we are talking about anger, which is a part of violence, do we look at anger in terms of righteous and unrighteous anger according to our own inclinations and environmental drive, or do we see only anger? Is there righteous anger ever? Or is there only anger? There is no good influence or bad influence, only influence, but when you are influenced by something which doesn't suit me I call it an evil influence.

The moment you protect your family, your country, a bit of coloured rag called a flag, a belief, an idea, a dogma, the thing that you demand or that you hold, that very protection indicates anger. So can you look at anger without any explanation or justification, without saying, 'I must protect my goods,' or 'I was right to be angry,' or 'How stupid of me to be angry'? Can you look at anger as if it were something by itself? Can you look at it completely objectively, which means neither defending it nor condemning it? Can you?

Can I look at you if I am antagonistic to you or if I am thinking what a marvellous person you are? I can see you only when I look at you with a certain care in which neither of these things is involved. Now, can I look at anger in the same way, which means that I am vulnerable to the problem, I do not resist it, I am watching this extraordinary phenomenon without any reaction to it?

It is very difficult to look at anger dispassionately because it is a part of me, but that is what I am trying to do. Here I am, a violent human being, whether I am black, brown, white or purple. I am not concerned with whether I have inherited this violence or whether society has produced it in me; all I am concerned with is whether it is at all possible to be free from it. To be free from violence means everything to me. It is more important to me than sex, food, position, for this thing is corrupting me. It is destroying me and destroying the world, and I want to understand it, I want to be beyond it. I feel responsible for all this anger and violence in the world. I feel responsible – it isn't just a lot of words – and I say to myself, 'I can do something only if I am beyond anger myself, beyond violence, beyond nationality.' And this feeling I have that I must understand the violence in myself brings tremendous vitality and passion to find out.

But to be beyond violence I cannot suppress it, I cannot deny it, I cannot say, 'Well, it is a part of me and that's that,' or 'I don't want it.' I have to look at it, I have to study it, I must become very intimate with it and I cannot become intimate with it if I condemn or justify it. We do condemn it, though; we do justify it. Therefore I am saying, stop for the time being condemning it or justifying it.

Now, if you want to stop violence, if you want to stop wars, how much vitality, how much of yourself, do you give to it? Isn't it important to you that your children are killed, that your sons go into the army where they are bullied and butchered? Don't you care? My God, if that doesn't interest you, what does? Guarding your money? Having a good time? Taking drugs? Don't you see that this violence in yourself is destroying your children? Or do you see it only as some abstraction?

All right then, if you are interested, attend with all your heart and mind to find out. Don't just sit back and say, 'Well, tell us all about it.' I point out to you that you cannot look at anger nor at violence with eyes that condemn or justify and that if this violence is not a burning problem to you, you cannot put those two things away. So first you have to learn how to look at anger, how to look at your husband, your wife, your children; you have to listen to the politician, you have to learn why you are not objective, why you condemn or justify. You have to learn that you condemn and justify because it is part of the social structure you live in, your conditioning as a German or an Indian or a Negro or an American or whatever you happen to have been born, with all the dulling of the mind that this conditioning results in. To learn, to discover something fundamental, you must have the capacity to go deeply. If you have a blunt instrument, a dull instrument, you cannot go deeply. So what we are doing is sharpening the instrument, which is the mind — the mind which has been made dull by all this justifying and condemning. You can penetrate deeply only if your mind is as sharp as a needle and as strong as a diamond.

It is no good just sitting back and asking, 'How am I to get such a mind?' You have to want it as you want your next meal, and to have it you must see that what makes your mind dull and stupid is this sense of invulnerability which has built walls round itself and which is part of this condemnation and justification. If the mind can be rid of that, then you can look, study, penetrate, and perhaps come to a state that is totally aware of the whole problem.

So let us come back to the central issue — is it possible to eradicate violence in ourselves? It is a form of violence to say, 'You haven't changed, why haven't you?' I am not doing that. It doesn't mean a thing to me to convince you of *anything*. It is your life, not my life. The way you live is your affair. I am asking whether it is possible for a human being living psychologically in any society to clear violence from himself inwardly. If it is, the very process will produce a different way of living in this world.

Most of us have accepted violence as a way of life. Two dreadful wars have taught us nothing except to build more and more barriers between human beings — that is, between you and me. But for those of us who want to be rid of violence, how is it to be done? I do not think anything is going to be achieved through analysis, either by ourselves or by a professional. We might be able to modify ourselves slightly, live a little more quietly with a little more affection, but in itself it will not give total perception. But I must know how to analyse, which means that in the process of analysis my mind becomes extraordinarily sharp, and it is that quality of sharpness, of attention, of seriousness, which will give total perception. One hasn't the eyes to see the whole thing at a glance; this clarity of the eye is possible only if one can see the details, *then jump*.

Some of us, in order to rid ourselves of violence, have used a concept, an ideal, called non-violence, and we think by having an ideal of the opposite to violence, non-violence, we can get rid of the fact, the actual — but we cannot. We have had ideals without number, all the sacred books are full of them, yet we are still violent — so why not deal with violence itself and forget the word altogether?

If you want to understand the actual you must give your whole attention, all your energy, to it. That attention and energy are distracted when you create a fictitious, ideal world. So can you completely banish the ideal? The man who is really serious, with the urge to find out what truth is, what love is, has no concept at all. He lives only in *what is*.

To investigate the fact of your own anger you must pass no judgement on it, for the moment you conceive of its opposite you condemn it and therefore you cannot see it as it is. When you say you dislike or hate someone that is a fact, although it sounds terrible. If you look at it, go into it completely, it ceases, but if you say, 'I must not hate; I must have love in my heart,' then you are living in a hypocritical world with double standards. To live completely, fully, in the moment is to live with what is, the actual, without any sense of condemnation or justification – then you understand it so totally that you are finished with it. When you see clearly the problem is solved.

But can you see the face of violence clearly – the face of violence not only outside you but inside you, which means that you are totally free from violence because you have not admitted ideology through which to get rid of it? This requires very deep meditation, not just a verbal agreement or disagreement.

You have now read a series of statements but have you really understood? Your conditioned mind, your way of life, the whole structure of the society in which you live, prevent you from looking at a fact and being entirely free from it *immediately*. You say, 'I will think about it; I will consider whether it is possible to be free from violence or not. I will try to be free.' That is one of the most dreadful statements you can make, 'I will try.' There is no trying, no doing your best. Either you do it or you don't do it. You are losing time while the house is burning. The house is burning as a result of the violence throughout the world and in yourself and you say, 'Let me think about it. Which ideology is best to put out the fire?' When the house is on fire, do you argue about the colour of the hair of the man who brings the water?

PART SEVEN

What Can I Do?

Besides simply reflecting on the nature of things, we can also bring change into the world, impressing reality with the stamp of action. Our inquiry would certainly be incomplete if we only considered thinking and did not explore the possibilities of action as well. What is the relationship between the two? Is action required of us? Do we have free choice?

Human action — as opposed to the action of molecules, rivers, winds, or the sun — involves intelligence. Where knowledge is missing, we say that an event has befallen us or happened to us, not that we *did* it. A second factor is intention. An act carries out or actualizes a desire, plan, or hope to change either ourselves or the world in some way, however small. If luck allows a beginner golfer to sink a hole in one, we say that it just happened that way. Acting so as to realize what one wants must be voluntary. If one pours a glass of water while sleep-walking, hypnotized, drugged or drunk the question arises of whether one's will is involved. The presence of a strong emotion like anger or jealousy also raises the question of will. Aristotle provides us with a clear analysis of the forms of ignorance and coercion and identifies action with rational, voluntary choice.

The concept of intelligent action is a strong current throughout Western thinking. We customarily precede action with a calculation about the consequences. In fact, the ability to predict the likely consequences of our actions is a measure of our intelligence. Conversely, where a person disregards the predictable results of, say, parking an unbraked car on a hillside, we judge him to be negligent, imprudent, uncaring, or unreasonable. Often several factors have to be taken into consideration. For instance, if one is trying to decide whether to buy a hat or a scarf, different considerations such as warmth, durability, and looks will have to be weighed.

Our common sense identifies 'good' with happiness. Developing this idea further, we tend to believe that, when deciding on a particular course of action, we should aim for the greatest possible happiness for the greatest number of people. Nevertheless this commonsense view is subject to question. Some say, for example, that concentrating on the *results* of an action removes the focus of attention from the act itself. This could cause us to lose track of present circumstances and focus entirely on what we expect to happen. We confuse what will be (which does not yet exist) with what is. Taken to the extreme, all action based on calculation of the future contains an irrational element. It takes us away from the centre of our power and into regions where our influence is unpredictable.

If, therefore, we are to concentrate on the action itself, rather than on its consequences, deciding what to do becomes largely a matter of ascertaining our own nature. Action then follows a harmonious resolution between external and internal demands; often this will mean renouncing our own desires and acting disinterestedly.

Is there then no place for human feeling in deciding our actions? Camus, who agrees that an obsession with consequences makes a realistic approach to action more difficult, gives an important role to passion. For Camus, the mind is constantly assigning meaning to a situation, but the reality outruns the attempt to comprehend it. This places a person in contradiction with himself or herself. The 'appetite for the absolute and for unity and the impossibility of reducing this world to a rational and reasonable principle' can never be reconciled. Yet we can no more deny the ego's thirst for familiar meanings than we can deny the world's lack of meaning. The need for action crystallizes the attention, focusing it on what is actually present. Action is a constant, passionate rejection of all attempts to categorize interpret, explain, or justify. Camus uses the myth of Sisyphus, who was condemned to push a boulder endlessly up a hillside, only to have it roll back down again, to symbolize the futility of man's endeavours. The effort to calculate consequences and assign values is inevitable, and must be endlessly rejected. According to Camus, then, to act is to struggle against the intellectual impediments to action.

We usually see action as depending on the exercise of choice. We choose what we want and act accordingly. A person's will is the cause of the act and of its effect. We believe that we are our deeds — 'What do you do?' has come to mean 'Who are you?' — to the extent that we hardly question the relationship between the two. We assume ourselves to be the authors of our undertakings. Is this so? A radically different understanding is presented in the *Bhagavad Gita*. There it is supposed that, though we refer to 'my action' in the same way as we refer to 'my pen', neither ownership nor possession is in fact involved. We do not have either will or the power of choice. Our identity as agents of our deeds and our destiny is in fact a fiction promulgated in the moment antecedent to an action by the thought, 'This is *my* act.' But the *Bhagavad Gita* says, 'While all kinds of work are done by the modes of nature, he whose soul is bewildered by the self-sense thinks, "I am the doer."' The self-concept, an invention of the ego, credits itself with events which in fact arise independently of choice. To see the effects of forces working through one's mind, body, and feelings as unwilled is to come to a new understanding of one's role in action. One is, the *Gita* suggests, not so much an actor as acted upon. One is an instrument to a supra-human intelligence, knowing only the present circumstances of an action and not what will ensue from it.

Henri Bergson also holds that a part of us gets in the way of our playing our true role. Our situation is that of an actor who suddenly gets the idea that since he is the playwright — which he is not – he can do as he chooses. Bergson holds that we can act in one of two conflicting ways: one free and readily adaptable to each new set of conditions, and one fixed and dependent on routine interpretation of our circumstances. Most actions, Bergson claims, 'owing to the solidification in memory of such and such sensations, feelings, or ideas . . . have many points of resemblance with reflex acts'. A reflex act, of course, involves no thought, while thought is an essential component of choice and of calculated action. To imbue action with intelligence, we must cease to believe that we make decisions and influence courses of action, and thrust ourselves more boldly into the present. Only thus can we partake fully of any possibility of change. Action, furthermore, demands that we be whole, that we express our entire selves, whereas we are normally distracted by habitual associations, images and evaluations; we must become, in Bergson's words, conscious automatons.

The suggestion that our attempts at decision-making get in the way of our acting independently of the coercive effects of habit is also expressed by Seng-st'an, the sixth-century Buddhist patriarch. Choice implies a comparison between options that are judged good or valuable. But making comparisons of this sort means taking into consideration how things were, might be or will be, rather than how they are. At a subtle level, contact with the real is lost. Seng-st'an claims that 'it is due to our choosing to accept or reject that we do not see the true nature of things'. We assume that things could be different. It is here that the problem of freedom of the will arises. But this concept distances us from the situation as it actually presents itself – we view action as a means of realizing the ideal rather than as an end in itself, in which the real is realized.

The question remains, what can be done? The suggestion which emerges is that we should move away from a discriminating attitude (differentiating right from wrong) to an open, responsive one (remaining sensitive to the actual occasion). The first step of the transformation involves an examination of our mental habits, and particularly of our aims. The way to a more active understanding is itself an activity, an action: the ending of illusions about our role as agents. It prepares the ground for us to be acted upon, as an organism is acted upon by the ecological whole of which it is a part. Only from a position of total engagement, of concern for the universal effects of our action, can we resolve to act as full human beings – members of a community, taking on the continuing support and maintenance of the cosmos. We shall inevitably fall short of this, but even our failures can help us to achieve a greater breadth of vision and better chances of success in the long run.

SENG-ST'AN, *HSIN HSIN MING* (*LECTURES ON THE FAITH-MIND*)

Seng-st'an (d. 606) was the third patriarch of Ch'an Buddhism, a Chinese form of Buddhism most widely known today through its Japanese development, Zen. Buddhism came to China from India in the sixth century. Few details of Seng-st'an's life are known. His only extant work is Hsin Hsin Ming, *or* Lectures of the Faith-Mind.

In his statement of the Middle Way of Buddhist thought and practice, Seng-st'an suggests that it is our habit of taking sides that creates difficulties for us. When we can free ourselves from the need to do so, personal preference becomes irrelevant. Then, things can be seen for what they are; the fact of their existence confers an intrinsic value on them. In this inner attitude, he suggests, lies a clue for an approach to action that goes beyond our preoccupation with our own ego.

The Great Way is not difficult
for those who have no preferences.
When love and hate are both absent
everything becomes clear and undisguised.
Make the smallest distinction, however,

and heaven and earth are set infinitely apart.
If you wish to see the truth
then hold no opinions for or against anything.
To set up what you like against what you dislike
is the disease of the mind.
When the deep meaning of things is not understood
the mind's essential peace is disturbed to no avail.

The Way is perfect like vast space
where nothing is lacking and nothing is in excess.
Indeed, it is due to our choosing to accept or reject
that we do not see the true nature of things.
Live neither in the entanglements of outer things,
nor in inner feelings of emptiness.
Be serene in the oneness of things
and such erroneous views will disappear by themselves.
When you try to stop activity to achieve passivity
your every effort fills you with activity.
As long as you remain in one extreme or the other
you will never know Oneness.

Those who do not live in the single Way
fail in both activity and passivity,
assertion and denial.
To deny the reality of things
is to miss their reality;
to assert the emptiness of things
is to miss their reality.
The more you talk and think about it,
the further astray you wander from the truth.
Stop talking and thinking,
and there is nothing you will not be able to know.
To return to the root is to find the meaning,
but to pursue appearances is to miss the source.

At the moment of inner enlightenment
there is a going beyond appearance and emptiness.
The changes that appear to occur in the empty world
    we call real only because of our ignorance.
Do not search for the truth;
only cease to cherish opinions.

Do not remain in the dualistic state;
avoid such pursuits carefully.
If there is even a trace
of this and that, of right and wrong,
the Mind-essence will be lost in confusion.
Although all dualities come from the One
do not be attached even to this One.
When the mind exists undisturbed in the Way,
nothing in the world can offend,
and when a thing can no longer offend,
it ceases to exist in the old way.

When no discriminating thoughts arise,
the old mind ceases to exist.
When thought objects vanish,
the thinking-subject vanishes,
as when the mind vanishes, objects vanish.
Things are objects because of the subject (mind);
the mind (subject) is such because of things (object).
Understand the relativity of these two
and the basic reality: the unity of emptiness.
In this Emptiness the two are indistinguishable
and each contains in itself the whole world.
If you do not discriminate between coarse and fine
you will not be tempted to prejudice and opinion.

To live in the Great Way

is neither easy nor difficult,
but those with limited views
are fearful and irresolute:
the faster they hurry, the slower they go,
and clinging (attachment) cannot be limited;
even to be attached to the idea of enlightenment
is to go astray.
Just let things be in their own way
and there will be neither coming nor going.

Obey the nature of things (your own nature),
and you will walk freely and undisturbed.
When thought is in bondage the truth is hidden,
for everything is murky and unclear,
and the burdensome practice of judging
brings annoyance and weariness.
What benefit can be derived
from distinctions and separations?

If you wish to move in the One Way
do not dislike even the world of senses and ideas.
Indeed, to accept them fully
is identical with true Enlightenment.
The wise man strives to no goals
but the foolish man fetters himself.
There is one Dharma, not many;
distinctions arise
from the clinging needs of the ignorant.
To seek Mind with the (discriminating) mind
is the greatest of all mistakes.

Rest and unrest derive from illusion;
with enlightenment there is no liking and disliking.
All dualities come from ignorant inference.

They are like dreams or flowers in air:
foolish to try to grasp them.
Gain and loss, right and wrong:
such thoughts must finally be abolished at once.

If the eye never sleeps,
all dreams will naturally cease.
If the mind makes no discriminations,
the ten thousand things
are as they are, of single essence.
To understand the mystery of this One-essence
is to be released from all entanglements.
When all things are seen equally
the timeless Self-essence is reached.
No comparisons or analogies are possible
in this causeless, relationless state.

Consider movement stationary
and the stationary in motion,
both movement and rest disappear.
When such dualities cease to exist
Openness itself cannot exist.
To this ultimate finality
no law or description applies.

For the unified mind in accord with the Way
all self-centred striving ceases.
Doubts and irresolutions vanish
and life in true faith is possible.
With a single stroke we are freed from bondage;
nothing clings to us and we hold to nothing.
All is empty, clear, self-illuminating,
with no exertion of the mind's power.
Here thought, feeling, knowledge, and imagination

are of no value.
In this world of Suchness
there is neither self nor other-than-self.

To come directly into harmony with this reality
just simply say when doubt arises, 'Not two.'
In this 'not two' nothing is separate,
nothing is excluded.
No matter when or where,
enlightenment means entering this truth.
And this truth is beyond extension or
    diminution in time or space;
in it a single thought is ten thousand years.

Emptiness here, Emptiness there,
but the infinite universe stands
always before your eyes.
Infinitely large and infinitely small;
no difference, for definitions have vanished
    and no boundaries are seen.
So too with Being and non-Being.
Don't waste time in doubts and arguments
that have nothing to do with this.

One thing, all things:
move among and intermingle,
without distinction.
To live in this realization
is to be without anxiety about non-perfection.
To live in this faith is the road to non-duality,
because the non-dual is one with the trusting mind.

words!
The Way is beyond language,

for in it there is

> no yesterday
> no tomorrow
> no today

CAMUS, *THE MYTH OF SISYPHUS*

From Albert Camus, *The Myth of Sisyphus and Other Essays*, translated by J. O'Brien, New York, Random House, and London, Hamish Hamilton, 1955

Albert Camus (1913–60), French thinker and novelist, explored a dynamic idea of existence, through essay, fiction, and philosophy. A fundamental notion was the groundlessness and absurdity of thought and action. He won the Nobel Prize in 1957. Novels include The Stranger *(1942) and* The Fall *(1956); he also published two major philosophical essays,* The Myth of Sisyphus *(1942) and* The Rebel *(1951).*

Camus unveils a vision of the basic contradiction of all action, the tension between desiring the absolute and the world's lack of finality. How is action possible on this basis? Advocating an approach made 'without appeal', he describes the growth of an awareness which begins to levy its own demands. It frees us from the concerns of daily life. It opens us to the question of how to go on. For Camus, this is the introduction of the element of passion, of commitment, so sorely lacking in our usual over-confident view of ourselves and our deeds.

Now the main thing is done, I hold certain facts from which I cannot separate. What I know, what is certain, what I cannot deny, what I cannot reject – this is what counts. I can negate everything of that part of me that lives on vague nostalgias, except this desire for unity, this longing to solve, this need for clarity and cohesion. I can refute everything in this world surrounding me that offends or enraptures me, except this chaos, this sovereign chance and this divine equivalence which springs from anarchy. I don't know whether this world has a meaning that transcends it. But I know that I do not know that meaning and that it is impossible for me just now to know it. What can a meaning outside my condition mean to me? I can understand only in human terms. What I touch, what resists me – that is what I understand. And these two certainties – my appetite for the absolute and for unity and the impossibility of reducing this world to a rational and reasonable principle – I also know that I cannot reconcile them. What other truth can I admit without lying, without bringing in a hope I lack and which means nothing within the limits of my condition?

If I were a tree among trees, a cat among animals, this life would have a meaning, or rather this problem would not arise, for I should belong to this world. I should *be* this world to which I am now opposed by my whole consciousness and my whole insistence upon familiarity. This ridiculous reason is what sets me in opposition to all creation. I cannot cross it out with a stroke of the pen. What I believe to be true I must therefore preserve. What seems to me so obvious, even against me, I must support. And what constitutes the basis of that conflict, of that break between the world and my mind, but the awareness of it? If therefore I want to preserve it, I can, through a constant awareness, ever revived, ever alert. This is what, for the moment, I must remember. At this moment the absurd, so obvious and yet so hard to win, returns to a man's life and finds its home there. At this moment, too, the mind can leave the arid, dried-up path of lucid effort. That path now emerges in daily life. It encounters the world of the anonymous impersonal pronoun 'one', but henceforth man enters in with his revolt and his lucidity. He has forgotten how to open. This hell of the present is his Kingdom at last. All problems recover their sharp edge. Abstract evidence retreats before the poetry of forms and colours. Spiritual conflicts become embodied and return to the abject and magnificent shelter of man's heart. None of them is settled. But all are transfigured. Is one going to die, escape by the leap, rebuild a mansion of ideas and forms to one's own scale? Is one, on the contrary, going to take up the heart-rending and marvellous wager of the absurd? Let's make a final effort in this regard and draw all our conclusions. The body, affection, creation, action, human nobility will then resume their places in this made world. At last man will again find there the wine of the absurd and the bread of indifference on which he feeds his greatness.

Let us insist again on the method: it is a matter of persisting. At a certain point on his path the absurd man is tempted. History is not lacking in either religions or prophets, even without gods. He is asked to leap. All he can reply is that he doesn't fully understand, that it is not obvious. Indeed, he does not want to do anything but what he fully understands. He is assured that this is the sin of pride, but he does not understand the notion of sin; that perhaps hell is in store, but he has not enough imagination to visualize that strange future; that he is losing immortal life, but that seems to him an idle consideration. An attempt is made to get him to admit his guilt. He feels innocent. To tell the truth, that is all he feels — his irreparable innocence. This is what allows him everything. Hence, what he demands of himself is to live *solely* with what he knows, to accommodate himself to what is, and to bring in nothing that is not certain. He is told that nothing is, but this at least is a certainty. And it is with this that he is concerned: he wants to find out if it is possible to live *without appeal* . . .

If I remain in that prearranged position which consists in drawing all the conclusions (and nothing else) involved in a newly dis-covered notion, I am faced with a second paradox. In order to remain faithful to that method, I have nothing to do with the problem of metaphysical liberty. Knowing whether or not man is free doesn't interest me. I can experience only my own freedom. As to it, I can have no general notions, but merely a few clear insights. The problem of 'freedom as such' has no meaning. For it is linked in quite a different way with the problem of God. Knowing whether or not man is free involves knowing whether he can have a master. The absurdity peculiar to this problem comes from the fact that the very notion that makes the problem of freedom possible also takes away all its meaning. For in the presence of God there is less a problem of freedom than a problem of evil. You know the alternative: either we are not free and God the all-powerful is responsible for evil. Or we are free and responsible but God is not all-powerful. All the scholastic subtleties have neither added anything nor subtracted anything from the acuteness of this paradox.

This is why I cannot get lost in the glorification or the mere definition of a notion which eludes me and loses its meaning as soon as it goes beyond the frame of reference of my individual experience. I cannot understand what kind of freedom would be given me by a higher being. I have lost the sense of hierarchy. The only conception of freedom I can have is that of the prisoner or the individual in the midst of the State. The only one I know is freedom of thought and action. Now if the absurd cancels all my chances of eternal freedom, it restores and magnifies, on the other hand, my freedom of action. That privation of hope and future means an increase in man's availability.

Before encountering the absurd, the everyday man lives with aims, a concern for the future or for justification (with regard to whom or what is not the question). He weighs his chances, he counts on 'some day', his retirement or the labour of his sons. He still thinks that something in his life can be directed. In truth, he acts as if he were free, even if all the facts make a point of contradicting that liberty. But after the absurd, everything is upset. That idea that 'I am', my way of acting as if everything has a meaning (even if, on occasion, I said that nothing has) — all that is given the lie in vertiginous fashion by the absurdity of a possible death. Thinking of the future, establishing aims for oneself, having preferences — all this presupposes a belief in the freedom, even if one occasionally ascertains that one doesn't feel it. But at that moment I am well aware that the higher liberty, that freedom *to be*, which alone can serve as basis for a truth, does not exist. Death is there as the only reality. After death the chips are down. I am not even free, either, to perpetuate myself, but a slave, and, above all, a slave without hope of an eternal revolution, without recourse to contempt. And who without revolution and without contempt can remain a slave? What freedom can exist in the fullest sense without assurance of eternity?

But at the same time the absurd man realizes that hitherto he was bound to that postulate of freedom on the illusion of which he was living. In a certain sense, that hampered him. To the extent to which he imagined a purpose to his life, he adapted himself to the demands of a purpose to be achieved and became the slave of his liberty. Thus I could not act otherwise than as the father (or the engineer or the leader of a nation, or the post-office sub-clerk) that I am preparing to be. I think I can choose to be that rather than something else. I think so unconsciously, to be sure. But at the same time I strengthen my postulate with the beliefs of those around me, with the presumptions of my human environment (others are so sure of being free, and that cheerful mood is so contagious!). However far one may remain from any presumption, moral or social, one is partly influenced by them and even, for the best among them (there are good and bad presumptions), one adapts one's life to them. Thus the absurd man realizes that he was not really free. To speak clearly, to the extent to which I hope, to which I worry about a truth that might be individual to me, about a way of being or creating, to the extent to which I arrange my life and prove thereby that I accept its having a meaning, I create for myself barriers between which I confine my life. I do like so many bureaucrats of the mind and heart who only fill me with disgust and whose only vice, I now see clearly, is to take man's freedom seriously.

The absurd enlightens me on this point: there is no future.

Henceforth this is the reason for my inner freedom. I shall use two comparisons here. Mystics, to begin with, find freedom in giving themselves. By losing themselves in their god, by accepting his rules, they become secretly free. In spontaneously accepted slavery they recover a deeper independence. But what does that freedom mean? It may be said, above all, that they *feel* free with regard to themselves, and not so much free as liberated. Likewise, completely turned towards death (taken here as the most obvious absurdity), the absurd man feels released from everything outside that passionate attention crystallizing in him. He enjoys a freedom with regard to common rules. It can be seen at this point that the initial themes of existential philosophy keep their entire value. The return to consciousness, the escape from everyday sleep represent the first steps of absurd freedom. But it is existential *preaching* that is alluded to, and with it that spiritual leap which basically escapes consciousness. In the same way (this is my second comparison) the slaves of antiquity did not belong to themselves. But they know that freedom which consists in not feeling responsible. Death, too, has patrician hands which, while crushing, also liberate.

Losing oneself in that bottomless certainty, feeling henceforth sufficiently remote from one's own life to increase it and take a broad view of it – this involves the principle of a liberation. Such new independence has a definite time limit, like any freedom of action. It does not write a cheque on eternity. But it takes the place of the illusions of *freedom*, which all stopped with death. The divine availability of the condemned man before whom the prison doors open in a certain early dawn, that unbelievable disinterestedness with regard to everything except for the pure flame of life – it is clear that death and the absurd are here the principles of the only reasonable freedom: that which a human heart can experience and live. This is a second consequence. The absurd man thus catches sight of a burning and frigid, transparent, and limited universe in which nothing is possible but everything is given, and beyond which all is collapse and nothingness. He can then decide to accept such a universe and draw from it his strength, his refusal to hope, and the unyielding evidence of a life without consolation . . .

Thus I draw from the absurd three consequences, which are my revolt, my freedom, and my passion. By the mere activity of consciousness I transform into a rule of life what was an invitation to death — and I refuse suicide. I know, to be sure, the dull resonance that vibrates throughout these days. Yet I have but a word to say: that it is necessary. When Nietzsche writes: 'It clearly seems that the chief thing in heaven and on earth is to *obey* at length and in a single direction: in the long run there results something for which it is worth the trouble of living on this earth as, for example, virtue, art, music, the dance, reason, the mind — something that transfigures, something delicate, mad, or divine,' he elucidates the rule of a really distinguished code of ethics. But he also points the way of the absurd man. Obeying the flame is both the easiest and the hardest thing to do. However, it is good for man to judge himself occasionally. He is alone in being able to do so.

'Prayer,' says Alain, 'is when night descends over thought.' 'But the mind must meet the night,' reply the mystics and the existentials. Yes, indeed, but not that night that is born under closed eyelids and through the mere will of man — dark, impenetrable night that the mind calls up in order to plunge into it. If it must encounter a night, let it be rather that of despair, which remains lucid — polar night, vigil of the mind, whence will arise perhaps that white and virginal brightness which outlines every object in the light of the intelligence. At that degree, equivalence encounters passionate understanding. Then it is no longer even a question of judging the existential leap. It resumes its place amid the age-old fresco of human attitudes. For the spectator, if he is conscious, that leap is still absurd. In so far as it thinks it solves the paradox, it reinstates it intact. On this score, it is stirring. On this score, everything resumes its place and the absurd world is reborn in all its splendour and diversity.

BHAGAVAD GITA

From Sir Sarvepalli Radhakrishnan and C. A. Moore, eds., *A Source Book in Indian Philosophy*, Princeton University Press and Oxford University Press, 1957

The Bhagavad Gita is an eighteen-chapter section of a vast Indian epic, the Mahabharata. It is centred on a historical battle, and concerns a dialogue between a warrior, Arjuna, and his divine chariot-driver, Krishna, which touches on the themes of good and evil, immortality, and transcendent knowledge. It was composed about 500 BC.

The fundamental question of the difference between action and inaction is raised by the Gita. The suggestion is that we normally believe that what is done stems from us. The idea, 'I am the doer', Krishna explains to Arjuna, causes us to latch on to a call to action that passes through us, and deflect it to that part of us that likes to take credit for things. This greatly diminishes our status, and cuts us off from our true source of power. When we are able to be more pure or non-attached, we see our part on the world's stage in a more objective way, and suffer less at what we call failure and success.

Be satisfied in the Self

17. But the man whose delight is in the Self alone, who is content with the Self, who is satisfied with the Self – for him there exists no work that needs to be done.

18. Similarly, in this world he has no interest whatever to gain by the actions that he has done and none to be gained by the

actions that he has not done. He does not depend on all these things for any interest of his.

19. Therefore, without attachment, perform always the work that has to be done, for man attains to the highest by doing work without attachment . . .

The Self is no doer

27. While all kinds of work are done by the modes of nature [gunas], he whose soul is bewildered by the self-sense thinks 'I am the doer.'

28. But he who knows the true character of the distinction of the soul from the modes of nature and then works, O mighty-armed [Arjuna], understanding that it is the modes which are acting on the modes themselves, does not get attached.

29. Those who are misled by the modes of nature get attached to the works produced by them. But let no one who knows the whole unsettle the minds of the ignorant who know only a part.

30. Resigning all thy works to Me, with thy consciousness fixed in the Self, being free from desire and egoism, fight, delivered from thy fever.

31. Those men, too, who, full of faith and free from cavil, constantly follow this teaching of Mine are released from the bondage of works.

32. But those who slight My teaching and do not follow it, know them to be blind to all wisdom, lost and senseless.

Nature and duty

33. Even the man of knowledge acts in accordance with his own nature. Beings follow their nature. What can repression accomplish?

34. For every sense-attachment and [every] aversion are fixed in regard to the objects of that sense. Let no one come under their sway, for they are his two enemies.

35. Better is one's own law though imperfectly carried out than the law of another carried out perfectly. Better is death in the fulfilment of one's own law, for to follow another's law is perilous.

The enemy is desire and anger

Arjuna said:

36. But by what is a man impelled to commit sin, as if by force, even against his will, O Varsneya [Krishna]?

The Blessed Lord said:

37. This is craving, this is wrath, born of the mode of passion, all devouring and most sinful. Know this to be the enemy here.

38. As fire is covered by smoke, as a mirror by dust, as an embryo is enveloped by the womb, so is this covered by that [passion].

39. Enveloped is wisdom, O Son of Kunti [Arjuna], by this insatiable fire of desire, which is the constant foe of the wise.

40. The senses, the mind, and the intelligence are said to be its seat. Veiling wisdom by these, it deludes the embodied soul.

41. Therefore, O Best of Bharatas [Arjuna], control thy senses from the beginning and slay this sinful destroyer of wisdom and discrimination.

42. The senses, they say, are great; greater than the senses is the mind; greater than the mind is the intelligence; but greater than the intelligence is he [the self].

43. Thus knowing him who is beyond the intelligence, steadying the [lower] self by the Self, smite, O Mighty-armed [Arjuna], the enemy in the form of desire, so hard to get at . . .

Action and inaction

16. What is action? What is inaction? As to this even the wise are bewildered. I will declare to thee what action is, knowing which thou shalt be delivered from evil.

17. One has to understand what action is, and likewise one has to understand what is wrong action, and one has to understand about inaction. Hard to understand is the way of work.

18. He who in action sees inaction and action in inaction – he is wise among men, he is a *yogin*, and he has accomplished all his work.

19. He whose undertakings are all free from the will of desire, whose works are burned up in the fire of wisdom – him the wise call a man of learning.

20. Having abandoned attachment to the fruit of works, ever content, without any kind of dependence, he does nothing though he is ever engaged in work.

21. Having no desires, with his heart and self under control, giving up all possessions, performing action by the body alone, he commits no wrong.

22. He who is satisfied with whatever comes by chance, who has passed beyond the dualities [of pleasure and pain], who is free from jealousy, who remains the same in success and failure – even when he acts, he is not bound . . .

Samkhya and Yoga lead to the same goal

Arjuna said:

1. Thou praisest, O Krishna, the renunciation of works and again their unselfish performance. Tell me for certain which one is the better of these two.

The Blessed Lord said:

2. The renunciation of works and their unselfish performance both lead to the soul's salvation. But of the two, the unselfish performance of works is better than their renunciation.*

3. He who neither loathes nor desires should be known as one who has ever the spirit of renunciation; for, free from dualities, he is released easily, O Mighty-armed [Arjuna], from bondage.

4. The ignorant speak of renunciation [Samkhya] and practice of works [Yoga] as different, not the wise. He who applies himself well to one gets the fruit of both.

5. The status which is obtained by men of renunciation is reached by men of action also. He who sees that the ways of renunciation and of action are one – he sees truly.

6. But renunciation, O Mighty-armed [Arjuna], is difficult to attain without *Yoga*; the sage who is trained in *Yoga* [the way of works] attains soon to the Absolute.

7. He who is trained in the way of works, and is pure in soul, who is master of his self and who has conquered the senses, whose soul becomes the self of all beings – he is not tainted by works, though he works.

8. The man who is united with the Divine and knows the truth thinks, 'I do nothing at all,' for in seeing, hearing, touching, smelling, tasting, walking, sleeping, breathing,

9. In speaking, emitting, grasping, opening and closing the eyes he holds that only the senses† are occupied with the objects of the senses.

10. He who works, having given up attachment, resigning his actions to God, is not touched by sin, even as a lotus leaf is untouched by water.

---

*The Samkhya method involves the renunciation of works and the Yoga insists on their performance in the right spirit. The two ways are not inconsistent. In Samkhya, might is emphasized. In Yoga, volitional effort is stressed. In one, we know the Self is thinking away the alien elements; in the other, we will them away. (Trans.)

†'Only the senses'; that is, not the self. (Trans.)

11. The *yogins* [men of action] perform works merely with the body, mind, understanding or merely with the senses, abandoning attachment, for the purification of their selves.

12. The self in union with the Divine attains to peace well-founded, by abandoning attachment to the fruits of works, but he whose self is not in union with the Divine is impelled by desire, and is attached to the fruit of action, and is therefore bound.

The enlightened self

13. The embodied self who has controlled his nature, having renounced all actions by the mind [inwardly], dwells at ease in the city of nine gates,* neither working nor causing work to be done.

14. The Sovereign Self does not create for the people agency, nor does He act. Nor does He connect works with their fruits. It is nature that works out these.

15. The All-pervading Spirit does not take on the sin or the merit of any. Wisdom is enveloped by ignorance; thereby creatures are bewildered.

16. But for those in whom ignorance is destroyed by wisdom — for them wisdom lights up the Supreme Self like the sun.

17. Thinking of That, directing one's whole conscious being to That, making That their whole aim, with That as the sole object of their devotion, they reach a state from which there is no return, their sins washed away by wisdom.

18. Sages see with an equal eye, a learned and humble *brahmin*, a cow, an elephant, or even a dog, or an outcaste.

19. Even here on earth the created world is overcome by those whose mind is established in equality. God is flawless and the same in all. Therefore are these persons established in God.

*The nine gates are the two eyes, the two ears, the two nostrils, the mouth, and the two organs of excretion and generation. (Trans.)

20. One should not rejoice on obtaining what is pleasant or sorrow on obtaining what is unpleasant. He who is thus firm of understanding and unbewildered — such a knower of God is established in God.

21. When the self is no longer attached to external contacts [objects], one finds the happiness that is in the Self. Such a one who is in union with God enjoys undying bliss.

22. Whatever pleasures are born of contacts with objects are only sources of pain: they have a beginning and an end, O Son of Kunti [Arjuna]; no wise man delights in them.

23. He who is able to resist the rush of desire and anger — even here before he gives up his body, he is a *yogin*, he is the happy man.

BERGSON, *TIME AND FREE WILL*

From H. Bergson, *Time and Free Will*, translated by F. L. Pogson, London, Allen & Unwin, 1960

Henri Bergson (1859–1941), French philosopher, concerned himself with questions of action, knowledge, and being which centred on the idea of evolution. He believed in a human freedom, separated intuition from intellect, and spoke of the open as opposed to the closed. He wrote Creative Evolution, Mind-Energy, *and* Time and Free Will.

For Bergson, there is a basic question concerning choice. Does it happen at all? Or, do we rather impute it to our actions when we take a backward glance at what has happened? In any event, he argues that we are free in what we undertake only when it comes from the whole of ourselves. Hence, to choose is always to choose oneself. Otherwise, our 'choices' are only partly willed, being rather the results of habitual tendencies.

Therefore, it is only an inaccurate psychology, misled by language, which will show us the soul determined by sympathy, aversion, or hate as though by so many forces pressing upon it. These feelings, provided that they go deep enough, each make up the whole soul, since the whole content of the soul is reflected in each of them. To say that the soul is determined under the influence of any one of these feelings is thus to recognize that it is self-determined. The associationist reduces the self to an aggregate of conscious states: sensations, feelings, and ideas. But if he sees in these various states no more than is expressed in their name, if he retains only their impersonal aspect, he may set them side by side for ever without getting anything but a phantom self, the shadow of the ego projecting itself into space. If, on the contrary, he takes these psychic states with the particular colouring which they assume in the case of a definite person, and which comes to each of them by reflection from all the others, then there is no need to associate a number of conscious states in order to rebuild the person, for the whole personality is in a single one of them, provided that we know how to choose it. And the outward manifestation of this inner state will be just what is called a free act, since the self alone will have been the author of it, and since it will express the whole of the self. Freedom, thus understood, is not *absolute*, as a radically libertarian philosophy would have it; it admits of degrees. For it is by no means the case that all conscious states blend with one another as raindrops with the water of a lake. The self, in so far as it has to do with a homogeneous space, develops on a kind of surface, and on this surface independent growths may form and float. Thus a suggestion received in the hypnotic state is not incorporated in the mass of conscious states, but, endowed with a life of its own, it will usurp the whole personality when its time comes. A violent anger roused by some accidental circumstance, an hereditary vice suddenly emerging from the obscure depths of the organism to the surface of consciousness, will act almost like a hypnotic suggestion. Alongside these independent elements there may be found more complex series, the terms of which do permeate one another, but which never succeed in blending perfectly with the whole mass of the self. Such is the system of feelings and ideas which are the result of an education not properly assimilated, an education which appeals to the memory rather than to the judgement. Here will be found, within the fundamental self, a parasitic self which continually encroaches upon the other. Many live this kind of life, and die without having known true freedom. But suggestion would become persuasion if the entire self assimilated it; passion, even sudden passion, would no longer bear the stamp of fatality if the whole history of the person were reflected in it, as in the indignation of Alceste;* and the most authoritative education would not curtail any of our freedom if it only imparted to us ideas and feelings capable of impregnating the whole soul. It is the whole soul, in fact, which gives rise to the free decision: and the act will be so much the freer the more the dynamic series with which it is connected tends to be the fundamental self.

Thus understood, free acts are exceptional, even on the part of those who are most given to controlling and reasoning out what they do. It has been pointed out that we generally perceive our own self by refraction through space, that our conscious states crystallize into words, and that our living and concrete self thus gets covered with an outer crust of clean-cut psychic states, which are separated from one another and consequently fixed. We added that, for the convenience of language and the promotion of social relations, we have everything to gain by not breaking through this crust and by assuming it to give an exact outline of the form of the object which it covers. It should now be added that our daily actions are called forth not so much by our feelings themselves, which are constantly changing, as by the unchanging images with which these feelings are bound up. In the morning, when the hour strikes at which I am accustomed to rise, I might

*In Molière's comedy *Le Misanthrope*. (Trans.)

receive this impression σὺν ὅλῃ τῇ ψυχῇ, as Plato says; I might let it blend with the confused mass of impressions which fill my mind; perhaps in that case it would not determine me to act. But generally this impression, instead of disturbing my whole consciousness like a stone which falls into the water of a pond, merely stirs up an idea which is, so to speak, solidified on the surface, the idea of rising and attending to my usual occupations. This impression and this idea have in the end become tied up with one another, so that the act follows the impression without the self interfering with it. In this instance I am a conscious automaton, and I am so because I have everything to gain by being so. It will be found that the majority of our daily actions are performed in this way and that, owing to the solidification in memory of such and such sensations, feelings, or ideas, impressions from the outside call forth movements on our part which, though conscious and even intelligent, have many points of resemblance with reflex acts. It is to these acts, which are very numerous but for the most part insignificant, that the associationist theory is applicable. They are, taken all together, the substratum of our free activity, and with respect to this activity they play the same part as our organic functions in relation to the whole of our conscious life. Moreover we will grant to determinism that we often resign our freedom in more serious circumstances, and that, by sluggishness or indolence, we allow this same local process to run its course when our whole personality ought, so to speak, to vibrate. When our most trustworthy friends agree in advising us to take some important step, the sentiments which they utter with so much insistence lodge on the surface of our ego and there get solidified in the same way as the ideas of which we spoke just now. Little by little they will form a thick crust which will cover up our own sentiments; we shall see how much we were mistaken. But then, at the very minute when the act is going to be performed, *something* may revolt against it. It is the deep-seated self rushing up to the surface. It is the outer crust bursting, suddenly giving way to an irresistible thrust. Hence in the depths of the self, below this most reasonable pondering over most reasonable pieces of advice, something else was going on – a gradual heating and a sudden boiling over of feelings and ideas, not unperceived, but rather unnoticed. If we turn back to them and carefully scrutinize our memory, we shall see that we had ourselves shaped these ideas, ourselves lived these feelings, but that, through some strange reluctance to exercise our will, we had thrust them back into the darkest depths of our soul whenever they came up to the surface. And this is why we seek in vain to explain our sudden change of mind by the visible circumstances which preceded it. We wish to know the reason why we have made up our mind, and we find that we have decided without any reason, and perhaps even against every reason. But, in certain cases, that is the best of reasons. For the action which has been performed does not then express some superficial idea, almost external to ourselves, distinct and easy to account for: it agrees with the whole of our most intimate· feelings, thoughts and aspirations, with that particular conception of life which is the equivalent of all our past experience, in a word, with our personal idea of happiness and of honour. Hence it has been a mistake to look for examples in the ordinary and even indifferent circumstances of life in order to prove that man is capable of choosing without a motive. It might easily be shown that these insignificant actions are bound up with some determining reason. It is at the great and solemn crisis, decisive of our reputation with others, and yet more with ourselves, that we choose in defiance of what is conventionally called a motive, and this absence of any tangible reason is the more striking the deeper our freedom goes.

But the determinist, even when he refrains from regarding the more serious emotions or deep-seated psychic states as forces, nevertheless distinguishes them from one another and is thus led to a mechanical conception of the self. He will show us this self hesitating between two contrary feelings, passing from one to the other and finally deciding in favour of one of them. The self and the feelings which stir it are thus treated as well-defined objects, which remain identical during the whole of the process. But if it is always the same self which deliberates, and if the two opposite feelings by which it is moved do not change, how, in virtue of this very principal of causality which determinism appeals to, will the self ever come to a decision? The truth is that the self, by the mere fact of experiencing the first feeling, has already changed to a slight extent when the second supervenes: all the time that the deliberation is going on, the self is changing and is consequently modifying the two feelings which agitate it. A dynamic series of states is thus formed which permeate and strengthen one another, and which will lead by a natural evolution to a free act. But determinism, ever craving for symbolical representation, cannot help substituting words for the opposite feelings which share the ego between them, as well as for the ego itself. By giving first the person and then the feelings by which he is moved a fixed form by means of sharply defined words, it deprives them in advance of every kind of living activity. It will then see on the one side an ego always self-identical, and on the other contrary feelings, also self-identical, which dispute for its possession; victory will necessarily belong to the stronger. But this mechanism, to which we have condemned ourselves in advance, has no value beyond that of a symbolical representation: it cannot hold good against the witness of an attentive consciousness, which shows us inner dynamism as a fact.

In short, we are free when our acts spring from our whole personality, when they express it, when they have that indefinable resemblance to it which one sometimes finds between the artist and his work. It is no use asserting that we are then yielding to the all-powerful influence of our character. Our character is still ourselves; and because we are pleased to split the person into two parts so that by an effort of abstraction we may consider in turn the self which feels or thinks and the self which acts, it would be very strange to conclude that one of the two selves is coercing the other. Those who ask whether we are free to alter our character lay themselves open to the same objection. Certainly our character is altering imperceptibly every day, and our freedom would suffer if these new acquisitions were grafted on to our self and not blended with it. But, as soon as this blending takes place, it must be admitted that the change which has supervened in our character belongs to us, that we have appropriated it. In a word, if it is agreed to call every act free which springs from the self and from the self alone, the act which bears the mark of our personality is truly free, for our self alone will lay claim to its paternity. It would thus be recognized that free will is a fact, if it were agreed to look for it in a certain characteristic of the decision which is taken, in the free act itself. But the determinist, feeling that he cannot retain his hold on this position, takes refuge in the past or the future. Sometimes he transfers himself in thought to some earlier period and asserts the necessary determination, from this very moment, of the act which is to come; sometimes, assuming in advance that the act is already performed, he claims that it could not have taken place in any other way. The opponents of determinism themselves willingly follow it on to this new ground and agree to introduce into their definition of our free act – perhaps not without some risk – the anticipation of what we might do and the recollection of some other decision which we might have taken. It is advisable, then, that we should place ourselves at this new point of view, and, setting aside all translation into words, all symbolism in space, attend to what pure consciousness alone shows us about an action that has come to pass or an action which is still to come. The original error of determinism and the mistake of its opponents will thus be grasped on another side, in so far as they bear explicitly on a certain misconception of duration.

THE EPIC OF GILGAMESH

From *The Epic of Gilgamesh*, translated by N. K. Sandars, Harmondsworth, Penguin Books, 1960

Gilgamesh, *probably recorded during the first centuries of the second millennium BC, existed in an earlier, oral form. It tells the story of the great king of Uruk in Mesopotamia, the search of a man to understand his life and the question of death and immortality.*

In this episode, Gilgamesh is about to set off on his search for knowledge, taking with him his faithful servant Enkidu. In the narrative, Shamash is the sun god, Uruk an important Babylonian city which Gilgamesh ruled.

The forest journey

Enlil of the mountain, the father of the gods, had decreed the destiny of Gilgamesh. So Gilgamesh dreamed and Enkidu said, 'The meaning of the dream is this. The father of the gods has given you kingship, such is your destiny, everlasting life is not your destiny. Because of this do not be sad at heart, do not be grieved or oppressed. He has given you power to bind and to loose, to be the darkness and the light of mankind. He has given you unexampled supremacy over the people, victory in battle from which no fugitive returns, in forays and assaults from which there is no going back. But do not abuse this power, deal justly with your servants in the palace, deal justly before Shamash.'

The lord Gilgamesh turned his thoughts to the Country of the Living; on the Land of Cedars the Lord Gilgamesh reflected. He said to his servant Enkidu, 'I have not established my name stamped on brick as my destiny decreed; therefore I will go to the country where the cedar is felled. I will set up my name in the place where the names of famous men are written, and where no man's name is yet written I will raise a monument to the gods.'

The eyes of Enkidu were full of tears and his heart was sick. He sighed bitterly and Gilgamesh met his eye and said, 'My friend, why do you sigh so bitterly?' But Enkidu opened his mouth and said, 'I am weak, my arms have lost their strength, the cry of sorrow sticks in my throat. Why must you set your heart on this enterprise?' Gilgamesh answered Enkidu, 'Because of the evil that is in the land, we will go to the forest and destroy the evil; for in the forest lives Humbaba whose name is "Hugeness", a ferocious giant.' But Enkidu sighed bitterly and said, 'When I went with the wild beasts ranging through the wilderness I discovered the forest; its length is ten thousand leagues in every direction. Enlil has appointed Humbaba to guard it and armed him with seven-fold terrors, terrible to all flesh is Humbaba. When he roars it is like the torrent of the storm, his breath is like fire, and his jaws are death itself. He guards the cedars so well that when the wild heifer stirs in the forest, though she is sixty leagues distant, he hears her. What man would willingly walk into the conntry and explore its depths? I tell you, weakness overpowers whoever goes near it: it is not an equal struggle when one fights with Humbaba; he is a great warrior, Gilgamesh, the watchman of the forest never sleeps.'

Gilgamesh replied: 'Where is the man who can clamber to heaven? Only the gods live for ever with glorious Shamash, but as for us men, our days are numbered, our occupations are a breath of wind. How is this, already you are afraid? I will go first although I am your lord, and you may safely call out, "Forward, there is nothing to fear!" Then if I fall I leave behind me a name that endures; men will say of me, "Gilgamesh has fallen in fight with ferocious Humbaba." Long after the child has been born in my house, they will say it, and remember.' Enkidu spoke again to Gilgamesh, 'O my lord, if you will enter that country, go first to the hero Shamash, tell the Sun God, for the land is his. The country where the cedar is cut belongs to Shamash.'

Gilgamesh took up a kid, white without spot, and a brown one with it; he held them against his breast, and he carried them into the presence of the sun. He took in his hand his silver sceptre and he said to glorious Shamash, 'I am going to that country, O Shamash, I am going; my hands supplicate, so let it be well with my soul and bring me back to the quay of Uruk. Grant, I beseech, your protection, and let the omen be good.' Glorious Shamash answered, 'Gilgamesh, you are strong, but what is the Country of the Living to you?'

'O Shamash, hear me, hear me, Shamash, let my voice be heard. Here in the city man dies oppressed at heart, man perishes with despair in his heart. I have looked over the wall and I see the bodies floating on the river, and that will be my lot also. Indeed I know it is so, for whoever is tallest among men cannot reach the heavens, and the greatest cannot encompass the earth. Therefore I would enter that country: because I have not established my name stamped on brick as my destiny decreed, I will go to the country where the cedar is cut. I will set up my name where the names of famous men are written; and where no man's name is written I will raise a monument to the gods.' The tears ran down his face and he said, 'Alas, it is a long journey that I must take to the Land of Humbaba. If this enterprise is not to be accomplished, why did you move men, Shamash, with the restless desire to perform it? How can I succeed if you will not succour me? If I die in that country I will die without rancour, but if I return I will make a glorious offering of gifts and of praise to Shamash.'

So Shamash accepted the sacrifice of his tears; like the compassionate man he showed him mercy. He appointed strong allies for Gilgamesh, sons of one mother, and stationed them in the mountain caves. The great winds he appointed: the north wind, the whirlwind, the storm and the icy wind, the tempest and the scorching wind. Like vipers, like dragons, like a scorching fire, like a serpent that freezes the heart, a destroying flood and the lightning's fork, such were they and Gilgamesh rejoiced.

He went to the forge and said, 'I will give orders to the

armourers; they shall cast us our weapons while we watch them.' So they gave orders to the armourers and the craftsmen sat down in conference. They went into the groves of the plain and cut willow and box-wood; they cast for them axes of nine score pounds, and great swords they cast with blades of six score pounds each one, with pommels and hilts of thirty pounds. They cast for Gilgamesh the axe 'Might of Heroes' and the bow of Anshan; and Gilgamesh was armed and Enkidu; and the weight of the arms they carried was thirty score pounds.

The people collected and the counsellors in the streets and in the market-place of Uruk; they came through the gate of seven bolts and Gilgamesh spoke to them in the market-place: 'I, Gilgamesh, go to see that creature of whom such things are spoken, the rumour of whose name fills the world. I will conquer him in his cedar wood and show the strength of the sons of Uruk, all the world shall know of it. I am committed to this enterprise: to climb the mountain, to cut down the cedar, and leave behind me an enduring name.' The counsellors of Uruk, the great market, answered him, 'Gilgamesh, you are young, your courage carries you too far, you cannot know what this enterprise means which you plan. We have heard that Humbaba is not like men who die, his weapons are such that none can stand against them; the forest stretches for ten thousand leagues in every direction; who would willingly go down to explore its depths? As for Humbaba, when he roars it is like the torrent of the storm, his breath is like fire and his jaws are death itself. Why do you crave to do this thing, Gilgamesh? It is no equal struggle when one fights with Humbaba.'

When he heard these words of the counsellors Gilgamesh looked at his friend and laughed, 'How shall I answer them; shall I say I am afraid of Humbaba, I will sit at home all the rest of my days?' Then Gilgamesh opened his mouth again and said to Enkidu, 'My friend, let us go to the Great Palace, to Egalmah, and stand before Ninsun the Queen. Ninsun is wise with deep knowledge, she will give us counsel for the road we must go.' They took each other by the hand as they went to Egalmah, and they went to Ninsun the great queen. Gilgamesh approached, he entered the palace and spoke to Ninsun. 'Ninsun, will you listen to me; I have a long journey to go, to the Land of Humbaba, I must travel an unknown road and fight a strange battle. From the day I go until I return, till I reach the cedar forest and destroy the evil which Shamash abhors, pray for me to Shamash.'

Ninsun went into her room, she put on a dress becoming to her body, she put on jewels to make her breast beautiful, she placed a tiara on her head and her skirts swept the ground. Then she went up to the altar of the Sun, standing upon the roof of the palace; she burnt incense and lifted her arms to Shamash as the smoke ascended: 'O Shamash, why did you give this restless heart to Gilgamesh, my son; why did you give it? You have moved him and now he sets out on a long journey to the Land of Humbaba, to travel an unknown road and fight a strange battle. Therefore from the day that he goes till the day he returns, until he reaches the cedar forest, until he kills Humbaba and destroys the evil thing which you, Shamash, abhor, do not forget him; but let the dawn, Aya your dear bride, remind you always, and when day is done give him to the watchman of the night to keep him from harm.' Then Ninsun the mother of Gilgamesh extinguished the incense, and she called to Enkidu with this exhortation: 'Strong Enkidu, you are not the child of my body, but I will receive you as my adopted son; you are my other child like the foundlings they bring to the temple. Serve Gilgamesh as a foundling serves the temple and the priestess who reared him. In the presence of my women, my votaries and hierophants, I declare it.' Then she placed the amulet for a pledge round his neck, and she said to him. 'I entrust my son to you; bring him back to me safely.'

And now they brought to them the weapons, they put in their hands the great swords in their golden scabbards, and the bow and the quiver. Gilgamesh took the axe, he slung the quiver from his shoulder, and the bow of Anshan, and buckled the sword to his belt; and so they were armed and ready for the journey. Now all the people came and pressed on them and said, 'When will you return to the city?' The counsellors blessed Gilgamesh and warned him, 'Do not trust too much in your own strength, be watchful, restrain your blows at first. The one who goes in front protects his companion; the good guide who knows the way guards his friend. Let Enkidu lead the way, he knows the road to the forest, he has seen Humbaba and is experienced in battles; let him press first into the passes, let him be watchful and look to himself. Let Enkidu protect his friend, and guard his companion, and bring him safe through the pitfalls of the road. We, the counsellors of Uruk, entrust our king to you, O Enkidu; bring him back safely to us.' Again to Gilgamesh they said, 'May Shamash give you your heart's desire, may he let you see with your eyes the thing accomplished which your lips have spoken; may he open a path for you where it is blocked, and a road for your feet to tread. May he open the mountains for your crossing, and may the night-time bring you the blessings of night, and Lugulbanda, your guardian god, stand beside you for victory. May you have victory in the battle as though you fought with a child. Wash your feet in the river of Humbaba to which you are journeying; in the evening dig a well, and let there always be pure water in your water-skin. Offer cold water to Shamash and do not forget Lugulbanda.'

PART EIGHT

The Mystery of Language

By means of words we communicate needs, hopes, fears, plans, memories, preferences, and so on. We formulate views on religion and politics, rebut criticism of art, disprove facts, and affirm our love and support for friends and associates. We also declare war, agree to truce, claim property, file suits, and vow fidelity. The power of words to form and influence our view of reality is without question.

We usually assume that our language is able to express what we think and experience. When words do not come easily, we tend to blame it on our lack of verbal ability or the inadequacy of our thought processes. Occasionally we also sense a failure in language itself: a dream that cannot be put into verbal form, a great painting whose meaning escapes language, or a felt wholeness which seems too fragile to be captured in words ('The sunset was indescribably beautiful.') Then we begin to wonder whether in fact words can always express adequately what we want to say. Does translation into words distort an experience? Is the web of our experience too delicate to put into words?

When we look closer, we may even ask whether the words we use denote anything outside our own thoughts. Locke makes a distinction between particular and general terms, between, say, the Rosetta Stone and stones in general. He argues that, while particular things exist, '*general* and *universal* belong not to the real existence of things; but are the inventions and creatures of the understanding . . .' Language has a strong tendency towards abstraction, veering away from the concrete towards a generalized version of experience. This bias breeds a real poverty of material, since our interest is diverted to the conceptual form and away from our actual impressions. We rely on what Locke calls 'a perfect arbitrary imposition' of our thought upon a virtually unknown reality.

In practice, we tend to look for general laws and universal principles. Hearing the sound of a bell, we wonder how to explain its tone in terms of causal relations that are true for all bells. Modern science is born of this impulse. It explains the bell sound as an instance of the complex laws of acoustic phenomena, phenomena which ultimately depend on the behaviour of electrons and protons. If Locke is right, the meaning that we give such entities derives ultimately from the particulars we can observe, and involves making large theoretical assumptions about them.

Another difficulty with Locke's approach is that it makes suspect whole realms of human endeavour. If words have meaning only when they pertain to particular facts, then ethics, aesthetics, religion, the fine and performing arts, psychotherapy, and even history involve aspects of language which are, strictly speaking, without meaning. At best they offer tentative hypotheses; at worst, they merely state preferences. It therefore follows that there can be no hope of resolving doubts or arguments objectively. An important strand of contemporary philosophy has remained sceptical of knowledge in these fields because of the pragmatic assumptions which have to be made about language. Wittgenstein, for example, suggests that 'whenever someone ... wanted to say something metaphysical', we should 'demonstrate to him that he had failed to give meaning to certain signs in his propositions'. On this basis, philosophy would be thoroughly precise, but greatly restricted. It would be scientific philosophy.

The desire for total clarity leads to language being seen as a kind of calculus. More than two centuries before Wittgenstein, Leibniz tried to devise a 'universal Algebra', a philosophical Esperanto, which would replace the imprecisions of ordinary speech with a language of mathematical exactitude. For some thinkers, the interest in devising an ideal language in order to express thought with precision has become central.

We do not always seek exactitude in language, however. Besides thinking about reality, we also feel and sense its presence. Poetry can sustain us through periods of self-doubt and inspire us with moments of wonder. Those who believe that the poet's use of language is just as valid as the scientist's discover a more extensive power of expression. 'Speech is an originating realm,' Merleau-Ponty says. The whole of us speaks. We speak through our entire organism, our body. Our attitudes, emotional nuances, hopes, and despairs all express something about us. Language articulates what Wittgenstein later came to call a 'form of life', a total approach to thinking and acting.

Philosophers approach expressive language either by dealing with it directly or by seeing what lies behind it, just as in music one person may hear the notes while another hears the pauses. When one is impressed by silence, then language in any form is a distraction. Many people have experienced a sense of unity with nature or harmony with another person or deep communion with a work of art, but find that to attempt to describe this verbally is to risk loss, to confine themselves to a smaller, more analytic portion of their minds. It may be that the non-verbal part of our minds is closer to reality, more attuned to the endless, undefinable variety of phenomena and their unnameable source. Some thinkers believe that the conventions of ordinary language and the forms they define are simply a convenient compromise. Lao Tzu, for instance, holds that 'The Tao that can be told of is not the eternal Tao;/ The name that can be named is not the eternal name.' In other words, we can choose to relinquish the hold words have on us and to search out a more direct approach.

If we agree that there are multiple levels of awareness, it may be that verbal expression is confined to only a few of these. Concepts fix thought. They categorize and classify our experience into discrete, repeatable units. Contrary to Locke's belief, however, they do have value: they impose a universal structure on the ever-changing flux appearing to our senses. Is there a power of thought both swift and sensitive enough to bear witness to this order of things? For Meister Eckhart, it must be 'free of all names and unconscious of any kind of forms'. To attain it, we must relinquish our attachment to words; we must stop mistaking the name for the thing. Do we need to take a vow of silence then? No, for the difficulty is not with words themselves, but with our assumption that we encompass reality with what we say. Eckhart suggests therefore that we need to be more aware of the silence which surrounds the words. When we communicate with the depth of our being we inevitably find words insufficient for our purpose. They are simply intermediaries, agents acting on our behalf, but they have no place in our search for wholeness.

Philosophers sometimes make the distinction between written and spoken language. With the spoken word come the overtones, nuances, and colorations that the voice imparts to our experience. To speak is to sound one's presence. The words themselves give only a portion of the meaning that is conveyed, for communication is as much a question of music as of linguistics and of listening as of speaking. Since much of what we say is not already composed, our music-making is 'experimental'. Speaking and listening, we engage in 'an act, the outcome of which is unknown'; we become disentangled from the mechanism of speaking and, as it were, allow our words to be said. When we are not so possessed by language, when we attend both to the word and to what lies beyond it, we are more aware of what cannot be said at all. Language is an important dimension of *shared* experience. It truly belongs to no one. We are all agents in keeping a language alive. If we no longer use a language for communication, it ceases to evolve and becomes a dead language, a language of grammarians and scholars. But a language in daily use, even when it lets us down – when we misunderstand each other – is still an instrument of communion and community, providing us with an important tool for surmounting the barriers separating us from one another.

WITTGENSTEIN, *TRACTATUS LOGICO-PHILOSOPHICUS*

From Ludwig Wittgenstein, *Tractatus Logico-Philosophicus*, translated by D.F. Pears and B.F. McGuiness, London, Routledge & Kegan Paul, 1961

Ludwig Wittgenstein (1889–1951), Viennese philosopher, was attracted while a young engineer to the ideas of mathematical logic and studied under Bertrand Russell. In the Tractatus Logico-Philosophicus *he proposed a new approach to the problems of philosophy. His later work,* Philosophical Investigations, *disavowed these discoveries, and opened up the field of linguistic study as a means of settling problems. This study has had a lasting effect on thought in the twentieth century.*

Wittgenstein presents us with a two-level view of language. There is the world of meaning, where thought can be formulated and put into words and propositions. Language at this level is assertive, saying, 'This is how things are.' Science and technology abound here. Then, there is another world of meaning, a higher one. Here, all matters of value exist. Although we can speak of their manifestations in the realm of language, such matters are themselves inexpressible. Only through silence are we able to comprehend them.

Even if all that we wish for were to happen, still this would only be a favour granted by fate, so to speak: for there is no *logical* connection between the will and the world which would guarantee it, and the supposed physical connection itself is surely not something that we could will.

Just as the only necessity that exists is *logical* necessity, so too the only impossibility that exists is *logical* impossibility.

For example, the simultaneous presence of two colours at the same place in the visual field is impossible, in fact logically impossible, since it is ruled out by the logical structure of colour.

Let us think how this contradiction appears in physics: more or less as follows – a particle cannot have two velocities at the same time; that is to say, it cannot be in two places at the same time; that is to say, particles that are in different places at the same time cannot be identical.

(It is clear that the logical product of two elementary propositions can neither be a tautology nor a contradiction. The statement that a point in the visual field has two different colours at the same time is a contradiction.)

All propositions are of equal value.

The sense of the world must lie outside the world. In the world everything is as it is, and everything happens as it does happen: *in* it no value exists – and if it did exist, it would have no value.

If there is any value that does have value, it must lie outside the whole sphere of what happens and is the case. For all that happens and is the case is accidental.

What makes it non-accidental cannot lie *within* the world, since if it did it would itself be accidental.

It must lie outside the world.

And so it is impossible for there to be propositions of ethics.

Propositions can express nothing that is higher.

It is clear that ethics cannot be put into words.

Ethics is transcendental.

(Ethics and aesthetics are one and the same.)

When an ethical law of the form, 'Thou shalt . . .,' is laid down, one's first thought is, 'And what if I do not do it?' It is clear, however, that ethics has nothing to do with punishment and reward in the usual sense of the terms. So our question about the *consequences* of an action must be unimportant. – At least those consequences should not be events. For there must be something right about the question we posed. There must indeed be some kind of ethical reward and ethical punishment, but they must reside in the action itself.

(And it is also clear that the reward must be something pleasant and the punishment something unpleasant.)

It is impossible to speak about the will in so far as it is the subject of ethical attributes.

And the will as a phenomenon is of interest only to psychology.

If the good or bad exercise of the will does alter the world, it can alter only the limits of the world, not the facts – not what can be expressed by means of language.

In short the effect must be that it becomes an altogether different world. It must, so to speak, wax and wane as a whole.

The world of the happy man is a different one from that of the unhappy man.

So too at death the world does not alter, but comes to an end.

Death is not an event in life: we do not live to experience death.

If we take eternity to mean not infinite temporal duration but timelessness, then eternal life belongs to those who live in the present.

Our life has no end in just the way in which our visual field has no limits.

Not only is there no guarantee of the temporal immortality of the human soul, that is to say of its eternal survival after death; but, in any case, this assumption completely fails to accomplish the purpose for which it has always been intended. Or is some riddle solved by my surviving for ever? Is not this eternal life itself as much of a riddle as our present life? The solution of the riddle of life in space and time lies *outside* space and time.

(It is certainly not the solution of any problems of natural science that is required.)

How things are in the world is a matter of complete indifference for what is higher. God does not reveal himself *in* the world.

The facts all contribute only to setting the problem, not to its solution.

It is not *how* things are in the world that is mystical, but *that* it exists.

To view the world *sub specie aeterni* is to view it as a whole — a limited whole.

Feeling the world as a limited whole — it is this that is mystical.

When the answer cannot be put into words, neither can the question be put into words.

The *riddle* does not exist.

If a question can be framed at all, it is also *possible* to answer it.

Scepticism is *not* irrefutable, but obviously nonsensical, when it tries to raise doubts where no questions can be asked.

For doubt can exist only where a question exists, a question only where an answer exists, and an answer only where something *can be said*.

We feel that even when *all possible* scientific questions have been answered, the problems of life remain completely untouched. Of course there are then no questions left, and this itself is the answer.

The solution of the problem of life is seen in the vanishing of the problem.

(Is not this the reason why those who have found after a long period of doubt that the sense of life became clear to them have then been unable to say what constituted that sense?)

There are, indeed, things that cannot be put into words. They *make themselves manifest*. They are what is mystical.

The correct method in philosophy would really be the following: to say nothing except what can be said, i.e. propositions of natural science — i.e. something that has nothing to do with philosophy — and then, whenever someone else wanted to say something metaphysical, to demonstrate to him that he had failed to give a meaning to certain signs in his propositions. Although it would not be satisfying to the other person — he would have the feeling that we were teaching him philosophy — *this* method would be the only strictly correct one.

My propositions serve as elucidations in the following way:
anyone who understands me eventually recognizes them as nonsensical, when he has used them – as steps – to climb up beyond
them. (He must, so to speak, throw away the ladder after he has
climbed up it.)

He must transcend these propositions, and then he will see the
world aright.

What we cannot speak about we must pass over in silence.

MERLEAU-PONTY, *THE PHENOMENOLOGY OF PERCEPTION*

**From Maurice Merleau-Ponty, *The Phenomenology of
Perception*, translated by C. Smith, Atlantic Highlands
(NJ), Humanities Press, and London, Routledge &
Kegan Paul, 1962**

*Maurice Merleau-Ponty (1908–61) was a French philosopher and
man of letters. His interests ranged from perception to Marxism,
from aesthetics to language. A chief concern throughout was the
measure of freedom in human experience. Important works are* The
Phenomenology of Perception *(1945),* Humanism and Terror *(1947),
and* Sense and Nonsense *(1948).*

*Merleau-Ponty refers thought regarding language back to its organic
milieu, our body. Our tendency is to picture speech as originating in a
talking machine, like Descartes's automata. But its power of expression
derives from its place in an incarnate being, ourselves. Merleau-Ponty
suggests here that language has a 'gestural meaning', that it operates like
a handshake or a nod of the head. And always, the body is an essential
aspect of the gesture.*

The realization that speech is an originating realm naturally comes
late. Here as everywhere, the relation of *having*, which can be seen

in the very etymology of the word 'habit', is at first concealed by relations belonging to the domain of *being*, or, as we may equally say, by ontic relations obtaining within the world.* The possession of language is in the first place understood as no more than the actual existence of 'verbal images', or traces left in us by words spoken or heard. Whether these traces are physical, or whether they are imprinted on an 'unconscious psychic life', is of little importance, and in both cases the conception of language is the same in that there is no 'speaking subject'. Whether the stimuli, in accordance with the laws of neurological mechanics, touch off excitations capable of bringing about the articulation of the word, or whether the states of consciousness cause, by virtue of acquired associations, the appearance of the appropriate verbal image, in both cases speech occurs in a circuit of third-person phenomena. There is no speaker, there is a flow of words set in motion independently of any intention to speak. The meaning of words is considered to be given with the stimuli or with the states of consciousness which it is simply a matter of naming; the shape of the word, as heard or phonetically formed, is given with the cerebral or mental tracks; speech is not an action and does not show up the internal possibilities of the subject: man can speak as the electric lamp can become incandescent. Since there are elective disturbances which attack the spoken language to the exclusion of the written one, or vice versa, and since language can disintegrate into fragments, we have to conclude that it is built up by a set of independent contributions, and that speech in the general sense is an entity of rational origin . . .

---

*This distinction of having and being does not coincide with M. G. Marcel's (*Être et Avoir*), although not incompatible with it. M. Marcel takes 'having' in the weak sense which the word has when it designates a proprietary relationship (I have a house, I have a hat) and immediately takes 'being' in the existential sense of belonging to . . ., or taking up (I am my body, I am my life). We prefer to take account of the usage which gives to the term 'being' the weak sense of existence as a thing, or that of predication (the table is, or is big), and which reserves 'having' for the relation which the subject bears to the term into which it projects itself (I have an idea, I have a desire, I have fears). Hence our 'having' corresponds roughly to M. Marcel's 'being', and our 'being' to his 'having'.(M. M.-P.)

In fact we shall once again see that there is a kinship between the empiricist or mechanistic psychologies and the intellectualist ones, and the problem of language is not solved by going from one extreme to the other. A short time ago the reproduction of the word, the revival of the verbal image, was the essential thing. Now it is no more than what envelops true denomination and authentic speech, which is an inner process. And yet these two conceptions are at one in holding that the word *has* no significance. In the first case this is obvious since the word is not summoned up through the medium of any concept, and since the given stimuli or 'states of mind' call it up in accordance with the laws of neurological mechanics or those of association, and that thus the word is not the bearer of its own meaning, has no inner power, and is merely a psychic, physiological or even physical phenomenon set alongside others, and thrown up by the working of an objective causality. It is just the same when we duplicate denomination with a categorical operation. The word is still bereft of any effectiveness of its own, this time because it is only the external sign of an internal recognition, which could take place without it, and to which it makes no contribution. It is not without meaning, since behind it there is a categorical operation, but this meaning is something which it does not *have*, does not possess, since it is thought which has a meaning, the word remaining an empty container. It is merely a phenomenon of articulation, of sound, or the consciousness of such a phenomenon, but in any case language is but an external accomplishment of thought. In the first case, we are on this side of the word as meaningful; in the second we are beyond it. In the first there is nobody to speak; in the second, there is certainly a subject, but a thinking one, not a speaking one. As far as speech itself is concerned, intellectualism is hardly any different from empiricism, and is no better able than the latter to dispense with an explanation in terms of involuntary action. Once the categorical operation is performed, the appearance of the word which completes the process still has to be explained, and this will still be done by recourse to a physiological or psychic mechanism, since the word is a passive shell. Thus we refute both intellectualism and empiricism by simply saying that *the word has a meaning*.

If speech presupposed thought, if talking were primarily a matter of meeting the object through a cognitive intention or through a representation, we could not understand why thought tends towards expression as towards its completion, why the most familiar thing appears indeterminate as long as we have not recalled its name, why the thinking subject himself is in a kind of ignorance of his thoughts so long as he has not formulated them for himself, or even spoken and written them, as is shown by the example of so many writers who begin a book without knowing exactly what they are going to put into it. A thought limited to existing for itself, independently of the constraints of speech and communication, would no sooner appear than it would sink into the unconscious, which means that it would not exist even for itself. To Kant's celebrated question, we can reply that it is indeed part of the experience of thinking, in the sense that we present our thought to ourselves through internal or external speech. It does indeed move forward with the instant and, as it were, in flashes, but we are then left to lay hands on it, and it is through expression that we make it our own. The denomination of objects does not follow upon recognition; it is itself recognition. When I fix my eyes on an object in the half-light, and say: 'It is a brush,' there is not in my mind the concept of a brush, under which I subsume the object and which moreover is linked by frequent association with the object, and which moreover is linked by frequent association with the word 'brush', but the word bears the meaning, and, by imposing it on the object, I am conscious of reaching that object. As has often been said,* for the child the thing is not known

*e.g. Piaget, *La Représentation du monde chez l'enfant*, pp. 60 and ff. (M.M.-P.)

until it is named, the name is the essence of the thing and resides in it on the same footing as its colour and its form. For pre-scientific thinking, naming an object is causing it to exist or changing it: God creates beings by naming them and magic operates upon them by speaking of them. These 'mistakes' would be unexplainable if speech rested on the concept, for the latter ought always to know itself as distinct from the former, and to know the former as an external accompaniment. If it is pointed out in reply that the child learns to know objects through the designations of language, that thus, given in the first place as linguistic entities, objects receive only secondarily their natural existence, and that finally the actual existence of a linguistic community accounts for childish beliefs, this explanation leaves the problem untouched, since, if the child can know himself as a member of a linguistic community before knowing himself as thinking about some Nature, it is conditional upon the subject's being able to overlook himself as universal thought and apprehend himself as speech, and on the fact that the word, far from being the mere sign of objects and meanings, inhabits things and is the vehicle of meanings. Thus speech, in the speaker, does not translate ready-made thought, but accomplishes it.* *A fortiori* must it be recognized that the listener receives thought from speech itself. At first sight, it might appear that speech heard can bring him nothing: it is he who gives to words and sentences their meaning, and the very combination of words and sentences is not an alien import, since it would not be understood if it did not encounter in the listener the ability spontaneously to effect it. Here, as everywhere, it seems at first sight true that consciousness can find in its experience only what it has itself put there. Thus the experience of communication

---

*There is, of course, every reason to distinguish between an authentic speech, which formulates for the first time, and second-order expression, speech about speech, which makes up the general run of empirical language. Only the first is identical with thought. (M.M.-P.)

would appear to be an illusion. A consciousness constructs — for x — that linguistic mechanism which will provide another consciousness with the chance of having the same thoughts, but nothing really passes between them. Yet, the problem being how, to all appearances, consciousness learns something, the solution cannot consist in saying that it knows everything in advance. The fact is that we have the power to understand over and above what we may have spontaneously thought. People can speak to us only a language which we already understand, each word of a difficult text awakens in us thoughts which were ours beforehand, but these meanings sometimes combine to form new thought which recasts them all, and we are transported to the heart of the matter, we find the source. Here there is nothing comparable to the solution of a problem, where we discover an unknown quantity through its relationship with known ones. For the problem can be solved only if it is determinate, that is, if the cross-checking of the data provides the unknown quantity with one or more definite values. In understanding others, the problem is always indeterminate* because only the solution will bring the data retrospectively to light as convergent, only the central theme of a philosophy, once understood, endows the philosopher's writings with the value of adequate signs. There is, then, a taking up of others' thought through speech, a reflection in others, an ability to think *according to others* which enriches our own thoughts. Here the meaning of words must be finally induced by the words themselves, or more exactly, their conceptual meaning must be formed by a kind of deduction from a *gestural meaning*, which is immanent in speech. And as, in a foreign country, I begin to understand the

---

*Again, what we say here applies only to first-hand speech — that of the child uttering its first word, of the lover revealing his feelings, of the 'first man who spoke', or of the writer and philosopher who reawaken primordial experience anterior to all traditions. (M.M.-P.)

meaning of words through their place in a context of action, and by taking part in a communal life – in the same way an as yet imperfectly understood piece of philosophical writing discloses to me at least a certain 'style' – either a Spinozist, criticist or phenomenological one – which is the first draft of its meaning. I begin to understand a philosophy by feeling my way into its existential manner, by reproducing the tone and accent of the philosopher. In fact, every language conveys its own teaching and carries its meaning into the listener's mind. A school of music or painting which is at first not understood, eventually, by its own action, creates its own public, if it really *says* something; that is, it does so by secreting its own meaning. In the case of prose or poetry, the power of the spoken word is less obvious, because we have the illusion of already possessing within ourselves, in the shape of the common property meaning of words, what is required for the understanding of any text whatsoever. The obvious fact is, however, that the colours of the palette or the crude sounds of instruments, as presented to us in natural perception, are insufficient to provide the musical sense of music, or the pictorial sense of a painting. But, in fact, it is less the case that the sense of a literary work is provided by the common property meaning of words, than that it contributes to changing that accepted meaning. There is thus, either in the man who listens or reads, or in the one who speaks or writes, a *thought in speech* the existence of which is unsuspected by intellectualism.

To realize this, we must turn back to the phenomenon of speech and reconsider ordinary descriptions which immobilize thought and speech, and make anything other than external relations between them inconceivable. We must recognize first of all that thought, in the speaking subject, is not a representation, that is, that it does not expressly posit objects or relations. The orator does not think before speaking, nor even while speaking; his speech is his thought. In the same way the listener does not form concepts on the basis of signs. The orator's 'thought' is empty while he is speaking and, when a text is read to us, provided that it is read with expression, we have no thought marginal to the text itself, for the words fully occupy our mind and exactly fulfil our expectations, and we feel the necessity of the speech. Although we are unable to predict its course, we are possessed by it. The end of the speech or text will be the lifting of a spell. It is at this stage that thoughts on the speech or text will be able to arise. Previously the speech was improvised and the text understood without the intervention of a single thought; the sense was everywhere present, and nowhere posited for its own sake. The speaking subject does not think of the sense of what he is saying, nor does he visualize the word which he is using. To know a word or a language is, as we have said, not to be able to bring into play any pre-established nervous network. But neither is it to retain some 'pure recollection' of the word, some faded perception. The Bergsonian dualism of habit-memory and pure recollection does not account for the near-presence of the words I know: they are behind me, like things behind my back, or like the city's horizon round my house, I reckon with them or rely on them, but without having any 'verbal image'. In so far as they persist within me, it is rather as does the Freudian Imago which is much less the representation of a former perception than a highly specific emotional essence, which is yet generalized, and detached from its empirical origins. What remains to me of the word once learnt is its style as constituted by its formation and sound. What we have said earlier about the 'representation of movement' must be repeated concerning the verbal image: I do not need to visualize external space and my own body in order to move one within the other. It is enough that they exist for me, and that they form a certain field of action spread around me. In the same way I do not need to visualize the word in order to know and pronounce it. It is enough that I possess its articulatory and acoustic style as one of the modulations, one of the possible uses of my body. I reach back for the word as my hand reaches towards the part of my body which is being pricked; the word has a certain location in my linguistic world, and is part of my equipment. I have only one means of representing it, which is uttering it, just as the artist has only one means of representing the work on which he is engaged: by doing it. When I imagine Peter absent, I am not aware of contemplating an image of Peter numerically distinct from Peter himself. However far away he is, I visualize him in the world, and my power of imagining is nothing but the persistence of the world around me. To say that I imagine Peter is to say that I bring about the pseudo-presence of Peter by putting into operation the 'Peter-behaviour-pattern'. Just as Peter in imagination is only one of the modalities of my being in the world, so the verbal image is only one of the modalities of my phonetic gesticulation, presented with many others in the all-embracing consciousness of my body. This is obviously what Bergson means when he talks about a 'motor framework' of recollection, but if pure representations of the past take their place in this framework, it is not clear why they should need it to become actual once more. The part played by the body in memory is comprehensible only if memory is not only the constituting consciousness of the past, but an effort to reopen time on the basis of the implications contained in the present, and if the body, as our permanent means of 'taking up attitudes' and thus constructing pseudo-presents, is the medium of our communication with time as well as with space. The body's function in remembering is the same function of projection which we have already met in starting to move: the body converts a certain motor essence into vocal form, spreads out the articulatory style of a word into audible phenomena, and arrays the former attitude, which is resumed, into the panorama of the past, projecting an intention to move into actual movement, because the body is a power of natural expression.

LAO TZU, *TAO-TE CHING*

**From *A Source Book in Chinese Philosophy*,
translated by Wing-Tsit Chan, Princeton
University Press, 1963**

Lao Tzu (6th century BC?), founder of Taoism, left a five-thousand-word work, the Tao-te Ching *(Classic of the Way and its Virtue), and very little else. The Tao is the idea of non-being, the mother of being. Virtue, or power, is that which is obtained, without possession, from the Tao.*

For Lao Tzu, reality exists and continues to exist at a level prior to all names. It is, simply, without qualification. The effect of language is to break up, fragment, and splinter what in itself remains unbroken. Although the word is somehow contained in the world, it is always on the verge of being a lie. It can be a guidepost only so long as we are careful not to mistake it for what is signified. Only when we are able to find the essence of language can it be useful to us in discovering what is real.

The Tao that can be told of is not the eternal Tao;
The name that can be named is not the eternal name.
The Nameless is the origin of Heaven and Earth;
The Named is the mother of all things.
Therefore let there always be non-being, so we may see
    their subtlety,
And let there always be being, so we may see their
    outcome.
The two are the same,
But after they are produced, they have different names.
They both may be called deep and profound.
Deeper and more profound,
The door of all subtleties!

Tao is empty (like a bowl).
It may be used but its capacity is never exhausted.

It is bottomless, perhaps the ancestor of all things.
It blunts its sharpness,
It unties its tangles.
It softens its light.
It becomes one with the dusty world.
Deep and still, it appears to exist forever.
I do not know whose son it is.
It seems to have existed before the Lord.

To hold and fill a cup to overflowing
    Is not as good as to stop in time.
Sharpen a sword-edge to its very sharpest,
    And the [edge] will not last long.
When gold and jade fill your hall,
    You will not be able to keep them.
To be proud with honour and wealth
    Is to cause one's own downfall.
Withdraw as soon as your work is done.
    Such is Heaven's Way.

The five colours cause one's eyes to be blind.
The five tones cause one's ears to be deaf.
The five flavours cause one's palette to be spoiled.
Racing and hunting cause one's mind to be mad.
Goods that are hard to get injure one's activities.

For this reason the sage is concerned with the belly and
    not the eyes.
Therefore he rejects the one but accepts the other.

Attain complete vacuity.
Maintain steadfast quietude.

All things come into being,
And I see thereby their return.

All things flourish,
But each one returns to its root.
This return to its root means tranquillity.
It is called returning to its destiny.
To return to destiny is called the eternal [Tao].
To know the eternal is called enlightenment.
Not to know the eternal is to act blindly to result in
    disaster.
He who knows the eternal is all-embracing.
Being all-embracing, he is impartial.
Being impartial, he is kingly [universal].
Being kingly, he is one with Nature.
Being one with Nature, he is in accord with Tao.
Being in accord with Tao, he is everlasting
And is free from danger throughout his lifetime.

The all-embracing quality of the great virtue follows
    alone from the Tao.
The thing that is called Tao is eluding and vague.
    Vague and eluding, there is in it the form.
    Eluding and vague, in it are things.
Deep and obscure, in it is the essence.
The essence is very real; in it are evidences.

From the time of old until now, its name
    [manifestations] ever remains.
By which we may see the beginning of all things.
How do I know that the beginnings of all things are so?
Through this [Tao].

Nature says few words.
For the same reason a whirlwind does not last a whole
    morning.
Nor does a rainstorm last a whole day.

What causes them?
It is Heaven and Earth [Nature].
If even Heaven and Earth cannot make them last long,
How much less can man?
Therefore he who follows Tao is identified with Tao.
He who follows virtue is identified with virtue.
He who abandons [Tao] is identified with the
   abandonment [of Tao].
He who is identified with Tao – Tao is also happy to
   have him.
He who is identified with virtue – virtue is also happy to
   have him.
And he who is identified with the abandonment [of Tao] –
   the abandonment [of Tao] is also happy to abandon him.
It is only when one does not have enough faith in others
   that others will have no faith in him.

LOCKE, *AN ESSAY CONCERNING HUMAN UNDERSTANDING*

From John Locke, *An Essay Concerning Human Understanding*, first published 1690

John Locke (1632–1704) was a thinker, political advisor, and theor-etician; his policies became the basis for both the Glorious Revolution of 1688 and the American Revolution. He also wrote at length on matters of knowledge and experience; his works include An Essay Concerning Human Understanding *and* Two Treatises of Government.

Locke informs us that a, or perhaps the, primary function of language is interpersonal communication. We are social creatures and need to speak together. The supposition of a common speech is agreement on what words stand for. Hence, Locke is chiefly interested in showing how we come to concur on the denotation or reference of words like 'table' or 'pen', and, furthermore, on how we form general and abstract terms like 'humanity' and 'virtue'. What he presents us with is a view of language which accords well with the special needs of science and other impersonal branches of knowledge.

Of words, or language in general

God, having designed man for a sociable creature, made him not only with an inclination, and under a necessity to have fellowship with those of his own kind, but furnished him also with language, which was to be the great instrument and common tie of society. Man, therefore, had by nature his organs so fashioned, so as to be fit to frame articulate sounds, which we call words. But this was not enough to produce language; for parrots, and several other birds, will be taught to make articulate sounds distinct enough, which yet by no means are capable of language.

Besides articulate sounds, therefore, it was further necessary that he should be able to use these sounds as signs of internal conceptions; and to make them stand as marks for the ideas within his own mind, whereby they might be made known to others, and the thoughts of men's minds be conveyed from one to another.

But neither was this sufficient to make words so useful as they ought to be. It is not enough for the perfection of language, that sounds can be made signs of ideas, unless those signs can be so made use of as to comprehend several particular things: for the multiplication of words would have perplexed their use, had every particular thing need of a distinct name to be signified by.

Besides these names which stand for ideas, there be other words which men make use of, not to signify any idea, but the want or absence of some ideas, simple or complex, or all ideas together; such as are *nihil* in Latin, and in English, *ignorance* and *barrenness*. All which negative or privative words cannot be said properly to belong to or signify no ideas: for then they would be perfectly insignificant sounds; but they relate to positive ideas, and signify their absence.

301

It may also lead us a little towards the original of all our notions and knowledge, if we remark how great a dependence our words have on common sensible ideas; and how those which are made use of to stand for actions and notions quite removed from sense have their rise from thence, and from obvious sensible ideas are transmitted to more abstruse significations, and made to stand for ideas that come not under the cognizance of our senses; e.g. to *imagine, apprehend, comprehend, adhere, conceive, instil, disgust, disturbance, tranquillity*, etc., are all words taken from the operations of sensible things, and applied to certain modes of thinking . . .

Man, though he have great variety of thoughts, and such from which others as well as himself might receive profit and delight; yet they are all within his own breast, invisible and hidden from others, nor can of themselves be made to appear. The comfort and advantage of society not being to be had without communication of thoughts, it was necessary that man should find out some external sensible signs, whereof those invisible ideas, which his thoughts are made up of, might be made known to others. For this purpose nothing was so fit, either for plenty or quickness, as those articulate sounds, which with so much ease and variety he found himself able to make. Thus we may conceive how *words*, which were by nature so well adapted to that purpose, came to be made use of by men as the signs of their ideas; not by any natural connection that there is between particular articulate sounds and certain ideas, for then there would be but one language amongst all men; but by a voluntary imposition, whereby such a word is made arbitrarily the mark of such an idea. The use, then, of words, is to be sensible marks of ideas; and the ideas they stand for are their proper and immediate signification.

The use men have of these marks being either to record their own thoughts, for the assistance of their own memory; or, as it were, to bring out their ideas, and lay them before the view of others: words, in their primary or immediate signification, stand for nothing but *the ideas in the mind of him that uses them*, how imperfectly soever or carelessly those ideas are collected from the things which they are supposed to represent. When a man speaks to another, it is that he may be understood: and the end of speech is, that those sounds, as marks, may make known his ideas to the hearer. That then which words are the marks of are the ideas of the speaker: nor can anyone apply them as marks, immediately, to anything else but the ideas that he himself hath: for this would be to make them signs of his own conceptions, and yet apply them to other ideas; which would be to make them signs and not signs of his ideas at the same time; and so in effect to have no signification at all. Words being voluntary signs, they cannot be voluntary signs imposed by him on things he knows not. That would be to make them signs of nothing, sounds without signification. A man cannot make his words the signs either of qualities in things, or of conceptions in the mind of another, whereof he has none in his own. Till he has some ideas of his own, he cannot suppose them to correspond with the conceptions of another man; nor can he use any signs for them: for thus they would be the signs of he knows not what, which is in truth to be the signs of nothing. But when he represents to himself other men's ideas by some of his own, if he consent to give them the same names that other men do, it is still to his own ideas; to ideas that he has, and not to ideas that he has not.

But though words, as they are used by men, can properly and immediately signify nothing but the ideas that are in the mind of the speaker; yet they in their thoughts give them a secret reference to two other things.

First, *they suppose their words to be marks of the ideas in the minds also of other men, with whom they communicate*: for else they should talk in vain, and could not be understood, if the sounds they applied to one idea were such as by the hearer were applied to another, which is to speak two languages. But in this men stand not usually to examine whether the idea they and those they discourse with have in their minds be the same: but think it enough that they use the word, as they imagine, in the common acceptation of that language; in which they suppose that the idea they make it a sign of is precisely the same to which the understanding men of that country apply that name.

Secondly, because men would not be thought to talk barely of their own imagination, but of things as really they are, therefore they often suppose their *words to stand also for the reality of things.* But this relating more particularly to substances and their names, as perhaps the former does to simple ideas and modes, we shall speak of these two different ways of applying words more at large, when we come to treat of the names of mixed modes and substances in particular: though give me leave here to say, that it is a perverting the use of words, and brings unavoidable obscurity and confusion into their signification, whenever we make them stand for anything but those ideas we have in our own minds.

Words, by long and familiar use, as has been said, come to excite in men certain ideas so constantly and readily, that they are apt to suppose a natural connection between them. But that they signify only men's peculiar ideas, and that *by a perfectly arbitrary imposition,* is evident, in that they often fail to excite in others (even that use the same language) the same ideas we take them to be signs of: and every man has so inviolable a liberty to make words stand for what ideas he pleases, that no one hath the power to make others have the same ideas in their minds that he has, when they use the same words that he does. And therefore the great Augustus himself, in the possession of that power which ruled the world, acknowledged he could not make a new Latin word: which was as much as to say, that he could not arbitrarily appoint what idea any sound should be a sign of, in the mouths and common language of his subjects. It is true, common use, by a tacit consent, appropriates certain sounds to certain ideas in all languages, which so far limits the signification of that sound, that unless a man applies it to the same idea, he does not speak properly; and let me add, that unless a man's words excite the same ideas in the hearer which he makes them stand for in speaking, he does not speak intelligibly. But whatever be the consequence of any man's using of words differently, either from their general meaning or the particular sense of the person to whom he addresses them, this is certain: their signification, in his use of them, is limited to his ideas, and they can be signs of nothing else.

MEISTER ECKHART, *THE SERMONS*

From Meister Eckhart, *Meister Eckhart*, translated by R. B. Blakney, New York, Harper & Row, 1941

Meister Eckhart (c. 1260–1328), German mystic, became superior-general of the Dominican order for the whole of Germany before portions of his work were declared heretical by Pope John XXII. Eckhart spoke of the continuous creation by God of the world in the 'eternal now'; he argues that this event takes place in the soul of each individual.

Are some names divine? In this extract, Meister Eckhart argues that they are not. There is, he feels, an element in him of such fineness that in its perpetual recreation it is identical with the unmanifested God. In other words, when God made us, he started with an atom of his own substance, which continues to exist in us to this moment. Such a particle is outside time and place. But a name occupies us, at least for a moment, so this element, like all divinity, must be free of names. Silence then is of the highest order.

I have often said before that there is an agent in the soul, untouched by time and flesh, which proceeds out of the Spirit and which remains for ever in the Spirit and is completely spiritual. In this agent, God is perpetually verdant and flowering with all the joy and glory that is in him. Here is joy so hearty, such inconceivably great joy that no one can ever fully tell it, for in this agent the eternal Father is ceaselessly begetting his eternal Son and the agent is parturient with God's offspring and is itself the Son, by the Father's unique power.

For this reason, if a person had a whole kingdom or all this world's goods and left it all solely for God's sake, to become the poorest man who ever lived on earth, and if then God gave him as much to suffer as he ever gave any man, and if this person suffered it out until he was dead, and if then, even for the space of a moment, God once let him see what he is in this agent of the soul, all his suffering and poverty would seem like a very little thing beside the joy of it, so great in that moment. Indeed, if afterwards God never gave him the Kingdom of Heaven at all, he would feel sufficiently repaid for all he had suffered, for God himself is in that agent of the soul in that eternal Now-moment.

If the spirit were only always united with God in this agent, a man could never grow old. For the Now-moment in which God made the first man, and the Now-moment in which the last man will disappear, and the Now-moment in which I am speaking are all one in God, in whom there is only one Now. Look! The person who lives in the light of God is conscious neither of time past nor of time to come but only of the one eternity. In fact, he is bereft of wonder, for all things are intrinsic in him. Therefore he gets nothing new out of future events, nor from chance, for he lives in the Now-moment that is, unfailingly, 'in verdure newly clad'. Such is the divine glory of this agent in the soul.

There is, however, still another agent, which also is not incarnate but which proceeds out of the spirit, yet remains in it and is always only spiritual. In this second agent, God glows and burns without ceasing, in all his fullness, sweetness, and rapture. Truly, it holds joy so great and rapture so unmeasured that no one can tell it or reveal it. Yet I say that if there were one person who could look into it for a moment and still keep his right mind, all he had ever suffered or that God wished him to suffer would be a very little thing indeed, nothing at all. Nay — I go even further — suffering would be to him always a joy and pleasure.

If you wish to know rightly whether your suffering is yours or of God, you can tell in the following way. If you are suffering because of yourself, whatever the manner, that suffering hurts and is hard to bear. If you suffer for God's sake and for God alone, that suffering does not hurt and is not hard to bear, for God takes the burden of it. If an hundredweight were loaded on my neck and then someone else took it at once on his neck, I had just as lief it were an hundred as one. It would not then be heavy to me and would not hurt me. To make a long story short, what one suffers through God and for God alone is made sweet and easy.

As I said in the first place, at the beginning of the sermon, 'Jesus went into a little castle and was received by a virgin who was a wife.' Why? It must needs be that she was a virgin and a wife and I have told you how he was received, but I have not yet told you what the little castle was, and that I shall do now.

I have said that there is one agent alone in the soul that is free. Sometimes I have called it the tabernacle of the Spirit. Other times I have called it the Light of the Spirit and again, a spark. Now I say that it is neither this nor that. It is something higher than this or that, as the sky is higher than the earth, and I shall call it by a more aristocratic name than I have ever used before, even though it disowns my adulation and my name, being far beyond both. It is free of all names and unconscious of any kind of forms. It is at once pure and free, as God himself is, and like him is perfect unity and uniformity, so that there is no possible way to spy it out.

God blossoms and is verdant in this agent of which I speak, with all the Godhead and spirit of God, and there he begets his only begotten Son as truly as if it were in himself. For he lives really in this agent, the Spirit together with the Father giving birth to the Son and in that light, he is the Son and the Truth. If you can only see with my heart, you may well understand what I am saying, for it is true and the Truth itself bespeaks my word.

Look and see: this little castle in the soul is exalted so high above every road [of approach], with such simplicity and uniformity, that the aristocratic agent of which I have been telling you is not worthy to look into it, even once for a moment. No, nor are the other agents, of which I have also spoken, ever able to peek in to where God glows and burns like a fire with all his abundance and rapture. So altogether one and uniform is this little castle, so high above all ways and agencies, that none can ever lead to it — indeed — not even God himself.

It is the truth as God lives. God himself cannot even peek into it for a moment — or steal into it — in so far as he has particular selfhood and the properties of a person. This is a good point to notice, for the onefold One has neither a manner nor properties. And therefore, if God is to steal into it [the little castle in the soul], it [the adventure] will cost him all his divine names and person-like properties; he would have to forgo all these if he is to gain entrance. Except as he is the onefold One, without ways or properties — neither the Father nor the Holy Spirit in this [personal] sense, yet something that is neither this nor that — See! — it is only as he is One and onefold that he may enter into that One which I have called the little castle of the soul. Otherwise he cannot get in by any means or be at home there, for in part the soul is like God — otherwise it would not be possible.

'THE WALL OF MYSTERY' — SUFI

Retold by Anne Twitty, in *Parabola*, Spring 1986

Genuine community of language or symbols can be achieved only through efforts that bring about community of activities under existing conditions. The ideal of scientific language is the construction of a system in which meanings are related to one another in inference and discourse and where the symbols are such as to indicate relationships.

Do the limits of language coincide with the limits of our experience? Are there any truly 'unspeakable' events? When we are able to say so much in language, why do we come up short on words with regard to certain areas of our life? This tale can remind us of these questions.

Far in the East there was once a wall of mystery. Few people approached it. Occasionally, however, someone more daring than the rest made his way to the wall and began to climb. It was not easy to climb to the top of the wall, but some persevered. Those who reached the top and looked over to the other side were seen to smile; then they slipped over the wall and were never seen again.

After a while, the people of that country learned to recognize the signs that told them someone was about to approach the wall. That person's eyes would begin to stare through and beyond his surroundings. He grew forgetful, and would often fail to answer questions put to him. He seemed absorbed in other questions that those about him could not understand.

The people of the country grew more and more curious. Although they did not want to risk climbing the wall themselves, they very much wanted to know what lay on the other side of it. Several of the men began to talk together. Then, the next time that they noticed someone with staring eyes and the look of inner vision, they brought chains and waited beside the wall. As the young man began to climb, they seized his feet and fastened chains to them. Still, he climbed upward, and at last reached the top of the wall.

He looked over. He smiled, just as the others had, a smile of rapture. The men at the foot of the wall, overcome with curiosity, pulled on the chains, and pulled him back. Eagerly, they began to question him. What was it like on the other side? But none of their questions were ever answered. By the time the young man's feet touched the ground, he had lost the power of speech.

PART NINE

Tomorrow

Any inquiry into the human condition inevitably confronts the dimension of time. Where do we come from? Where are we going? What have we inherited from the past? What is the future we are moving towards? In our turbulent age, we crave security. We wish to know that the challenges of the present will give way tomorrow to greater understanding, compassion, communication, and responsibility. If we are pessimistic, we suspect that the outlook in the future will seem even bleaker than it does today. To some, nuclear weapons seem to have placed us on the knife-edge of annihilation. Then the question becomes, has man a future? For the first time in history, the continuation of our species is in question.

When philosophers think about man's future, they rarely think in terms of finality. They see change and transformation rather than the end of everything. Some people say that this is naïve, in the face of the horrors of possible nuclear destruction, eco-catastrophe, overpopulation, famine, or simply a gradual lowering of the genetic strength of the species. Others argue that it is in the nature of thought that it cannot conceive of its own cessation. None the less, philosophers of many persuasions believe that we do have a future. This conviction comes from their study of past and present, which reveals not a linear but a cyclical movement to history. Appearance, disappearance, reappearance: in any event, it is difficult to point to a single moment that is terminal. Completing one phase provides the beginning of the next one. This seems especially true where life is concerned.

Does man have to make his own future or is it awaiting him,

unavoidably, like a fate or a destiny? Do we belong to the future as individuals, as members of a species (*Homo sapiens*), or as creatures on a planet? Do we all belong equally to a future or is there something non-egalitarian about the way the future comes to each of us?

Evolution, since Darwin, has come to mean a biological force that operates indiscriminately up and down the scale of organic life. Man lives under the same laws of evolution as the jellyfish, the house-fly, or the swallow. Evolution, according to this view, proceeds automatically, as does gravitation, radioactive decay, or harmonic resonance. Not all philosophers hold this position, however. For some, man possesses attributes and capacities which differentiate him from the rest of the animal kingdom. He is qualitatively different, as well as having a larger brain mass. The unique factor is consciousness. Bergson maintains that there exists a radical difference between animal and human consciousness. The latter 'is synonymous with invention and with freedom'. In moments of consciousness, freedom, the opposite of automatism, opens a person to another kind of evolution, one that is, in Bergson's view, creative. This power is not merely creative – it is self-creative, both in the sense that it is through acts of freedom that a self is brought into being, and also in the sense that they require our conscious participation. We must balance our intellectual functions, employing our intuitive, non-analytic powers just as much as our critical, judgemental ones. To evolve, we must begin to think in a new way.

Nietzsche also discusses the idea of individual evolution. For him, each person is a promise that is empty until enacted; each is, in Nietzsche's words, 'fragment and riddle and dreadful accident'. Personal evolution presupposes work and resolve, in order to transform one's relation to one's own past: 'to redeem those who lived in the past and to re-create all "it was" into a "thus I willed it"'. Ordinarily, the past is what happened to us; we remain passive towards it; we regard it as an impersonal weight which bears us down. The past is, for each individual, the conditioning with which he meets the present. To inject will into the past, to live with our own past willingly, we need to neutralize the influence of habit. This imposes a unity of purpose on the different, unrelated habits that have hitherto prevented the refinement of our energies. When we finally release our impeded energies, we can create or re-create the unity to which belongs the future of humanity.

There is another point of view, however. We may agree that a purely biological force of evolution is inadequate to illuminate man's relation to the future and may also believe that consciousness is the *sine qua non* for man's further development. But we may nevertheless object to placing the individual at the centre of conscious progress. We could say that each person is an element only in the mass of planetary consciousness and that no special participation is required, other than to develop their capacities to the full. The evolution of the higher human potential will proceed inevitably and independently of our wills.

Does evolution in fact take a single direction or have a single meaning? Is everyone under the same 'law' of evolution? Ouspensky believes that the answer is not simple. Speaking of one evolutionary tree is misleading. One has to discern different levels in a process, each level exhibiting a consciousness special to itself. An investigation of man's future must be based on consciousness not only of human beings, but also of those beings above and below us. Ouspensky concludes that evolution is the 'consequence of the incursion into the given plane of properties and characteristics of some higher plane'. The truly 'evolutionary' moments of a person's awareness are literally uplifting. They bring that person into contact with a reality normally closed to him because it belongs to another level.

Either the future will proceed in the same way as the present or it is the means of transformation. What is transformation? It differs from mere change in the way that the predictable event differs from the truly unexpected one. If we do not experience a new being, involving our thinking, feeling, and physical aspects, then we have not transformed ourselves. This journey requires us to cross unknown territory, to leave behind the familiar and become receptive to what is offered us. 'How can I know that this is true?' The sceptic in each of us, Idries Shah reminds us, in his parable 'The Tale of the Sands', must be acknowledged before we can progress. Doubt must give place to a less critical attitude; when doubt has been discarded, the way forward will be revealed.

As regards the future of man, it may be useful to think in terms of myth, which offers a larger, cosmological rather than anthropocentric, perspective. Zimmer suggests, in the myth of Markandeya, the ancient Vedic sage, that the process of evolution is linked to that of dissolution. New creation accompanies and is necessarily accompanied by destruction of what is past. Our own search and striving for a way to be constitutes a single thin thread in the fabric of world-maintenance. The larger picture must also be considered; the 'significant insignificance' of our own development then takes on a new dimension.

The cosmic dream of the god Vishnu is seen as containing past and future in a single moment; Markandeya, who escapes from this dream for a while, had until then taken the dream for reality. Dreams have frequently been regarded as forecasting the future, but how can we know what a dream means when our language is geared to the concepts, judgements, and thoughts which define what we call waking reality? One is reminded of Heraclitus' idea that nature speaks in signs. To read a dream for pointers to the future is a problem of interpretation – the extract from the Book of Daniel is a good example of this. We may also ponder how our waking reality differs from the dream state. Could it be that we could read the signs of our future in our workaday world if we were more sensitive to its language? We should remember, however, that we frequently desire to know the unknowable and we tend to allow our imagination full play in 'reading' the future in dreams. It may be that the future will sometimes announce itself to us in a dream, but we need to know ourselves very well to be able to winnow the true message from our own wishful interpretations.

NIETZSCHE, *THUS SPOKE ZARATHUSTRA*

From *The Portable Nietzsche*, edited and translated by Walter Kaufmann, New York, Viking Press, 1954

According to Nietzsche (see also p. 181), we are at present incomplete, fragmented. Our lives are a series of accidents, with only an accidental unity. Does the future hold in store more of the same? In Nietzsche's view, the answer is no. We have the unused capacity to affirm ourselves in such a way as to transform the contingent nature of our activity into an intentional, essential one. Through the exercise of this kind of willing, we embrace our fate, and become makers of our own selves. We redeem ourselves.

When Zarathustra crossed over the great bridge one day the cripples and beggars surrounded him, and a hunchback spoke to him thus: 'Behold, Zarathustra. The people too learn from you and come to believe in your doctrine; but before they will believe you entirely one thing is still needed: you must first persuade us cripples. Now here you have a fine selection and, verily, an opportunity with more than one handle. You can heal the blind and make the lame walk; and from him who has too much behind him you could perhaps take away a little. That, I think, would be the right way to make the cripples believe in Zarathustra.'

But Zarathustra replied thus to the man who had spoken: 'When one takes away the hump from the hunchback one takes away his spirit – thus teach the people. And when one restores his eyes to the blind man he sees too many wicked things on earth, and he will curse whoever healed him. But whoever makes the lame walk does him the greatest harm: for when he can walk his vices run away with him — thus teach the people about cripples. And why should Zarathustra not learn from the people when the people learn from Zarathustra?

'But this is what matters least to me since I have been among men: to see that this one lacks an eye and that one an ear and a third a leg, while there are others who have lost their tongues or their noses or their heads. I see, and have seen, what is worse, and many things so vile that I do not want to speak of everything; and concerning some things I do not even like to be silent: for there are human beings who lack everything, except one thing of which they have too much — human beings who are nothing but a big eye or a big mouth or a big belly or anything at all that is big. Inverse cripples I call them.

'And when I came out of my solitude and crossed over this bridge for the first time I did not trust my eyes and looked and looked again, and said at last, "An ear! An ear as big as a man!" I looked still more closely — and indeed, underneath the ear something was moving, something pitifully small and wretched and slender. And, no doubt of it, the tremendous ear was attached to a small, thin stalk — but this stalk was a human being! If one used a magnifying glass one could even recognize a tiny envious face; also, that a bloated little soul was dangling from the stalk. The people, however, told me that this great ear was not only a human being, but a great one, a genius. But I never believed the people when they spoke of great men; and I maintained my belief that it was an inverse cripple who had too little of everything and too much of one thing.'

When Zarathustra had spoken thus to the hunchback and to those whose mouthpiece and advocate the hunchback was, he turned to his disciples in profound dismay and said: 'Verily, my friends, I walk among men as among the fragments and limbs of men. This is what is terrible for my eyes, that I find man in ruins and scattered as over a battlefield or a butcher-field. And when my eyes flee from the now to the past, they always find the same:

fragments and limbs and dreadful accidents – but no human beings.

'The now and the past on earth – alas, my friends, that is what I find most unendurable; and I should not know how to live if I were not also a seer of that which must come. A seer, a willer, a creator, a future himself and a bridge for the future – and alas, also, as it were, a cripple at this bridge: all this is Zarathustra.

'And you too have often asked yourselves, Who is Zarathustra to us? What shall we call him? And, like myself, you replied to yourselves with questions. Is he a promiser? or a fulfiller? A conqueror? or an inheritor? An autumn? or a ploughshare? A physician? or one who has recovered? Is he a poet? or truthful? A liberator? or a tamer? Good? or evil?

'I walk among men as among the fragments of the future – that future which I envisage. And this is all my creating and striving, that I create and carry together into One what is fragment and riddle and dreadful accident. And how could I bear to be a man if man were not also a creator and guesser of riddles and redeemer of accidents?

'To redeem those who lived in the past and to re-create all "it was" into a "thus I willed it" – that alone should I call redemption. Will – that is the name of the liberator and joy-bringer; thus I taught you, my friends. But now learn this too: the will itself is still a prisoner. Willing liberates; but what is it that puts even the liberator himself in fetters? "It was" – that is the name of the will's gnashing of teeth and most secret melancholy. Powerless against what has been done, he is an angry spectator of all that is past. The will cannot will backwards; and that he cannot break time and time's covetousness, that is the will's loneliest melancholy.

'Willing liberates; what means does the will devise for himself to get rid of his melancholy and to mock his dungeon? Alas, every prisoner becomes a fool; and the imprisoned will redeems himself foolishly. That time does not run backwards, that is his wrath; "that which was" is the name of the stone he cannot move. And so he moves stones out of wrath and displeasure, and he wreaks revenge on whatever does not feel wrath and displeasure as he does. Thus the will, the liberator, took to hurting; and on all who can suffer he wreaks revenge for his inability to go backwards. This, indeed this alone, is what *revenge* is: the will's ill will against time and its "it was".

'Verily, a great folly dwells in our will; and it has become a curse for everything human that this folly has acquired spirit.

'*The spirit of revenge*, my friends, has so far been the subject of man's best reflection; and where there was suffering, one always wanted punishment too.

'For "punishment" is what revenge calls itself; with a hypocritical lie it creates a good conscience for itself.

'Because there is suffering in those who will, inasmuch as they cannot will backwards, willing itself and all life were supposed to be – a punishment. And now cloud upon cloud rolled over the spirit, until eventually madness preached. "Everything passes away; therefore everything deserves to pass away. And this too is justice, this law of time that it must devour its children." Thus preached madness.

'"Things are ordered morally according to justice and punishment. Alas, where is redemption from the flux of things and from the punishment called existence?" Thus preached madness.

'"Can there be redemption if there is eternal justice? Alas, the stone *It was* cannot be moved: all punishments must be eternal too." Thus preached madness.

'"No deed can be annihilated: how could it be undone by punishment? This, this is what is eternal in the punishment called existence, that existence must eternally become deed and guilt again. Unless the will should at last redeem himself, and willing should become not willing." But, my brothers, you know this fable of madness.

'I led you away from these fables when I taught you, "The will is a creator." All "it was" is a fragment, a riddle, a dreadful accident

— until the creative will says to it, "But thus I willed it." Until the creative will says to it, "But thus I will it; thus shall I will it."

'But has the will yet spoken thus? And when will that happen? Has the will been unharnessed yet from his own folly? Has the will yet become his own redeemer and joy-bringer? Has he unlearned the spirit of revenge and all gnashing teeth? And who taught him reconciliation with time and something higher than any reconciliation? For that will which is the will to power must will something higher than any reconciliation; but how shall this be brought about? Who could teach him also to will backwards?'

BERGSON, *CREATIVE EVOLUTION*

From Henri Bergson, *Creative Evolution*, translated by A. Mitchell, New York, Holt, Rinehart & Winston, 1944

Bergson (see also p. 267) sees life as a wave spreading from the centre of organic life on earth. It encompasses the human species, but man plays a unique role in the process. In man is found the possibility of consciousness. Consciousness is the fleeting vision that appears in moments of intuition, and lights up the possibility of a higher evolution of life than that which currently takes man along with it. We can investigate this possibility only by turning from conceptual, analytical thinking towards consciousness, which is an evolutionary force.

Radical therefore, also, is the difference between animal consciousness, even the most intelligent, and human consciousness. For consciousness corresponds exactly to the living being's power of choice; it is coextensive with the fringe of possible action that surrounds the real action: consciousness is synonymous with invention and with freedom. Now, in the animal, invention is never anything but a variation on the theme of routine. Shut up in the habits of the species, it succeeds, no doubt, in enlarging them by its individual initiative; but it escapes automatism only for an instant, for just the time to create a new automatism. The gates of its prison close as soon as they are opened; by pulling at its chain its succeeds only in stretching it. With man, consciousness breaks the chain. In man, and in man alone, it sets itself free. The whole history of life until man has been that of the effort of consciousness to raise matter, and of the more or less complete overwhelming of consciousness by the matter which has fallen back on it. The enterprise was paradoxical, if, indeed, we may speak here otherwise than by metaphor of enterprise and of effort. It was to create with matter, which is necessity itself, an instrument of freedom, to make a machine which should triumph over mechanism, and to use the determinism of nature to pass through the meshes of the net which this very determinism had spread. But, everywhere except in man, consciousness has let itself be caught in the net whose meshes it tried to pass through: it has remained the captive of the mechanisms it has set up. Automatism, which it tries to draw in the direction of freedom, winds about it and drags it down. It has not the power to escape, because the energy it has provided for acts is almost all employed in maintaining the infinitely subtle and essentially unstable equilibrium into which it has brought matter. But man not only maintains his machine, he succeeds in using it as he pleases. Doubtless he owes this to the superiority of his brain, which enables him to build an unlimited number of motor mechanisms, to oppose new habits to the old ones unceasingly, and, by dividing automatism against itself, to rule it. He owes it to his language, which furnishes consciousness with an immaterial body in which to incarnate itself and thus exempts it from dwelling exclusively on material bodies, whose flux would soon drag it along and finally swallow it up. He owes it to social life, which stores and preserves efforts as language stores thought, fixes thereby a mean level to which individuals must raise themselves at the outset, and by this initial stimulation prevents the average man from slumbering and drives the superior man to mount still higher. But our brain, our society, and our language are only the external and various signs of one and the same internal superiority. They tell, each after its manner, the unique, exceptional success which life has won at a given moment of its evolution. They express the difference of kind, and not only of degree, which separates man from the rest of the animal world. They let us guess that, while at the end of the vast springboard from which life has taken its leap, all the others have stepped down, finding the cord stretched too high, man alone has cleared the obstacle.

It is in this quite special sense that man is the 'term' and the 'end' of evolution. Life, we have said, transcends finality as it transcends the other categories. It is essentially a current sent through matter, drawing from it what it can. There has not, therefore, properly speaking, been any project or plan. On the other hand, it is abundantly evident that the rest of nature is not for the sake of man: we struggle like the other species, we have struggled against other species. Moreover, if the evolution of life had encountered other accidents in its course, if, thereby, the current of life had been otherwise divided, we should have been, physically and morally, far different from what we are. For these various reasons it would be wrong to regard humanity, such as we have it before our eyes, as prefigured in the evolutionary move-ment. It cannot even be said to be the outcome of the whole of evolution, for evolution has been accomplished on several diverg-ent lines, and while the human species is at the end of one of them, other lines have been followed with other species at their end. It is in a quite different sense that we hold humanity to be the ground of evolution.

From our point of view, life appears in its entirety as an immense wave which, starting from a centre, spreads outwards, and which on almost the whole of its circumference is stopped and converted into oscillation: at one single point the obstacle has been forced, the impulsion has passed freely. It is this freedom that the human form registers. Everywhere but in man, consciousness has had to come to a stand; in man alone it has kept on its way. Man, then, continues the vital movement indefinitely, although he does not draw along with him all that life carries in itself. On other lines of evolution there have travelled other tendencies which life implied, and of which, since everything interpenetrates, man has, doubtless, kept something, but of which he has kept only very little. *It is as if a vague and formless being, whom we may call, as we will,* man *or* superman, *had sought to realize himself, and had succeeded only by abandoning a part of himself on the way*. The losses are represented by the rest of the animal world, and even by the vegetable world, at least in what these have that is positive and above the accidents of evolution.

From this point of view, the discordances of which nature offers us the spectacle are singularly weakened. The organized world as a whole becomes as the soil on which was to grow either man himself or a being who morally must resemble him. The animals, however distant they may be from our species, however hostile to it, have been none the less useful travelling companions, on whom consciousness has unloaded whatever encumbrances it was dragging along, and who have enabled it to rise, in man, to heights from which it sees an unlimited horizon open again before it.

It is true that it has not only abandoned cumbersome baggage on the way; it has also had to give up valuable goods. Consciousness, in man, is pre-eminently intellect. It might have been, it ought, so it seems, to have been also intuition. Intuition and intellect represent two opposite directions of the work of consciousness: intuition goes in the very direction of life, intellect goes in the inverse direction, and thus finds itself naturally in accordance with the movement of matter. A complete and perfect humanity would be that in which these two forms of conscious activity should attain their full development. And, between this humanity and ours, we may conceive any number of possible stages, corresponding to all the degrees imaginable of intelligence and of intuition. In this lies the part of contingency in the mental structure of our species. A different evolution might have led to a humanity either more intellectual still or more intuitive. In the humanity of which we are a part, intuition is, in fact, almost completely sacrificed to intellect. It seems that to conquer matter, and to reconquer its own self, consciousness has had to exhaust the best part of its power. This conquest, in the particular conditions in which it has been accomplished, has required that consciousness should adapt itself to the habits of matter and concentrate all its attention on them, in fact determine itself more especially as intellect. Intuition is there, however, but vague and above all discontinuous. It is a lamp almost extinguished, which only glimmers now and then, for a few moments at most. But it glimmers wherever a vital interest is at stake. On our personality, on our liberty, on the place we occupy in the whole of nature, on our origin and perhaps also on our destiny, it throws a light feeble and vacillating, but which none the less pierces the darkness of the night in which the intellect leaves us.

These fleeting intuitions, which light up their object only at distant intervals, philosophy ought to seize, first to sustain them, then to expand them and so unite them together. The more it advances in this work, the more will it perceive that intuition is mind itself, and, in a certain sense, life itself: the intellect has been cut out of it by a process resembling that which has generated matter. Thus is revealed the unity of the spiritual life. We recognize it only when we place ourselves in intuition in order to go from intuition to the intellect, for from the intellect we shall never pass to intuition.

Philosophy introduces us thus into the spiritual life. And it shows us at the same time the relation of the life of the spirit to that of the body. The great error of the doctrines on the spirit has been the idea that by isolating the spiritual life from all the rest, by suspending it in space as high as possible above the earth, they were placing it beyond attack, as if they were not thereby simply exposing it to be taken as an effect of mirage! Certainly they are right to listen to conscience when conscience affirms human freedom; but the intellect is there, which says that the cause determines its effect, that like conditions like, that all is repeated and that all is given. They are right to believe in the absolute reality of the person and in his independence towards matter; but science is there, which shows the interdependence of conscious life and cerebral activity. They are right to attribute to man a privileged place in nature, to hold that the distance is infinite between the animal and man; but the history of life is there, which makes us witness the genesis of species by gradual transformation, and seems thus to reintegrate man into animality. When a strong instinct assures the probability of personal survival, they are right not to close their ears to its voice; but if there exist 'souls' capable of an independent life, whence do they come? When, how and why do they enter into this body which we see arise, quite naturally, from a mixed cell derived from the bodies of its two parents? All these questions will remain unanswered, a philosophy of intuition will be a negation of science, will be sooner or later swept away by science, if it does not resolve to see the life of the body just where it really is, on the road that leads to the life of the spirit. But it will then no longer have to do with definite living beings. Life as a whole, from the initial impulsion that thrust it into the world, will appear as a wave which rises, and which is opposed by the descending movement of matter. On the greater part of its surface, at different heights, the current is converted by matter into a vortex. At one point alone it passes freely, dragging with it the obstacle which will weigh on its progress but will not stop it. At this point is humanity; it is our privileged situation. On the other hand, this rising wave is consciousness, and, like all consciousness, it includes potentialities without number which interpenetrate and to which consequently neither the category of unity nor that of multiplicity is appropriate, made as they both are for inert matter. The matter that it bears along with it, and in the interstices of which it inserts itself, alone can divide it into distinct individualities. On flows the current, running through human generations, subdividing itself into individuals. This subdivision was vaguely indicated in it, but could not have been made clear without matter. Thus souls are continually being created, which, nevertheless, in a certain sense pre-existed. They are nothing else than the little rills into which the great river of life divides itself, flowing through the body of humanity. The movement of the stream is distinct from the river bed, although it must adopt its winding course. Consciousness is distinct from the organism it animates, although it must undergo its vicissitudes. As the possible actions which a state of consciousness indicates are at every instant beginning to be carried out in the nervous centres, the brain underlies at every instant the motor indications of the state of consciousness; but the interdependency of consciousness and brain is limited to this; the destiny of consciousness is not bound up on that account with the destiny of cerebral matter. Finally, consciousness is essentially free; it is freedom itself; but it cannot pass through matter without settling on it, without adapting itself to it: this adaptation is what we call intellectuality; and the intellect, turning itself back towards active, that is to say free, consciousness, naturally makes it enter into the conceptual forms into which it is accustomed to see matter fit. It will therefore always perceive freedom in the form of necessity; it will always neglect the part of novelty or of creation inherent in the free act; it will always substitute for action itself an imitation artificial, approximative, obtained by compounding the old with the old and the same with the same. Thus, to the eyes of a philosophy that attempts to reabsorb intellect in intuition, many difficulties vanish or become light. But such a doctrine does not only facilitate speculation; it gives us also more power to act and to live. For, with it, we feel ourselves no longer isolated in humanity, humanity no longer seems isolated in the nature that it dominates. As the smallest grain of dust is bound up with our entire solar system, drawn along with it in that undivided movement of descent which is materiality itself, so all organized beings, from the humblest to the highest, from the first origins of life to the time in which we are, and in all places as in all times, do but evidence a single impulsion, the inverse of the movement of matter, and in itself indivisible. All the living hold together, and all yield to the same tremendous push. The animal takes its stand on the plant, man bestrides animality, and the whole of humanity, in space and in time, is one immense army galloping beside and before and behind each of us in an overwhelming charge able to beat down every resistance and clear the most formidable obstacles, perhaps even death.

DAUMAL, *MOUNT ANALOGUE*

From René Daumal, *Mount Analogue*, translated by Roger Shattuck, New York, Random House, 1959

René Daumal (1908–44), French Sanskrit scholar, poet, and philosopher, remained relatively unknown until his works appeared after his death. A vision of the unified and harmonious person pervades his writing; his most famous books are Mount Analogue *and* A Night of Serious Drinking.

René Daumal gives us a revealing allegory of the work of the artist. The artist is someone who wants to express, in some medium or other, the truth of what is. But this truth 'disappears' in the face of a lie, even the most petty. The artist must work to acquire a sense of this tendency to be untruthful to oneself. Art then is vigilance towards lying, together with the vivid awareness that we do not know the truth of things.

The history of the Hollow-Men and the Bitter-Rose

The Hollow-Men live in solid rock and move about in it in the form of mobile caves or recesses. In ice they appear as bubbles in the shape of men. But they never venture out into the air, for the wind would blow them away.

They have houses in the rock whose walls are made of emptiness, and tents in the ice whose fabric is of bubbles. During the day they stay in the stone, and at night they wander through the ice and dance during the full moon. But they never see the sun, or else they would burst.

They eat only the void, such as the form of corpses; they get drunk on empty words and all the meaningless expressions we utter.

Some people say they have always existed and will exist for ever. Others say they are the dead. And others say that as a sword has its scabbard or a foot its imprint, every living man has in the mountain his Hollow-Man, and in death they are reunited.

In the village of Hundred-Houses there lived an old priest-magician Hunoes and his wife, Hulay-Hulay. They had two sons, two identical twins who could not be told apart, called Mo and Ho. Even their mother got them mixed up. To tell them apart, the day of name giving they had put on Mo a necklace bearing a little cross and on Ho a necklace bearing a little ring.

Old Hunoes had one great unconfessed worry. According to custom his eldest son should succeed him. But which was his elder son? Did he even have an elder son?

At the age of adolescence Mo and Ho were already accomplished mountaineers. They came to be called the two mountain goats. One day, their father told them, 'To whichever one of you brings back to me the Bitter-Rose I shall hand on the great knowledge.' The Bitter-Rose is found only at the summit of the highest peaks. Whoever eats of it finds that whenever he is about to tell a lie, aloud or to himself, his tongue begins to burn. He can still tell falsehoods, but he has been warned. A few people have seen the Bitter-Rose: according to what they say, it looks like a large multicoloured lichen or a swarm of butterflies. But no one has ever been able to pick it, for the tiniest tremor of fear anywhere close by alerts it, and it disappears into the rock. Even if one desires it, one is a little afraid of possessing it, and it vanishes.

To describe an impossible action or an absurd undertaking, they say: 'It's like looking for night in broad daylight,' or 'It's like wanting to throw light on the sun in order to see it better,' or 'It's like trying to catch the Bitter-Rose.'

Mo has taken his ropes and pick and hatchet and iron hooks. At sunrise he is already high up on a peak called Cloudy Head. Like a lizard, sometimes like a spider, he inches upwards across the high red precipice, between white snow below and the blue-black sky. Little swift-moving clouds envelop him from time to time and then expose him suddenly to the light again. And now at last, a little distance above him, he sees the Bitter-Rose, shimmering with unearthly tints. He repeats to himself unceasingly the charm that his father had taught him to ward off fear.

He's going to need a screw ring here, with a rope sling, in order to straddle this outcropping of rock like a rearing horse. He strikes with his hammer, and his hand breaks through into a hole. There is a hollow under the stone. Shattering the crust around it, he sees that the hollow is in the form of a man: torso, legs, arms, and little tubes in the shape of fingers spread in terror. He has split the head with the blow of his pick.

An icy wind passes across the stone. Mo has killed a Hollow-Man. He has shuddered, and the Bitter-Rose has retreated into the rock.

Mo climbs back down to the village and tells his father, 'I killed a Hollow-Man. But I saw the Bitter-Rose, and tomorrow I shall go to look for it.'

Old Hunoes became grave. Far off he saw one misfortune after another coming in procession. He said: 'Watch out for the Hollow-Men. They will seek vengeance. They cannot enter our world, but they can come up to the surface of things. Beware of the surface of things.'

At dawn the next day Hulay-Hulay gave a great cry, rose up, and ran towards the mountain. At the foot of the red cliff Mo's garments, his ropes and hatchet, and his medal with the cross. His body was no longer there.

'Ho,' she cried, running back. 'They've killed your brother. They've killed my son.'

Ho rises up with his teeth clenched and the skin tightening on his scalp. He takes his hatchet and prepares to set out. His father says to him: 'First, listen to me. This is what you have to do. The Hollow-Men have taken your brother and changed him into a Hollow-Man. He will try to escape. He will go in search of light to the seracs of the Clear Glacier. Put his medal around your neck as well as your own. Go to him and strike at his head. Enter the form of his body, and Mo will live again among us. Do not fear to kill a dead man.'

Ho gazes wide-eyed into the blue ice of the Clear Glacier. Is the light playing tricks on him, are his eyes deceiving him, or is he really seeing what he sees? He watches silvery forms with arms and legs, like greased divers under water. There is his brother, Mo, his hollow shape fleeing from a thousand Hollow-Men in pursuit. But they are afraid of the light. Mo's form seeks the light and rises in a large blue serac, turning around and around as if in search of a door. Despite his bursting heart and the blood clotting in his veins, Ho steps forward. To his blood and to his heart he says, 'Do not fear to kill a dead man.' Then he strikes the head, shattering the ice. Mo's form becomes motionless; Ho opens the ice of the serac and enters his brother's form like a sword fitted into its sheath, a foot into its imprint. He moves his elbows and works himself into place, then draws his legs back out of the mould of ice. And he hears himself saying words in a language he has never spoken. He feels he is Ho, and that he is Mo at the same time. All

Mo's memories have entered his mind – the way up Cloudy Head and where the Bitter-Rose has its habitation.

With the circle and the cross around his neck, he comes to Hulay-Hulay. 'Mother, you will have no more trouble telling us apart. Mo and Ho are now in the same body; I am your only son, Moho.'

Old Hunoes shed a few tears, and his face showed happiness. But there was still one doubt he wished to dispel. He said to Moho, 'You are my only son; Ho and Mo can no longer be distinguished.'

Moho told him with conviction, 'Now I can reach the Bitter-Rose. Mo knows the way; Ho knows the right gesture. Master of my fears, I shall have the flower of discernment.'

He picked the flower, he received the teaching, and old Hunoes was able to leave this world peacefully.

ZIMMER, *MYTHS AND SYMBOLS IN INDIAN ART AND CIVILIZATION*

From Heinrich Zimmer, *Myths and Symbols in Indian Art and Civilization*, ed. Joseph Campbell, Princeton University Press, 1971

Heinrich Zimmer (1890–1943), German ideologist and thinker, saw throughout the great diversity of Indian thought a search for one unity. His study of the visual arts of India covered the grounds of metaphysics, ethics, and the theory of knowledge. His works include Philosophies of India, The King and the Corpse, *and* Myths and Symbols in Indian Art and Civilization.

Zimmer relates the myth of illusion, or Maya. Markandeya, a great sage, enjoys a moment of awakening to the timeless truth of reality. Until that moment, he remained completed absorbed in the dream of Vishnu, the figure of universal creative force in Hindu mythology. He took the dream for reality. In the moment of his separation, another sort of vision took place, one which greatly disturbed him before he was swallowed by the dream again. The suggestion is that at any time we too may find ourselves in a new, startling relation to what is real.

Vishnu sleeps. Like a spider that has climbed up the thread that once issued from its own organism, drawing it back into itself, the god has consumed again the web of the universe. Alone upon the immortal substance of the ocean, a giant figure, submerged partly, partly afloat, he takes delight in slumber. There is no one to behold him, no one to comprehend him; there is no knowledge of him, except within himself.

This giant, 'Lord of Maya', and the cosmic ocean on which he is recumbent, are dual manifestations of a single essence; for the ocean, as well as the human form, is Vishnu. Furthermore, since in Hindu mythology the symbol for water is the serpent (*naga*), Vishnu is represented, normally, as reposing on the coils of a prodigious snake, his favourite symbolic animal, the serpent Ananta, 'Endless'. So that, not only the gigantic anthropomorphic form and the boundless elemental, but the reptile too is Vishnu. It is on a serpent ocean of his own immortal substance that the Cosmic Man passes the universal night.

Inside the god is the cosmos, like an unborn babe within the mother; and here all is restored to its primal perfection. Though without there exists only darkness, within the divine dreamer an ideal vision thrives of what the universe should be. The world, recovering from decline, confusion, and disaster, runs again the harmonious course.

And now, it is during this spellbound interlude that there occurs – according to the tale – a fantastic event:

A holy man, Markandeya by name, is wandering inside the god, over the peaceful earth, as an aimless pilgrim, regarding with pleasure the edifying sight of the ideal vision of the world. This

Markandeya is a well-known mythical figure, a saint endowed with life unending. He is many thousands of years old, yet of unageing strength and alert mind. Wandering now through the interior of Vishnu's body, he is visiting the holy hermitages, gratified by the pious pursuits of the sages and their pupils. At shrines and holy places he pauses to worship, and his heart is made glad by the piety of the people in the countries through which he roams.

But now an accident occurs. In the course of his aimless, unending promenade, the sturdy old man slips, inadvertently, out through the mouth of the all-containing god. Vishnu is sleeping with lips a little open; breathing with a deep, sonorous, rhythmical sound, in the immense silence of the night of Brahma. And the astonished saint, falling from the sleeper's giant lip, plunges head-long into the cosmic sea.

At first, because of Vishnu's Maya, Markandeya does not behold the sleeping giant, but only the ocean, utterly dark, stretching far in the all-embracing, starless night. He is seized by despair, and fears for his life. Splashing about in the dark water, he becomes presently pensive, ponders, and begins to doubt. 'Is it a dream? Or am I under the spell of an illusion? Forsooth, this circumstance, utterly strange, must be the product of my imagination. For the world as I know it, and as I observed it in its harmonious course, does not deserve such annihilation as it seems now suddenly to have suffered. There is no sun, no moon, no wind; the mountains have all vanished, the earth has disappeared. What manner of universe is this in which I discover myself?'

These searching reflections of the saint are a kind of commentary on the idea of Maya, the problem 'What is real?' as conceived by the Hindu. 'Reality' is a function of the individual. It is the result of the specific virtues and limitations of individual consciousness. While the saint had been wandering about the interior of the cosmic giant he had perceived a reality which had seemed to him congenial to his nature, and he had regarded it as solid and substantial. Nevertheless, it had been only a dream or vision within the mind of the sleeping god. Contrariwise, during the night of nights, the reality of the primal substance of the god appears to the human consciousness of the saint as a bewildering mirage. 'It is impossible,' he ponders, 'it cannot be real.'

The aim of the doctrines of Hindu philosophy and of the training in yoga practice is to transcend the limits of individualized consciousness. The mythical tales are meant to convey the wisdom of the philosophers and to exhibit in a popular, pictorial form the experiences or results of yoga. Appealing directly to intuition and imagination, they are accessible to all as an interpretation of existence. They are not explicitly commented upon or elucidated. The dialogues and speeches of the principal figures contain moments of philosophical exposition and interpretation, yet the story itself is never explained. There is no explicit commentary on the meaning of the mythological action. The tale goes straight to the listener through an appeal to his intuition, to his creative imagination. It stirs and feeds the unconscious. By an eloquence rather of incident than of word, the mythology of India serves its function as the popular vehicle of the esoteric wisdom of yoga experience and of orthodox religion.

An immediate effect is assured, because the tales are not the products of individual experiences and reactions. They are produced, treasured, and controlled by the collective working and thinking of the religious community. They thrive on the ever-renewed assent of successive generations. They are refashioned, reshaped, laden with new meaning, through an anonymous creative process and a collective, intuitive acceptance. They are effective primarily on a subconscious level, touching intuition, feeling, and imagination. Their details impress themselves on the memory, soak down, and shape the deeper stratifications of the psyche. When brooded upon, their significant episodes are capable of revealing various shades of meaning, according to the experiences and life-needs of the individual . . .

The saint, forlorn in the vast expanse of the waters and on the very point of despair, at last became aware of the form of the sleeping god; and he was filled with amazement and a beatific joy. Partly submerged, the enormous shape resembled a mountain range breaking out of the waters. It glowed with a wonderful light from within. The saint swam nearer, to study the presence; and he had just opened his lips to ask who this was, when the giant seized him, summarily swallowed him, and he was again in the familiar landscape of the interior.

Thus abruptly restored to the harmonious world of Vishnu's dream, Markandeya was filled with extreme confusion. He could only think of his brief yet unforgettable experience as a kind of vision. Paradoxically, however, he himself, the human being unable to accept any reality that transcended the interpretative powers of his limited consciousness, was not contained within that divine being, as a figure of its universal dream. And yet to Markandeya, who had been suddenly blessed with a vision of the Supreme Existence – in and by itself, in its all-containing solitude and quietude – that revelation likewise had been but a dream.

Markandeya, back again, resumed his former life. As before, he wandered over the wide earth, a saintly pilgrim. He observed yogis practising austerities in the woods. He nodded assent to the kingly donors who performed costly sacrifices, with lavish gifts for the brahmins. He watched brahmins officiating at sacrificial rituals and receiving generous fees for their effective magic. All castes he saw piously devoted to their proper tasks, and the holy sequence of the Four Stages of Life he observed in full effect among men. Graciously pleased with this ideal state of affairs, he wandered in safety for another hundred years.

But then, inadvertently, once again, he slipped from the sleeper's mouth and tumbled into the pitch-black sea. This time, in the dreadful darkness and water-desert of silence, he beheld a luminous babe, a godlike boy beneath a fig tree, peaceful in slumber. Then again, by the effect of Maya, Markandeya saw the lonely little boy cheerfully at play, undismayed amidst the vast ocean. The saint was filled with curiosity, but his eyes could not stand the dazzling splendour of the child, and so he remained at a comfortable distance, pondering as he kept himself afloat on the pitchy deep. Markandeya mused: 'Something of this kind I seem to remember having beheld once before – long, long ago.' But then his mind became aware of the fathomless depth of the shoreless ocean and was overcome with a freezing fear.

The god, in the guise of the divine child, gently addressed him. 'Welcome, Markandeya!' The voice had the soft deep tone of the melodious thundering of an auspicious rain cloud. The god reassured him: 'Welcome, Markandeya! Do not be afraid, my child. Do not fear. Come hither.'

The hoary, ageless saint could not recall a time when anyone had presumed either to address him as 'child', or to name him simply by his first name without any respectful appellation referring to his saintliness and birth. He was profoundly offended. Though weary, pained with fatigue, and at a very great disadvantage, he burst into a display of temper. 'Who presumes to ignore my dignity, my saintly character, and to make light of the treasure of magic power stored in me through my ascetic austerities? Who is this who slights my venerable age, equal to a thousand years – as the gods count years? I am not accustomed to this sort of insulting treatment. Even the highest gods regard me with exceptional respect. Not even Brahma would dare to approach me in this irreverent manner. Brahma addresses me courteously: "O Long-lived one", he calls me. Who now courts disaster, flings himself blindly into the abyss of destruction, casts away his life, by naming me simply Markandeya? Who merits death?'

When the saint had thus expressed his wrath, the divine child resumed his discourse, unperturbed. 'Child, I am thy parent, thy father and elder, the primeval being who bestows all life. Why do you not come to me? I knew your sire well. He practised severe austerities in bygone times in order to beget a son. He gained my grace. Pleased with his perfect saintliness, I granted him a gift, and he requested that you, his son, should be endowed with inexhaustible life-strength and should never grow old. Your father knew the secret core of his existence, and you stem from that core. That is why you are now privileged to behold me, recumbent on the primal, all-containing cosmic waters, and playing here as a child beneath the tree.'

Markandeya's features brightened with delight. His eyes grew wide, like opening blossoms. In humble surrender, he made as if to bow and he prayed: 'Let me know the secret of your Maya, the secret of your apparition now as child, lying and playing in the infinite sea. Lord of the Universe, by what name are you known? I believe you to be the Great Being of all beings; for who else could exist as you exist?'

Vishnu replied: 'I am the Primeval Cosmic Man, Narayana. He is the waters; he is the first being; he is the source of the universe. I have a thousand heads. I manifest myself as the holiest of holy offerings; I manifest myself as the sacred fire that carries the offerings of men on earth to the gods in heaven. Simultaneously, I manifest myself as the Lord of Waters. Wearing the garb of Indra, the king of gods, I am the foremost of the immortals. I am the cycle of the year, which generates everything and again dissolves it. I am the divine yogi, the cosmic juggler or magician, who works wonderful tricks of delusion. The magical deceptions of the cosmic yogi are the yugas, the ages of the world. This display of the mirage of the phenomenal process of the universe is the work of my creative aspect; but at the same time I am the whirlpool, the destructive vortex, that sucks back whatever has been displayed and puts an end to the procession of the yugas. I put an end to everything that exists. My name is Death of the Universe.'

OUSPENSKY, *TERTIUM ORGANUM*

**From P. D. Ouspensky, *Tertium Organum*, translated
by N. Bessaraboff and C. Bragdon, New York,
Random House, 1970**

P. D. Ouspensky (1878–1947), Russian mathematician and philosopher, was attracted at an early age to the idea of the fourth dimension. Roused by the great questions of life and of man's place in the scheme of things, he searched, in particular and theoretical ways, for an adequate basis of being and knowing. His major books are Tertium Organum, A New Model of the Universe, *and* In Search of the Miraculous.

Ouspensky raises the question of the vehicle through which the force of evolution works. Darwin showed that the species is the organ of evolving nature; others, like Spencer, argue that human culture is also capable of evolution. Ouspensky maintains that only the individual person can evolve because consciousness alone provides the means, and consciousness is an attribute of the individual. He then goes on to ask whether evolution, the transformation of individual consciousness, is an event to be awaited in the future, or whether it can occur in the present.

The living world of nature (including man) is analogous to man; and it is more correct and more convenient to regard the different forms of consciousness in different divisions and strata of living nature as belonging to one organism and performing different, but related functions, than as separate, and evolving from one another. Then the necessity disappears for all this naïve theorizing on the subject of evolution. We do not regard the organs and members of the body of man as evolved one from another *in a given individual* and we should not be guilty of the same error with relation to the organs and members of the body of living nature.

I do not deny the law of evolution, but the application of it to the explanation of many phenomena of life is in great need of correction.

Firstly, if we accept the idea of one common evolution, after all it is necessary to remember that the types which develop slower, the remnants of evolution, may not continue to follow after, and at a slow pace, *the same* evolution, but may begin an evolution of their own, developing in many cases exactly those properties on account of which they were thrown out from basic evolution.

Secondly, though we accept the law of evolution, there is no necessity to regard all existing forms as having been developed one from another (like man from the ape, for example). In such cases it is more correct to regard them all as the *highest types* in *their own* evolution. The absence of intermediate forms makes this view much more probable than that which is usually accepted, and which gives such rich material for discussions about the obligatory and inevitable perfection of all — 'perfection' from our standpoint.

The views propounded here are indeed more difficult than the usual evolutionary point of view, just as the conception of the living world as an *entire* organism is more difficult; but this difficulty must be surmounted. I have said already that the real world must be illogical from the usual points of view, and by no means can it be made simple and comprehensible to one and all. The theory of evolution is in need of many corrections, additions, and much development. If we consider the existing forms on any given plane, it will be quite impossible to declare that all these forms evolved from the simplest forms on the plane. Some undoubtedly evolved from the lowest ones; others resulted from the process of degeneration of the higher ones; a third class developed from the remnants of some evolved form — while a fourth class resulted as a consequence of the incursion into the given plane of the properties and characteristics of some higher plane. It is certainly impossible to regard those complex forms as developed by an evolutionary process upon the given plane.

The classification below will show more clearly this correlation of forms of manifestation of consciousness, or of different states of consciousness.

First form. A sense of one-dimensional space in relation to the other world. Everything transpires on a line, as it were. Sensations are not differentiated. Consciousness is immersed in itself, in its work of nutrition, digestion and assimilation of food, etc. This is the state of the cell, the group of cells, of tissues and organs of the body of an animal, of plants and lower organisms. In a man this is the 'instinctive mind'.

Second form. A sense of two-dimensional space. This is the state of the animal. That which is for us the third dimension, for it is motion. It already senses, feels, but does not think. Everything that it sees appears to it as genuinely real. Emotional life and flashes of thought in a man.

Third form. A sense of three-dimensional space. Logical thinking. Philosophical division into I and Not-I. Dogmatic religions or dualistic spiritism. Codified morality. Division into spirit and matter. Positivistic science. The idea of evolution. A mechanical universe. The understanding of cosmic ideas as metaphors. Imperialism, 'historical materialism', socialism, etc. Subjection of the personality to society and law. Automatism. Death as the extinction of the personality. Intellect and flashes of self-consciousness.

Fourth form. Beginning of the understanding of four-dimensional space. A new concept of time. The possibility of more prolonged self-consciousness. Flashes of cosmic consciousness. The idea and sometimes the sensation of a living universe. A striving towards the wondrous. Sensation of infinity. Beginning of self-conscious will and moments of cosmic consciousness. Possibility of personal immortality.

Thus the third form includes that 'man' whom science studies. But the fourth form is characteristic of the man who is beginning to pass out of the field of observation of positivism and logical understanding . . .

Evolution or culture?

The most interesting and important questions arising with regard to cosmic consciousness may be summed up as follows: (1) Is the manifestion of cosmic consciousness a problem of the distant future, and of other generations — i.e., must cosmic consciousness appear as the result of an evolutionary process, after centuries and millennia, and will it then become a common property or a property of the majority? And (2) Can cosmic consciousness make its appearance *now* in contemporary man, i.e., at least as the result of a certain education and self-development which will aid the unfolding in him of dominant forces and capabilities, i.e., as the result of a certain *culture*?

It seems to me with regard to this, the following ideas are tenable:

The possibility of the appearance or development of cosmic consciousness belongs to the few.

But even in the case of those men in whom cosmic consciousness may appear, certain quite definite inner and outer conditions are requisite for its manifestation — a certain *culture*, the education of those elements congenial to cosmic consciousness, and the elimination of those hostile to it.

The distinguishing signs of those men in whom cosmic consciousness is likely to manifest are not studied at all.

The first of these signs is the constant or frequent sensation that the world is not at all as it appears; that what is most important in it is not at all what is considered most important. The quest of the wondrous, sensed as the only real and true, results from this impression of the unreality of the world and everything related thereto.

High mental culture, high intellectual attainments, are not necessary conditions at all. The example of many *saints*, who were not intellectual, but who undoubtedly attained cosmic consciousness, shows that cosmic consciousness may develop in purely emotional

339

soil, i.e., in the given case, as a result of religious emotion. Cosmic consciousness is also possible of attainment through the emotion attendant upon creation – in painters, musicians and poets. Art in its highest manifestations is a path to cosmic consciousness.

But equally in all cases the unfoldment of cosmic consciousness demands a certain *culture*, a correspondent life. From all the examples cited by Dr Bucke, and all others that one might add, it would not be possible to select a single case in which cosmic consciousness unfolded in conditions of inner life adverse to it, i.e., in moments of absorption by the *outer* life, with its struggles, its emotions and interests.

For the manifestation of cosmic consciousness it is necessary that the centre of gravity of *everything* shall lie for man in the inner world, in self-consciousness, and not in the outer world at all.

If we assume that Dr Bucke himself had been surrounded by entirely different conditions than those in which he found himself at the moment of experiencing cosmic consciousness, then in all probability his illumination would not have come at all.

He spent the evening reading poetry in the company of men of high intellectual and emotional development, and was returning home full of the thoughts and emotions of the evening.

But if instead of this he had spent the evening playing cards in the society of men whose interests were common and whose conversation was vulgar, or at a political meeting, or had he worked a night shift in a factory at a turning-lathe or written a newspaper editorial in which he himself did not believe and nobody else would believe – then we may declare with certainty that no cosmic consciousness would have appeared in him at all. For it undoubtedly demands a great freedom, and concentration on the inner world.

This conclusion in regard to the necessity for special culture and definitely favourable inner and outer conditions does not necessarily mean that cosmic consciousness is likely to manifest in *every man* who is put in these conditions. There are men, probably an enormous majority of contemporary humanity, in whom exists no such possibility at all. And in those who do not possess it in some sort already, it cannot be created by any culture whatever, in the same way that no kind or amount of culture will make an animal speak the language of man. The possibility of the manifestation of cosmic consciousness cannot be inoculated artificially. A man is either born with or without it. This possibility can be throttled or developed, but it cannot be created.

Not all can learn to discern the real from the false; but he who can will not receive this gift of discernment free. This is a thing of great labour, a thing of great work, which demands boldness of thought and boldness of feeling.

THE BOOK OF DANIEL

From the Book of Daniel, Authorized Version

The Book of Daniel belongs to the Old Testament collection of writings of the Prophets.

We can dream about the future; we can also prophesy, have premonitions, intimations, foreknowledge, depending on the clarity of vision. What allows us to see what is not yet in existence? The Old Testament gives many examples of prophecy. The Book of Daniel is a good one. In this brief selection, Nebuchadnezzar, the king of Babylon, gives Daniel a dream by which to interpret the future. Daniel's understanding gives us all pause for thought.

Chapter IV

4. I Nebuchadnezzar was at rest in mine house, and flourishing in my palace:

5. I saw a dream which made me afraid, and the thoughts upon my bed and the vision of my head troubled me.

6. Therefore made I a decree to bring in all the wise men of Babylon before me, that they might make known unto me the interpretation of the dream.

7. Then came in the magicians, the astrologers, the Chaldeans, and the soothsayers: and I told the dream before them; but they did not make known unto me the interpretation thereof.

8. But at the last Daniel came in before me, whose name was Belteshazzar, according to the name of my god, and in whom is the spirit of the holy gods: and before him I told the dream, saying,

9. O Belteshazzar, master of the magicians, because I know that the spirit of the holy gods is in thee, and no secret troubleth thee, tell me the visions of my dream that I have seen, and the interpretation thereof.

10. Thus were the visions of mine head in my bed; I saw, and behold a tree in the midst of the earth, and the height thereof was great.

11. The tree grew, and was strong, and the height thereof reached unto heaven, and the sight thereof to the end of all the earth:

12. The leaves thereof were fair, and the fruit thereof much, and in it was meat for all: the beasts of the field had shadow under it, and the fowls of the heaven dwelt in the boughs thereof, and all flesh was fed of it.

13. I saw in the visions of my head upon my bed, and, behold, a watcher and an holy one came down from heaven;

14. He cried aloud, and said thus, Hew down the tree, and cut off his branches, shake off his leaves, and scatter his fruit: let the beasts get away from under it, and the fowls from his branches:

15. Nevertheless leave the stump of his roots in the earth, even with a band of iron and brass in the tender grass of the field; and let it be wet with the dew of heaven, and let his portion be with the beasts in the grass of the earth:

16. Let his heart be changed from man's, and let a beast's heart be given unto him; and let seven times pass over him.

17. This matter is by the decree of the watchers, and the demand by the word of the holy ones: to the intent that the living may know that the most High ruleth in the kingdom of men, and giveth it to whomsoever he will, and setteth up over it the basest of men.

18. This dream I king Nebuchadnezzar have seen. Now thou, O Belteshazzar, declare the interpretation thereof, forasmuch as all the wise men of my kingdom are not able to make known unto me the interpretation: but thou art able; for the spirit of the holy gods is in thee.

19. Then Daniel, whose name was Belteshazzar, was astonied for one hour, and his thoughts troubled him. The king spake, and said, Belteshazzar, let not the dream, or the interpretation thereof, trouble thee. Belteshazzar answered and said, My lord, the dream be to them that hate thee, and the interpretation thereof to thine enemies.

20. The tree that thou sawest which grew, and was strong, whose height reached unto the heaven, and the sight thereof to all the earth;

21. Whose leaves were fair, and the fruit thereof much, and in it was meat for all; under which the beasts of the field dwelt, and upon whose branches the fowls of the heaven had their habitation:

22. It is thou, O king, that art grown and become strong: for thy greatness is grown, and reacheth unto heaven, and thy dominion to the end of the earth.

23. And whereas the king saw a watcher and an holy one coming down from heaven, and saying, Hew the tree down, and destroy it; yet leave the stump of the roots thereof in the earth, even with a band of iron and brass, in the tender grass of the field; and let it be wet with the dew of heaven, and let his portion be with the beasts of the field, till seven times pass over him;

24. This is the interpretation, O king, and this is the decree of the most High, which is come upon my lord the king:

25. That they shall drive thee from men, and thy dwelling shall be with the beasts of the field, and they shall make thee to eat grass as oxen, and they shall wet thee with the dew of heaven, and seven times shall pass over thee, till thou know that the most High ruleth in the kingdom of men, and giveth it to whomsoever he will.

26. And whereas they commanded to leave the stump of the tree roots; thy kingdom shall be sure unto thee, after that thou shalt have known that the heavens do rule.

27. Whereof, O king, let my counsel be acceptable unto thee, and break off thy sins by righteousness, and thine iniquities by shewing mercy to the poor; if it may be a lengthening of thy tranquillity.

28. All this came upon the king Nebuchadnezzar.

29. At the end of twelve months he walked in the palace of the kingdom of Babylon.

30. The king spake, and said, Is not this great Babylon, that I have built for the house of the kingdom by the might of my power, and for the honour of my majesty?

31. While the word was in the king's mouth there fell a voice from heaven, saying, O king Nebuchadnezzar, to thee it is spoken; The kingdom is departed from thee.

32. And they shall drive thee from men, and thy dwelling shall be with the beasts of the field: they shall make thee to eat grass as oxen, and seven times shall pass over thee, until thou know that the most High ruleth in the kingdom of men, and giveth it to whomsoever he will.

33. The same hour was the thing fulfilled upon Nebuchadnezzar: and he was driven from men, and did eat grass as oxen, and his body was wet with dew of heaven, till his hairs were grown like eagles' feathers, and his nails like birds' claws.

RILKE, *DUINO ELEGIES*

**From *The Selected Poetry of Rainer Maria Rilke*,
translated by Stephen Mitchell, New York, Random
House, 1982**

*Rainer Maria Rilke (1875–1926), German poet, aimed to express the
inward reality with immediacy and intensity. Influenced by artists of his
time, such as Rodin and Picasso, he wrote of human alienation and the
search to return to an all-encompassing unity.* His most important
works are the *Duino Elegies,* Sonnets to Orpheus, *and* The Note-
books of Malte Laurids Brigge.

*Rilke evokes a poetic image of nature in which humans occupy a
critical place. The world is a world of ceaseless change, and we too are
constantly subject to change. Yet, he suggests, we have a kind of sense,
within ourselves, by which we grasp a thing and transform it into
something real and enduring. Without this, everything would be trans-
itory; with it, Rilke says, we have the possibility of fulfilling ourselves,
and nature too may be fulfilled.*

The Ninth Elegy

Why, if this interval of being can be spent serenely
in the form of a laurel, slightly darker than all
other green, with tiny waves on the edges
of every leaf (like the smile of a breeze) —: why then
have to be human — and, escaping from fate,
keep longing for fate? . . .

Oh *not* because happiness *exists*,
that too-hasty profit snatched from approaching loss.
Not out of curiosity, not as practice for the heart, which
would exist in the laurel too . . .

But because *truly* being here is so much; because
    everything here
apparently needs us, this fleeting world, which in some
    strange way
keeps calling to us. Us, the most fleeting of all.
Once for each thing. Just once; no more. And we too,
just once. And never again. But to have been
this once, completely, even if only once:
to have been at one with the earth, seems beyond
    undoing.

And so we keep pressing on, trying to achieve it,
trying to hold it firmly in our simple hands,
in our overcrowded gaze, in our speechless heart.
Trying to become it. — Whom can we give it to? We
    would
hold on to it all, forever . . . Ah, but what can we take
    along
into that other realm? Not the art of looking,
which is learned so slowly, and nothing that happened
    here.
    Nothing.
The sufferings, then. And, above all, the heaviness,
and the long experience of love, — just what is wholly
unsayable. But later, among the stars,
what good is it — *they* are *better* as they are: unsayable.
For when the traveller returns from the mountain-slopes
    into the valley,
he brings, not a handful of earth, unsayable to others, but
    instead
some word he has gained, some pure word, the yellow
    and blue
gentian. Perhaps we are *here* in order to say: house,
bridge, fountain, gate, pitcher, fruit-tree, window —

at most: column, tower . . . But to *say* them, you must
    understand,
oh to say them *more* intensely than the Things
    themselves
ever dreamed of existing. Isn't the secret intent
of this taciturn earth, when it forces lovers together,
that inside their boundless emotion all things may shudder
    with joy?
Threshold: what it means for two lovers
to be wearing down, imperceptibly, the ancient threshold
    of their door —
they too, after the many who came before them
and before those to come . . ., lightly.

Here is the time for the *sayable, here* is its homeland.
Speak and bear witness. More than ever
the Things that we might experience are vanishing, for
what crowds them out and replaces them is an imageless
    act.
An act under a shell, which easily cracks open as soon as
the business inside outgrows it and seeks new limits.
Between the hammers our heart
endures, just as the tongue does
between the teeth and, despite that,
still is able to praise.

Praise this world to the angel, not the unsayable one,
you can't impress *him* with glorious emotion; in the
    universe
where he feels more powerfully, you are a novice. So
    show him
something simple which, formed over generations,
lives as our own, near our hand and within our gaze.
Tell him of Things. He will stand astonished; as *you* stood

by the rope-maker in Rome or the potter along the Nile.
Show him how happy a Thing can be, how innocent and
    ours,
how even lamenting grief purely decides to take form,
serves as a Thing, or dies into a Thing –, and blissfully
escapes far beyond the violin. – And these Things,
which live by perishing, know you are praising them;
    transient,
they look to us for deliverance: us, the most transient of
    all.
They want us to change them, utterly, in our invisible
    heart,
within – oh endlessly – within us! Whoever we may be at
    least.

Earth, isn't this what you want: to arise within us,
invisible? Isn't it your dream
to be wholly invisible someday? – Oh Earth: invisible!
What, if not transformation, is your urgent command?
Earth, my dearest, I will. Oh believe me, you no longer
need your springtimes to win me over – one of them,
ah, even one, is already too much for my blood.
Unspeakably I have belonged to you, from the first.
You were always right, and your holiest inspiration
is our intimate companion, Death.

Look, I am living. On what? Neither childhood nor future
grows any smaller . . . Superabundant being
wells up in my heart.

ARKANA – NEW-AGE BOOKS FOR MIND, BODY AND SPIRIT

With over 150 titles currently in print, Arkana is the leading name in quality new-age books for mind, body and spirit. Arkana encompasses the spirituality of both East and West, ancient and new, in fiction and non-fiction. A vast range of interests is covered, including Psychology and Transformation, Health, Science and Mysticism, Women's Spirituality and Astrology.

If you would like a catalogue of Arkana books, please write to:

Arkana Marketing Department
Penguin Books Ltd
27 Wright's Lane
London W8 5TZ

ARKANA - NEW-AGE BOOKS FOR MIND, BODY AND SPIRIT

A selection of titles already published or in preparation

The TM Technique Peter Russell

Through a process precisely opposite to that by which the body accumulates stress and tension, transcendental meditation works to produce a state of profound rest, with positive benefits for health, clarity of mind, creativity and personal stability. Peter Russell's book has become the key work for everyone requiring a complete mastery of TM.

The Development of the Personality: Seminars in Psychological Astrology Volume I Liz Greene and Howard Sasportas

Taking as a starting point their groundbreaking work on the cross-fertilization between astrology and psychology, Liz Greene and Howard Sasportas show how depth psychology works with the natal chart to illuminate the experiences and problems all of us encounter throughout the development of our individual identity, from childhood onwards.

Homage to the Sun: The Wisdom of the Magus of Strovolos Kyriacos C. Markides

Homage to the Sun continues the adventure into the mysterious and extraordinary world of the spiritual teacher and healer Daskalos, the 'Magus of Strovolos'. The logical foundations of Daskalos' world of other dimensions are revealed to us – invisible masters, past-life memories and guardian angels, all explained by the Magus with great lucidity and scientific precision.

The Year I: Global Process Work Arnold Mindell

As we approach the end of the 20th century, we are on the verge of planetary extinction. Solving the planet's problems is literally a matter of life and death. Arnold Mindell shows how his famous and groundbreaking process-orientated psychology can be extended so that our own sense of global awareness can be developed and we – the whole community of earth's inhabitants – can comprehend the problems and work together towards solving them.

ARKANA – NEW-AGE BOOKS FOR MIND, BODY AND SPIRIT

A selection of titles already published or in preparation

Encyclopedia of the Unexplained
Edited by Richard Cavendish   Consultant: J. B. Rhine

'Will probably be the definitive work of its kind for a long time to come' – *Prediction*

The ultimate guide to the unknown, the esoteric and the unproven: richly illustrated, with almost 450 clear and lively entries from Alchemy, the Black Box and Crowley to faculty X, Yoga and the Zodiac.

Buddhist Civilization in Tibet   Tulku Thondup Rinpoche

Unique among works in English, *Buddhist Civilization in Tibet* provides an astonishing wealth of information on the various strands of Tibetan religion and literature in a single compact volume, focusing predominantly on the four major schools of Buddhism: Nyingma, Kagyud, Sakya and Gelug.

The Living Earth Manual of Feng-Shui   Stephen Skinner

The ancient Chinese art of Feng-Shui – tracking the hidden energy flow which runs through the earth in order to derive maximum benefit from being in the right place at the right time – can be applied equally to the siting and layout of cities, houses, tombs and even flats and bedsits; and can be practised as successfully in the West as in the East with the aid of this accessible manual.

In Search of the Miraculous: Fragments of an Unknown Teaching   P. D. Ouspensky

Ouspensky's renowned, vivid and characteristically honest account of his work with Gurdjieff from 1915–18.

'Undoubtedly a *tour de force*. To put entirely new and very complex cosmology and psychology into fewer than 400 pages, and to do this with a simplicity and vividness that makes the book accessible to any educated reader, is in itself something of an achievement' – *The Times Literary Supplement*